:e.

WOMAN
of ROME

Also by LILY TUCK

FICTION

The News from Paraguay

Limbo, and Other Places I Have Lived

Siam, or the Woman Who Shot a Man

The Woman Who Walked on Water

Interviewing Matisse, or the Woman Who Died Standing Up

WOMAN
of ROME

A *Life of*
* ELSA MORANTE *

LILY TUCK

HARPER

An Imprint of HarperCollins*Publishers*
www.harpercollins.com

HarperCollins books may be purchased for educational, business, or sales promotional use. For information, please write: Special Markets Department, HarperCollins Publishers, 10 East 53rd Street, New York, NY 10022.

An extension of this copyright appears on page 264.

FIRST EDITION

Designed by Leah Carlson-Stanisic

Library of Congress Cataloging-in-Publication Data
Tuck, Lily.
Woman of Rome: a life of Elsa Morante / Lily Tuck.
p.   cm.
ISBN: 978-0-06-147256-5
1. Morante, Elsa, ca. 1912–1985.   2. Authors, Italian—20th century—Biography.   3. Women authors, Italian—20th century—Biography.
I. Title.
PQ4829.O615Z896   2008

853'.912—dc22   [B] 2007044647

08 09 10 11 12 WBC/RRD 10 9 8 7 6 5 4 3 2 1

CONTENTS

WOMAN

of ROME

·INTRODUCTION

Elsa Morante was not amiable, she was not genial, she was not sweet or always nice. She was not a woman with whom one could have a casual conversation or speak about mundane things. She took offense easily, she made quick and final judgments, she constantly tested her friends. A truth teller, she tended to say hurtful things. She was immensely talented, passionate, often impossible, courageous, quarrelsome, witty, ambitious, generous. She loved Mozart, she loved children, animals—especially, cats, Siamese cats. She detested any sort of artifice, posturing, falsehood, she detested the misuse of power. She once admitted that she detested biography. The biographer, she claimed, always divulged what one is not.

On a warm, sunny day in April 2005, I begin my search for Elsa and for the people who knew her by ringing the bell for the *portiere* of the nondescript, modern, yellow brick building at via dell'Oca 27, just off the Piazza del Popolo, where Elsa Morante once lived. It takes the *portiere* a while to answer me through the intercom.

"*Chi è? Chi è?*" she shouts. I try to explain in my halting Italian that I want to ask her something.

"*Momento,*" she finally says.

Looking up, I can see Elsa Morante's penthouse terrace, which is filled with potted plants: bougainvillea, oleander and lemon trees whose branches are falling over with fruit. Pigeons strut confidently on the sidewalk close to my feet and across the street a restaurant with an outdoor seating area is starting to fill up with noontime luncheon customers.

At last the *portiere* opens the front door for me.

"*Buon giorno, signora,*" I say. I also say that I hope I am not disturbing her before I go on to tell her that I am writing about Elsa Morante and ask if it would be possible for me to see the apartment where she lived.

The mention of Elsa Morante's name fills the *portiere* with sudden indignation. Rage, even. Her hands on her hips, she stands in front of me and shouts that yes, Elsa Morante lived in the building but she knows nothing about Elsa Morante! She has nothing to do with Elsa Morante! She could not care less about Elsa Morante! And moreover, she adds, can I not see that it is lunchtime? Still furious, she slams shut the front door of the building.

Of course, Elsa Morante is well-known in Italy but until recently—when there was a renewal of interest on the twentieth anniversary of her death—few Italians actually read much of her work. In some high schools, students are now obliged to read a few chapters of *La Storia (History)*, her best-known and longest novel. There are also the finely edited and handsome two volumes of her collected work published by Meridiani Mondadori. But, there is, to date, only one full-length study devoted to Morante's work (in English) and, until now, there has been no biography (in any language). It has been suggested that the reason for this is that Italy does not concern itself with the paraphernalia of literature: the correspondence, letters, the gossip about literary figures. It has also been pointed out that had Elsa Morante and her husband, Alberto Moravia, been French, they would have been as much celebrated as Jean-Paul Sartre and Simone de Beauvoir. Sadly, it is not surprising then that there is no plaque on Elsa Morante's apartment door, no monument to her, no street named after her. There is small comfort to be had in the knowledge that when Alberto Moravia—despite the fact that of the two writers, he was by far the more famous and enjoyed a great reputation throughout the world—was asked who was the most important writer of his generation, he was always quick to answer: Elsa Morante.

I first went to Rome as a child. In 1948, after the war, the film industry played a large role—far larger than literature—in determining the cultural life of the Eternal City, attracting film producers, directors, actors and technicians from all over the world to Rome. My father was such a person. Growing up, I loved spending my summers with my bachelor father. I loved the lack of supervision. I loved that I went horseback riding every afternoon at an elegant equestrian center on via Cassia. Once, briefly, I met Alberto Moravia. I had lunch at his house on the beach in Fregene. I don't remember the exact circumstances, only that I drove out with a friend, a young Chilean named Sergio, who knew Moravia or knew someone who knew him. It was a hot, overcast day and I went swimming. Afterward, as I was changing out of my bathing suit and standing naked about to step into my underwear, Moravia barged into the room without knocking. As far as I know (I am sure I would remember if I had), I never met Elsa Morante. However, I would like to think that our paths might have crossed at least once or twice: we might have passed each other on a street in Trastevere where ripe oranges drop from trees and bougainvillea bloom from terraces; we could have stood

browsing together, almost rubbing elbows, looking at the new
novels in Lion's, the English bookstore near Piazza di Spagna or
crossed each other on the Spanish Steps on the way to Trinità dei
Monti; or better yet, on warm summer evenings, we might have
sat at nearby tables at the Café de Paris, on the via Veneto, eating
our *gelato* and participating in that typical Roman pastime—
watching people go by.

I read *Arturo's Island*, Elsa Morante's second novel, when it was
first translated into English in 1959 while I was sunbathing on the
beach in Capri (and, who knows, Elsa, who loved to sunbathe,
might have been there as well)—not far from the island of
Procida, where the novel is set. Right away *Arturo's Island* became
a sort of cult book among many American college students as well
as one of my favorites. And although I did not necessarily iden-
tify with Arturo the protagonist—my life was primarily urban
and quite different from his—the book struck a deep chord. Also
the novel surprised and shocked me, I had never read anything
quite like it, and it made me curious about the author. I imagined
that she was mysterious and strange and very beautiful, which
Elsa Morante was—I think she had the sort of face which changes
constantly so that at times she appeared beautiful and at others
less so. And, finally, already as a young woman I knew that I
wanted to become a writer. A writer like Elsa Morante.

When I began this book, I did not immediately realize how
much, as a consequence of writing about Elsa, the years I lived in
Rome would affect and color these pages and that such a large
Pandora's box filled with my own memories would all of a sudden
open. Memories that have been made still more vivid by my many
recent visits to Rome—a city that has remained remarkably un-

changed and unmarked by the passage of time and where, to my immense pleasure, I have been able to recapture a part of my own past.

In the United States, Elsa Morante is virtually unknown. This book—an effort to re-create her life by means of research, interviews and a close reading of her work—attempts to bring more attention to her and to her oeuvre and to open that door which the *portiere*, whom I unwittingly disturbed during the sacred *ora di pranzo*, so rudely closed in my face.

one

TWO UNCLES

The year of Elsa Morante's birth is well known. But, as a
favor, in an autobiographical piece she wrote in 1960,
she has asked that her biographer not mention the date—not because
she is vain but because, for her, one year is as good as the next and she
would prefer to remain ageless.[1] It is the same year that the *Titanic* set
out on its doomed maiden voyage with 2,224 passengers and crew
members on board; the same year that Germany, the Austro-
Hungarian Empire and Italy renewed the Triple Alliance; the year
of the outbreak of the Balkan War, which set the stage for World
War I; the year the Olympic games were held in Stockholm and the
twenty-four-year-old Native American Jim Thorpe won both the
pentathlon and decathlon (he was later stripped of his medals when it
was learned that he had played semiprofessional baseball); in the
United States, the year that New Mexico and Arizona became states;
the year that the German geologist and meteorologist Alfred Lothar
Wegener proposed his theory of continental drift, arguing that the
earth's continents had once been a single large landmass and were
still in the process of change; and, finally, in Rome, the year that
the first activities of the Italian Boy Scouts, founded by Carlo Colombo and known as Giovani Esploratori Italiani, took place.

In a poem Elsa Morante wrote many years later, she claimed to
have been born of a "difficult love" at that "bitter hour at midday /
under the sign of Leo / on a Christian feast day."[2] She also claimed

in "Our Brother Antonio," a newspaper piece she published in
1939, that from the very day of their birth, she and her brothers all
showed themselves to be extraordinary paragons of virtue. She for
example was born with a crown of gold hair so thick and so long
that, immediately, the attending nurse who delivered her had to
braid and tie it with a blue ribbon.[3] (Photos, however, always show
Elsa with short, dark hair—so what, one wonders, could she have
been thinking of? And what, one also wonders, is true?) At the
time of Elsa's birth, the Morante family lived at via Anicia 7 but,
soon after, they moved to a small, squalid apartment on via
Amerigo Vespucci 42, located in the Testaccio, which was then a
working-class district of Rome. Later, Elsa Morante said she grew
up in the company of both poor and rich children (the latter no
doubt the children of the friends of Elsa's rich godmother, Donna
Gonzaga) and thus she learned not to judge anyone by social class
but by his or her kindness instead. In fact, the cruelest child she ever
met, who made her drink gasoline, was the son of a butler while the
nicest was a young patient at Gabelli (a famous Roman hospital
which treated only venereal diseases), which, in retrospect, made her
wonder what sort of pervert he may have been. Elsa learned the al-
phabet and learned to write at the same time. She claimed to have
composed her first poem when she was two and a half years old:

> *Un povero galletto*
> *che stava alla finestra*
> *gli casca giù la testa*
> *e va e va e va.*
> *Un gallo piccolino*
> *che stava alla finestra*
> *gli casca giù la testa*
> *e non vede più e più*

A little rooster
who was at the window
fell down on his head
and went and went and went.
A small little rooster
who was at the window
fell down on his head
and he nothing nothing sees.

Not only was Elsa Morante a self-taught prodigy, she invented herself. At an early age, too, Elsa Morante imagined herself as other, as a boy. A boy, she thought, could be heroic; a girl could not.

Elsa Morante was the oldest of four surviving children. An older brother, Mario, whom Elsa always inexplicably referred to as Antonio and to whom, later, she addressed her diary, died shortly after he was born. According to Elsa, this Mario/Antonio opened his eyes and saw the light and was so disgusted that he quickly closed them again. According to Elsa's mother, who spoke of him often, comparing him to a famous king, had Mario/Antonio lived, he would most certainly have become a prophet or a genius and brought honor to the family.[4] Elsa described her brother Aldo, who was two years younger, as lively and rebellious; she also said that Aldo had a large black birthmark on his forehead (but there is no sign of the birthmark on any of the photographs of him nor does Aldo's son, Paolo Morante, recall seeing a birthmark on his father's forehead[5]). Marcello, the younger brother, was timid and shy and, early on, according still to Elsa, was prone to amorous attachments; five or six minutes after he was born he developed one for the nurse who delivered him, grasping her finger and not letting go. Finally, there was Maria, the youngest child—younger than Elsa by ten years.

Elsa's mother, Irma Poggibonsi,* came from the town of Modena in northern Italy; she was a schoolteacher and had literary aspirations. She was also Jewish and since she was terrified of being discovered to be Jewish, she made sure her children got a Catholic education. (When World War II broke out, she changed her name to Bisi and went into hiding in Padua, taking the youngest, Maria, with her. Marcello was sent to Tuscany: Aldo was interned in a concentration camp; Elsa, by then, was living on her own in Rome.) Little is known of Irma's family. Her father was a hunchback whom everyone in the family was deeply ashamed of; Irma's mother had repeated breakdowns that manifested themselves in various ways: locking herself up in the bedroom and running back and forth, battering her head against the walls until either her head cracked open or she was knocked unconscious.

Irma's husband, Augusto Morante, was a Sicilian and the children's legal father. He worked as a probation officer at Aristide Gabelli, a boys' reform school located at Porta Portese, in Trastevere. Augusto Morante was deeply in love with Irma Poggibonsi and while he was courting her, he wrote her a little love song:

> *Irmina mia bella Irmina*
> *Irmina mia bella Irmina*
> *innamorato io son di te*

>> Irma my beautiful little Irma,
>> Irma my beautiful little Irma,
>> I am in love with you[6]

---

* Sometimes her surname is spelled Poggibonzi.

Unfortunately, in bed, he proved to be impotent. On their wedding night and on many of the subsequent nights, poor Augusto tried all sorts of positions, all kinds of arrangements, turning Irma this way and that. All to no avail. Irma made him pay dearly for this. (Asked later why she did not leave him, Irma answered that if she had, Augusto would have killed himself.) Not only did Irma treat Augusto with contempt, she humiliated him: making him sleep alone in a small room in the basement of the house and making him eat his meals separately from the rest of the family (Augusto ate lunch at eleven and dinner at five, the rest of the family ate lunch at one and dinner at eight). He was excluded from all family functions and social gatherings and holidays; his attempts to become part of the family were mocked and considered inappropriate. As a result, he grew more and more silent and solitary, his appearance grew shabbier and shabbier, and his body gave off a bad odor. Augusto's only pleasure (except the one Irma always accused him of and the reason, she also claimed, he was so hunched over) was cultivating the little land around the house and growing vegetables and flowers.

The origins of Elsa Morante's real father can only be guessed at.

But growing up, the Morante children had two uncles, both of whom were called Ciccio, the nickname for Francesco. The two uncle Ciccios were easy to tell apart. One Ciccio was tall, handsome and elegant, with bright blue eyes, and spoke in a musical baritone; the other Ciccio was ugly and had a large nose that dripped. The ugly Ciccio was a police officer and Augusto's brother, and he was known as the "true" uncle. The handsome Ciccio was not a relative but a family friend; he was known as the "false" uncle.

Of course, the "false" uncle turned out to be the children's real father.

The family secret—and the one she never admitted to—was that Irma fell in love with the handsome, "false" uncle. Difficult to resist him—his good looks, his sense of humor. And when he came to visit, usually once a month—sometimes, he even spent the night on the living room sofa—Ciccio brought the family expensive biscuits and sang them songs, genuine songs, not silly made-up ones, in his lovely baritone voice. Years later, after her husband, Augusto, had died, Irma tried to force Ciccio to come back to her but she only succeeded in blackmailing him into giving Aldo and Marcello money. The two boys remembered meeting Ciccio for coffee on Piazza della Rotonda. Eventually, Irma was told that Ciccio had committed suicide (this may or may not have been a ruse on his part to stop her from pursuing him).

The "false" uncle was Sicilian and his real name was Francesco Lo Monaco. Long before Irma confessed to the children, Elsa had guessed that he was her father. In any event, years before she learned the truth, Elsa, half joking, half serious, told everyone that she knew who her real father was—he was the Duke of Aosta.[7]*

Save for her large, dark, luminous eyes, Irma was not especially good-looking. She had short legs and a protruding stomach; worse, as she grew older, her face was covered with facial hair. More than anything, however, Irma had wanted a secure, settled life, a nice family and children. When this proved to be

---

* Morante was probably referring to Duke Emmanuel Philibert Aosta (1869–1931), who was one of Italy's most dashing and competent generals during World War I. He was the son of King Amadeo of Spain and the cousin of the Italian king Victor Emmanuel III.

impossible with her husband, she agreed to take on a surrogate partner, even though she claimed that the sexual act filled her with nausea. In fact, Irma forbade any reference to sex or to bodily functions in the family. She herself would go to the toilet only in the middle of the night when everyone was asleep, so that no one would hear her pee.

However, as a teacher, Irma had the reputation of being both dedicated and compassionate. She made a point of helping failing students and, when necessary, gave private lessons after school at no cost. At home, she did almost everything herself: cooking, cleaning, ironing. (For short periods of time, she hired servant girls but soon found fault with them and fired them.) As a result, Marcello, the youngest son, complained that the house was always dusty, dirty even, the clothes and linen never properly ironed. Irma's best efforts were reserved for her cooking.[8] When she was in a good mood, she liked to make up songs: one of them was about her children (Maria was not yet born); it began:

> *Della mia Elsuccia*
> *roseo è il colore*
> *Marcello è un angelo*
> *Aldo è un amore.*

> Of my little Elsa
> pink is the color
> Marcello is an angel
> Aldo is a darling[9]

Yet according to "the angel," Marcello, who wrote a family memoir, *Maledetta benedetta (Accursed and Blessed)*, which was published in 1986,* Irma was a shouter. She had violent, loud arguments with the children, with Aldo in particular. She made Aldo clean the rooms and do the heavy housework and not only did Aldo resent this but, suspecting that his mother thought him less intelligent than Elsa and Marcello, he was jealous. According to Marcello, the walls of the Monteverde house never ceased to reverberate with screams, insults and threats. Often, Irma and Aldo did not speak to each other for days, which resulted in Irma having to say something like "Elsa, can you tell Aldo that he must . . ." Or they left angry notes for each other on the kitchen table.† By most accounts, Irma's strategy was to make the children feel guilty by telling them all she was sacrificing for their sake; then, when they still appeared ungrateful, she would grow belligerent, even hysterical. The older she got, the worse her rages became. Often she was the one who threatened suicide. After a particularly violent outburst, Marcello recalled how he chased upstairs after his mother to her room, where he found her with a mouth full of pills.[10]

Aldo and Marcello had their fights too. One time, according to Marcello, Aldo kept his head painfully pressed to a step on the stairs for an entire afternoon. Elsa tried to protect Marcello, who was four years younger and timid. She included him in a club she

---

* This memoir, published shortly after Elsa's death, proved to be very divisive among the Morante family—the extended Morante family as well. It was how the children of the "true" Uncle Ciccio, the Morante children's cousins, learned that they were in fact not related to Elsa and her siblings. Maria Morante apparently did not speak to her brother Marcello for a year. She took the position that the book was "evil" and that it also completely misrepresented her mother.

† The antagonistic relationship between mother and son is contradicted by Paolo Morante's testimony. Likewise, Maria Morante remembers a mother who was both caring and compassionate.

had founded for her classmates, Club della Primavera, and took him on early morning walks while he admired and daydreamed about her. Later, Marcello admitted to being in love with Elsa as a child and fantasizing about her. For a long time, he hoped that Elsa reciprocated his feelings and it was not until one day when, sitting next to her on a bus, his body pressed up against hers, he finally understood that Elsa's affection for him was only sisterly.[11]

Elsa remained more or less immune to family quarrels and jealousies. For one thing, she had her own room. No one was supposed to enter her room, which was always very untidy. Elsa never bothered to make her bed, she left her clothes scattered on the floor. Irma protected her. She was proud of her daughter's precocity and was always pushing her forward and had gone as far as to seek the patronage of a wealthy aristocrat named Donna Maria Guerrieri Gonzaga.* Elsa went to live with Donna Gonzaga for months at a time in her villa in the elegant Roman district of Nomentano; in addition to a beautiful villa, Donna Gonzaga had an expensive car, a chauffeur, several servants and a pedigreed dog.[12] It seems she had taken a fancy to the child, whom Irma was determined to raise above her social station and determined to turn into someone special.

But talk of any kind of happy childhood for the three older Morante children seems almost incidental—for Marcello, especially, who remembered his childhood as a time filled with gloom and unhappiness, which marred the rest of his life.[13]

In 1922 the family moved to Monteverde, to via Camillo de

---

* It is not clear how Donna Gonzaga became Elsa Morante's godmother. Marcello Morante suggests in his memoir that perhaps his mother had met her through a Jesuit priest, Father Tacchi-Venturi.

Lellis 10. Situated in the middle of a block in what now looks to be a relatively poor neighborhood that is dominated by a large municipal hospital complex, the Morante family house is a three-story, orange stucco building surrounded by a high wall. The house looks shabby and neglected and it has been divided up into four apartments. Peering through the gate, one can see a small garden shaded by a very tall palm tree, the sole distinctive and decorative sight on the street. But when the Morante family lived there, according to Elsa's sister, Maria, the house had a large garden and was surrounded by fields. Maria Morante also recalled how Elsa would often take her on walks through those fields and, to keep her from flagging or complaining—Maria was only four or five years old at the time—Elsa would tell her stories. Maria remembered one story in particular, since she was its inspiration. The story was about how babies, before they are born, have no hearts and live on stars—except for one particular baby who got a heart from a nightingale, just before the bird died. It began: "This story was told to me by Mariolina" (Mariolina was Elsa's nickname for her sister). In addition, Maria Morante remembers how, when the story was published, Elsa, who had already left home and was living alone in a small room, supporting herself, spent the 1000 lire—a substantial amount at the time— she was paid for the story on a huge Christmas tree, which was so tall the top had to be chopped off so that it could fit inside the Monteverde house, and on presents for everyone in the family, as well as for all of Maria's friends.[14]

During our visit, Maria Morante showed me a photo that dates from around that period. Maria Morante, aged four or five, sits on Elsa's lap; their two brothers stand on either side of them, and over a dozen children, probably the rest of Maria's school class, are seated all around them. One cannot make out Elsa Morante's face, as Elsa has scratched it out—no doubt it was not a flattering photograph.

Now in her mideighties, Maria Morante lives alone in a modest apartment in the Monte Sacro district of Rome. When she opened the door, I was immediately struck by her physical resemblance to Elsa—the broad shape of her face and wide mouth. Although seemingly still robust, quite garrulous and disposed to be hospitable, she was not very forthcoming about her sister. Her remarks were cautious and protective. She did, however, praise Elsa's enormous capacity for generosity and spoke of how Elsa was able to observe and describe children and how, although childless herself, she understood their most intimate thoughts. Maria said her own son, Luca, three years old at the time, was the model for Giuseppe in Elsa's novel *History*, recalling the way he spoke baby talk and the peculiar way he waved his arms to say hello.

Irma, Maria maintained, was a serious, dedicated mother and teacher. She was a good friend of Maria Montessori and taught her methods in school (to this day, apparently, Irma's pupils still telephone Maria to tell her how fondly they remember her mother as a teacher). The fact that Irma had a full-time job, four children and little household help meant that she was not able to pursue her own career of choice, which was that of a journalist. But more important, she loved her children and if she could be faulted at all it would be that she loved Elsa and Aldo more than she loved Marcello and Maria—the two younger children were relegated to a second tier. And only at the end of our interview together did Maria Morante allow how as a family things changed for them as they grew older. Although they continued to love one another as brothers and sisters, they each led separate lives and no strong bond existed to keep them together.[15]

As for Elsa's brother Marcello, his eldest son, Daniele,

remembered how Elsa used to bring gifts for everyone at Christmas until one year she suddenly stopped coming. The reason, Daniele Morante guesses, was that she realized that Marcello had literary ambitions—he was a writer and he wrote several plays, which were actually well received and won prizes—and he was very competitive. Although not jealous or threatened by him, Elsa sensed that Marcello was in competition with her and this more than anything deeply disturbed her. Also, it did not correspond to the image she had of him as a younger brother. However, when in 1973 Marcello traveled from his home in Tuscany to undergo major surgery, Elsa was very attentive. Nevertheless, they soon fell out once again when Marcello wanted to introduce Elsa to a painter friend and, misconstruing this, Elsa accused Marcello of trying to take advantage of her and her artist friends. As a result, they did not see each other often. Despite the ups and downs, Daniele Morante was Elsa Morante's favorite nephew and one can see why. He is a gentle and mild-mannered man who is also very soft-spoken—so soft, in fact, that later I had trouble hearing him on my tape recorder.[16]

Although accounts vary on how affected or preoccupied she was by it, Elsa Morante's attitude toward her family throughout her life seems to have remained conflicted—especially, not surprisingly, her attitude to her mother. Apparently Elsa often spoke about her mother and yet it is clear from what she said that she wanted her mother to be different. She wanted her mother to be more refined in her bearing as well as her appearance, which was shabby and ordinary. Elsa had an expectation that was not fulfilled by the reality and this made for a complicated relationship. In addition, Elsa was afraid of her mother because she felt Irma's envy, which manifested itself as an ambivalence that Elsa could not bear—a feeling of both love and hate that today would be called passive-aggressive. No doubt, Marcello, especially, and Maria as well shared these ambivalent feelings toward their more well-known sister. Always Elsa maintained that she would have preferred to be either loved or hated and that uncertainty troubled her. She could not stand people who were falsely humble or felt disappointed in their lives. That was the reason probably she always loved her brother Aldo—not because he was successful but because he was satisfied with his life and was not jealous of hers. In other words, she wanted to have a different sort of family, a magnificent and happy family.[17]

Monteverde, where the Morante family lived, is located on the west bank of the Tiber River and remains much the same as it was in Elsa's childhood, except that it is more built up and populated. The nondescript apartment houses are, for the most part, cheaply built; the few older stucco-walled villas and their gardens are protected by high cement walls and imposing iron gates, but a lot of them, like the Morante house, are now divided into apartments. The more affluent-looking streets are lined with oleander trees and the general feeling one gets from Monteverde is middle-class respectability. A few minutes' walk away, through Porta San Pancrazio, stands the Gianicolo or Janiculum Hill, a favorite destination for both visitors and locals. Here are embassies, diplomatic residences, academies and large romantic-looking villas that can be glimpsed behind high walls and perfectly trimmed hedges. Surely, on warm spring Sunday afternoons when the Roman sky was a cloudless Canaletto blue, poor Augusto, in one of his many awkward attempts to establish an affectionate relationship, took the children for a walk along the Aurelian Wall and down the Passagio del Gianicolo to show them the imposing equestrian monument of Giuseppe Garibaldi, the hero (along with Cavour and Mazzini) of the Italian unification known as the Risorgimento.

(The monument to his wife, Anita, who fought bravely by his side, also depicted on horseback and set a few yards below him, would not be erected for several more years.) Standing there on the large open piazza, they would have had a splendid view of the city spread out below them—from Castel Sant'Angelo, to the great white mass of the newly built Law Courts, to the dome of San Giovanni dei Fiorentini, the two belfries of the Trinità dei Monti, the Quirinal Place behind the dome of the Pantheon all the way to the church of San Pietro in Montorio. The children would probably have gotten a treat, as well, a *gelato*. For them, no doubt, like for Manuel, the protagonist in Elsa Morante's last novel, *Aracoeli*, the appearance of the ice cream wagon was "hailed with acclaim and rejoicing, almost as if an altar on four wheels were presented before us." The ice cream vendor, too, was described as a poet and he expressed himself with this rhyme:

> *Qui c'è il Regno del Gelo ʒuccherato!*
> *Tutto crema e cioccolato!*
> *Chi vuole il Cono!*
> *Corri ch'è buono!*

> This is the kingdom of sugar and ice,
> Vanilla and chocolate and everything nice!
> Romans, fulfill your dream
> With a cone of Norge ice cream![18]

From there, Augusto and the Morante children must have walked back past the Villa Doria Pamphili, now a vast park, and continued around the corner where the road opens onto a wide crossing and where Porta Aurelia, which marked the beginning of the Aurelian Way, once stood. Porta Aurelia was rebuilt and renamed Porta San Pancrazio in 1854 (after the nearby church of St.Pancras) and was the site of the 1849 battle between Garibaldi and his Roman troops against the French as they attempted to defend the short-lived Roman Republic. When the time came to go home, Augusto was pleased and proud to make use of the single name he had invented to call the three children: *"Marcelsado! Marcelsado!"*[19]

Augusto would die shortly after the Second World War. During his final illness, Irma, his wife, allowed him to move upstairs and sleep on the living room sofa, where he breathed his last. The children rarely came to visit him—for instance, Elsa did just once. After his death, Irma sold the Monteverde house and moved into an apartment in the same building where Maria and her husband resided. Irma lived to be nearly eighty-three and died, probably of stomach cancer, in a nursing home in Viterbo, in 1963. Again, the children—all but Maria—hardly ever went to visit her there. During one of Elsa's rare visits, a nun at the clinic complained to Elsa about her "indecent" clothes (Elsa was wearing trousers). After her mother died, Elsa organized a very elaborate and expensive funeral, using up much of her mother's money and justifying it by saying that that was what Irma would have wanted.

Aldo married twice and was a successful economist and banker. He spent many years living and working abroad: first in Mexico, then in Venezuela, where he opened a branch of the Banca Commerciale Italiana; and finally opening another branch in Beijing (apparently he lived in an apartment right off Tiananmen Square and witnessed the shootings in 1989; some of the bullets went through his windows). According to his son, Paolo, Aldo had an almost photographic memory and he could recite *The Divine Comedy* by heart; he also always maintained a very cordial relation with Elsa.[20] Marcello took up several professions, including the law, journalism, politics and the theater; he had ten children (one of whom is the actor Laura Morante). Maria married and divorced and had one child, Luca. She is a member of the Communist Party and until recently was an active union leader.

two

SECRET GAMES

At the age of five, Elsa Morante wrote out her poems in a little blue-lined school notebook. Her handwriting is sure and tidy, her letters are perfectly formed. Never once does she deviate from the lines on the page that indicate the height of the capitals or of the lowercase letters, no errors or erasures can be seen. Verses like:

> *Senti mamina*
> *Disse Celestina*
> *quanto torna del lavoro*
> *portami un bel drappo d'oro*

> Listen mother dear
> Said Celestina
> when you return from work
> bring me a beautiful cloth of gold

scan and rhyme perfectly and are illustrated with colorful and intricately drawn little figures of people and animals. In addition, Elsa—no fool—indicated the price for her book on its cover: 3.5 lire. The notebook is an exquisite piece of childish art and it is also surprisingly sophisticated. Turning the pages, it is hard to believe that it is the work of such a young child and right away, too, one is struck by both Elsa Morante's imagination and her thoroughness. Even more surprising is the fact that the child was completely self-taught—she did not attend elementary school. Her intention, she said, to become a writer originated with her birth. Later, she confessed that she also had once dreamt of being a dancer, a ballerina. A dream, she said, she never told anyone about as, her whole life, she was a terrible dancer.[1]

After the Morante family moved to Monteverde in 1922, Elsa was enrolled in the local middle school, where she wrote a musical play. When the headmistress introduced the play, she was so filled with emotion she could hardly speak. The headmistress did, however, manage to say how the words the audience members were about to hear were written by a child who was in the room and that they, the audience, were in the presence of a genius.[2] Marcello, Elsa's youngest brother, was supposed to have a part in the play, but at the last moment he got stage fright and wet his pants.

Elsa Morante was always first in her class and the other children gave her presents, sweets and bits of chocolate, so that they could copy her work. In spite of all the attention, Elsa was never quite satisfied. She considered herself awkward, ugly and too thin. She was in fact anemic. She described her face as being as pale as a washed-out doll's and the curly hair that framed it as being as black as a crow's wing. Her blue eyes too were always ringed with dark circles. At school, she was jealous of one girl in particular, a wealthy classmate named Giacinta. Giacinta was not very smart but she was very pretty and athletic. She also had a closet full of clothes, while Elsa's own clothes were always in disarray, missing a button or the hem of her dress was falling down. But since, as Elsa would explain later, she had a hypocritical and devious heart, she pretended to like Giacinta—to her face she was nice to Giacinta but behind her back she made fun of her. One time, for example, Elsa forced poor Giacinta to play a game in which she had to extract herself from hell, go to purgatory, then on to paradise by obeying Elsa's arbitrary commands, which consisted of repeating the word *misericordia* three hundred times. This and other bits of childish cruelty would prompt the adult Elsa to write, "Still today, if I think of my poor victim, who, like a meek and gentle lamb, had to endure torture, I am overcome by remorse. Forgive me, Giacinta."[3]

Games played an important role in Elsa Morante's early life. At home, with Aldo and Marcello, she invented the "Game of Gentlemen." The three children swore one another to secrecy and to tell no one—not even their mother. Elsa assigned each of them a role: Elsa played the leading character, a noble, handsome count named Villa Guidicini; Aldo played a gentleman and Marcello played a servant or the cook. Fascinated by the traditions of old aristocratic families, their mansions, their antiques and their silver, Elsa made up the episodes along those themes. She wrote and directed a draft each day, like a soap opera, and the children would then improvise. The game included a newspaper in which Elsa published poems and in which Marcello, the cook, published recipes. For a time, Aldo and Marcello obeyed her completely. After two years, however, Aldo grew bored and began a parallel game of his own, without Elsa. Lying in bed at night, he and Marcello fantasized about women. According to Marcello, Aldo got all the beautiful ones and he, Marcello, got the ugly ones; in one game, a woman named Ileana was so beautiful that Marcello was not even allowed to speak to her. In view of the contentious atmosphere in the Morante household, it is not difficult to imagine how these games may have provided the means for the three Morante children to explore forbidden subjects.

"Il gioco secreto" ("The Secret Game"), written by Elsa in 1941, appears to illustrate this. In the story, three aristocratic children named Antonietta, Pietro and Giovanni (who are the same number of years apart as were Elsa, Aldo and Marcello) invent a parallel life. The game is played at night in secret and when, too excited, the children cannot sleep. During one particularly sleepless night, Antonietta and Giovanni kiss and are transformed: Antonietta's dark hair turns into beautiful blond tresses, her shabby nightgown becomes a sumptuous robe, her purse is transformed into gold, while Giovanni is grown tall, his pallid, sickly cheeks are a rosy, healthy pink. But all of sudden the mother walks into the room and discovers them; the game is over and all that is left is ordinary reality: "three ugly children."

Growing up, Elsa always maintained that she would have preferred to have been born a boy. The reason, too, she gave much later in a 1957 letter to a friend (at the same time that she warned him "not to laugh"), for writing her novel *Arturo's Island* was her "old, incurable desire to be a boy . . . and to return to the condition I once had loved and lost and which I seem to remember."[4] A boy, according to Elsa Morante—and no doubt at the time she was right—had a greater spirit of adventure and a greater opportunity to be heroic. She preferred the company of boys to that of girls, although this did not mean that she felt more solidarity with one over the other. Her feeling of solidarity, she claimed, encompassed all humans worthy of respect without having to distinguish their gender. Also, she was aware that there existed a kind of sexism toward women. In France and the United States, for example, women, she pointed out, not only give up their last names but are known by the name of their husbands: Mrs. Robert Smith. In Switzerland, women still did not have the vote. Another distinction she strongly disapproved of was that between *scrittori* and *scrittici*; why then, she asked, were there not other categories like: blond and brunette writers, fat and thin ones?[5]

Until she was fifteen, Elsa Morante wrote poems and stories for children, which she illustrated and which were later collected and published under the title *Le bellissime avventure di Caterì dalla trecciolina e altre storie (The Marvelous Adventures of Cathy with the Long Tresses and Other Stories)*. Her favorite poet then was Baudelaire and to read his poems, she taught herself French. She attended the prestigious, avant-garde high school Visconti e Mamiani in the city center, where she received an excellent classical education and learned, along with other subjects, how to read both ancient Greek and Latin. During that time, she was often sent away from home for months at a time to stay with her rich godmother, Donna Gonzaga, in her elegant Nomentano villa. However if, on some occasions, Donna Gonzaga appeared derelict in her duties or if she momentarily forgot about Elsa, Elsa's mother was quick to remind her and quick also to solicit financial support from her. First Irma would write Donna Gonzaga a warm letter filled with expressions of trust, which ended with a request for money. If no answer or money seemed to be forthcoming, Irma would write a second letter describing her poverty and Elsa's poor health. Finally, as a last resort, Irma would write angrily and threateningly, reminding Donna Gonzaga of her duty as a Christian and as Elsa's godmother (perhaps she even threatened to spread malicious gossip about her) so that, in the end, Donna Gonzaga always had to give in.[6] Poor Donna Gonzaga. Except for a dream in which Donna Gonzaga seems to be testing Elsa to see if she has stolen one of her rings, she is rarely ever mentioned or acknowledged during Elsa Morante's adult life. It is as if the woman or her kindnesses had never existed.

As an adolescent, Elsa spent her summers at various seaside

resorts. Each year the resorts grew more luxurious, thanks to Irma's frantic efforts (and to Donna Gonzaga's generosity) to try to organize a pleasant environment for children who were bored and frustrated and did not want to participate in any of the summer activities. Elsa always loved the sea although she never learned to swim. She loved to sunbathe and later in life, on various trips to the islands of Ponza and Procida, she often hired a boat to take her to a deserted beach so that she could sunbathe nude in privacy. On the cover of Marcello Morante's memoir, *Maledetta benedetta*, there is a photograph showing the four children in their bathing suits. Elsa looks to be fifteen or sixteen; she wears a woolen maillot and has a long strand of pearls around her neck. With one hand she is coquettishly holding her hat, she is smiling and seems to be clowning for the photographer. Marcello has his arms folded over his bare chest and is looking down, a half smile on his face. Maria stands between Elsa and Marcello, looking small and childish, her arms behind her back, her face solemn, nearly expressionless (for some reason, she has pulled down the top of her bathing suit so that she too is bare chested and could be mistaken for a little boy). Finally, there is Aldo, who sits on the ground at the others' feet, looking stern and handsome (there is no sign of the black birthmark on his forehead).

By the time the last family summer holiday was spent on the Argentario peninsula at elegant Porto Santo Stefano, both Elsa and Aldo had become very independent; they came and went whenever and at whatever time they liked. Elsa was seeing a wealthy, well-born boy and when, later that year, he came to visit her in the house in Monteverde, Marcello was proud to be made the lookout and an accomplice to her illicit affair.[7] Also, during that last holiday, Irma managed to introduce Elsa to a man named Guelfo Civinini who was an editor at the newspaper *Corriere della*

Sera. Later, however, when Civinini lost interest in Elsa for reasons that are unclear, Irma, who was always determined to play a role in Elsa's career as well as earn her daughter's gratitude, threatened to blackmail him by accusing him of sleeping with Elsa. Thanks to him, however, Elsa was able to publish her first piece, "Story of Children and of Stars," in an important paper. She was eighteen at the time.

By then, too, Elsa Morante had begun to distance herself from her mother while her mother, no doubt aware that she was losing control over her precocious daughter, became even more tenacious. In an attempt perhaps to compete with Elsa, Irma wrote a story called "Sogna e Vita" ("Dream and Life") that was published in a magazine called *La Scuola (The School)*. Irma, clearly, wanted to live through her daughter although at the same time her envy may have taken the form of wanting Elsa to live primarily for her. Meanwhile, feeling more and more oppressed by her mother's constant interference, Elsa stayed away from home as often as she could. One night Elsa did not come home at all and her mother, in a panic, telephoned a friend to find out where Elsa was—although Elsa had expressly forbidden her to do so. This precipitated a terrible scene between the two women. When Irma had finally gone to bed, still angry, Elsa wrote the word *maledetta* (accursed) on a piece of paper and slipped it under her mother's door; a few hours later, she must have had a change of heart, for she wrote *benedetta* (blessed) on another piece of paper, which she also slipped under her mother's door. These two words were to become the title of Marcello Morante's memoir and also, no doubt, were apt indications of Elsa's complicated feelings toward her mother, a subject she would often return to in her fiction.

At eighteen, without ever attending university, Elsa left home for good. She rented a furnished room near Piazza Venezia, in corso Umberto. Carlo Levi, the author of *Christ Stopped at Eboli*, visited her there once after Elsa had published two stories in the newspaper *Meridiano di Roma*. He described her room as being very small and her bed enormous. As for Elsa, he said that she was not yet a woman: "what with her violet eyes, her small, wide face, her timid smile which uncovered her tiny gapped teeth, and her gray hair, ruffled and disorderly."[8] Alberto Moravia, her future husband, who met Elsa soon thereafter, described her in similar terms—"She had had white hair since adolescence, a big mushroom of hair above her round face"—and since all the photos of Elsa, except those taken in the last years of her life, show her with very dark hair, she must have begun dyeing her hair when she was very young. Italo Calvino, in fact, used to joke that he knew Elsa when she *still* had white hair. "She was very nearsighted," Moravia continued; "she had beautiful eyes with the dreamy gaze of the near-sighted. She had a little nose, and a big willful mouth. A rather childish face."[9] On another occasion Moravia compared Elsa Morante's face to an apple.

The next ten years were not an easy time for Elsa Morante. In fact, it is hard to imagine how she was able to survive at all on her own in a Catholic country where extremely conservative values were still the norm. Young Italian middle-class women lived at home with their parents and not in apartments alone, they waited to get married and did not try to pursue a career on their own. Their lives were defined by their family, and especially by their father (or a male who assumed the role of patriarch) who ruled absolutely at the same time that he protected his wife and children. Who, one wonders, protected Elsa Morante during that time? Even in the early fifties when I first spent time in Rome, a young woman could not walk down the street, ride a bus, without some predatory man following and accosting her. One cannot help but imagine how Elsa, a teenager still, living alone and nearly penniless, must have fallen prey to all kinds of unsavory and opportunistic characters and disagreeable situations. And who, one also wonders, were the models she turned to for guidance? It would appear that during this period she relied almost entirely on literature for her ideas and for the life she was struggling to create for herself.

To make matters more difficult, Italy was suffering the effects of the Great Depression, which included a recession and inflation due in part to Italy's lack of industry. The political climate in the 1930s was volatile, as well as increasingly repressive. Fascism had taken root—particularly after the Italian victory over Ethiopia—and Fascist customs and Fascist language were being enforced: a salute replaced a handshake, the familiar *tu* replaced the more formal *lei*; bands of Blackshirts prowled the city, marching with the exaggerated high step they called *passo romano* (not unlike the German goose step). The diplomatic relationship between Italy, Britain and France deteriorated while the relationship between Mussolini and Hitler solidified into a military alliance, primarily to ensure Franco's victory in Spain as well as to guarantee territorial concessions from France and Britain in the Mediterranean and in North Africa. And, finally, in 1938, there was the enactment of the racial laws in Italy that forbade racial intermarriage and excluded Jews from government offices and certain professions.

A diary Elsa Morante kept at that time recorded her dreams. Although the entries are intermittent, they illustrate how socially vulnerable and inadequate she felt and how lonely—so lonely, in fact, that she claimed she had to resort to telephoning the number that gives the correct time in order to hear the sound of a human voice. She did, however, have many love affairs. She identifies her lovers in her diary only by their initials and very few of them seemed to have brought her any pleasure or satisfaction. One man is identified: blond Willy Coppens, who may have been the father of a child Elsa had to abort. This unfortunate experience has never been confirmed nor have more details emerged; the only thing certain on the subject is that all her life Elsa Morante either claimed she regretted not having had children or said she could not have any (again, perhaps, the result of a botched abortion).

Mostly she was very poor and often went hungry. To help support herself, she gave Latin and Italian lessons. Later, Morante also acknowledged quite openly—without shame or remorse and only to describe the dire necessity of it—having occasionally resorted to prostitution for money. She felt neither sullied nor emotionally scarred by this experience. Nevertheless, it must have played an important role in how Morante understood the lives of the poor, the underprivileged and the powerless.

Remarkably, she also managed to write stories that appeared regularly in such popular magazines and weekly newspapers as *Corriere dei Piccoli*, *Oggi* and *Meridiano di Roma*. Most of these stories—about 120 in all—are no longer than a page or two and must have been written for immediate publication; in fact, many read like essays, particularly those written under her pseudonym, Antonio Carrera. In "I fidanzati" ("The Betrothed"), for instance, she describes different types of engaged couples, among whom the male is known in some circles as a *scalasedia* or "seat warmer," as his role is to sit quietly and patiently and wait for the girl to come and sit next to him. Another short piece, "Parenti serpenti" ("Snake Relatives"), describes the author's ambivalent feelings toward *his* numerous, disparate relatives, saying, for instance, that his great-aunt Stefania's dyed black hair, small face and tiny eyes remind him of a fly.

The early stories written under Elsa Morante's own name seem more like fables. However, unlike most fables, their moral is ambiguous. In the story, "Il soldato del re" ("The King's Soldier"), neither the king nor his faithful soldier, who is sent to look for the perfect girl to be the king's wife, ends up with the perfect girl (whom the soldier does, in fact, find). In "La vigna" ("The Vineyard"), events are again turned upside down: the baby named in honor of his uncle, the owner of the vineyard, does not inherit the vineyard as hoped—precisely because he was named after his uncle—and the vineyard is left abandoned and its sour grapes are harvested by the birds. Among these early stories, one in particular stands out: "Qualcuno bussa alla porta" ("Someone Is Knocking at the Door"), not only for its odd title (although with each new section, someone does come a-knocking) but also for its length (at 25,000 words, it was more like a novella). Published in installments in *I Diritti della Scuola* (The School Dues), this tale within a tale within another tale tells the story (among many others) of Michele Wogau, a handsome, reclusive aristocrat. Overly possessive and jealous of his beautiful young wife, he kills her, a deed for which he can never forgive himself. Meanwhile a young woman, Mirtilla, falls in love with a handsome ne'er-do-well and becomes pregnant; after the ne'er-do-well abandons her, she abandons the child. The child, Lucia, is adopted by Wogau and raised in virtual isolation in an elegant large house and garden; although Lucia does not love her foster reclusive father, she respects him. She falls in love with Franco, a poor young pianist, whom she marries. Their life together is difficult but in the end Franco composes a masterpiece. In the last installment, Lucia, on a feast day, is drawn almost magically to a beautiful island, leaving behind her husband and her newborn child (it is not clear whether she does so for good). On the island, she meets a gypsy who is singing and dancing in the village square—her mother, Mirtilla.

The importance of this rather loose-ended, predictable but confused story lies in the many themes it introduces that will reappear in Elsa Morante's novels: the abandoned children raised in isolation in semimagical places, the destructive power of possessive parental love and the not so redemptive quality of conjugal love. Her repeated use of certain settings, too, will become familiar: islands as paradise, beautiful gardens, the sea, certain animals who take on human traits (dogs and roosters in particular) and her attaching significance and making much of the contrast between dark and blue eyes, and black and blond hair.[10]

Fifteen very, very short and slight stories (most of them autobiographical) appeared in the weekly newspaper *Oggi* and included "Prima della classe" ("First in Her Class"), an account of how although she was first in her class, none of the children really liked her except for one little boy whose name, coincidentally, was Amore and who loved Elsa not for her brain but for her beautiful curly hair. Another, "Lettere d'amore" ("A Love Letter"), is an amusing description of how she once wrote a letter to Charles Lindbergh, the aviator, that attempted to lure him with a promise of a trip, for just the two of them, to a deserted island where a house with a piano awaited, as well as a vegetable garden and some chickens. "Domestiche" ("The Servants") is a candid and telling look at the Morante family's servants and also corroborates Marcello Morante's account of how inept and insensitive their mother, Irma, was in dealing with them: "Like noisy birds who land on the windowsill to pick up some crumbs and then after a flutter and a chirp vanish again into the horizon, so did our servants pass through our lives. Filled with the zest for life, vivacious and plump, they presented themselves full of good intentions. We could hear them singing while they did the dishes. . . . After a week, all our maids had become thin, thin. Some would sob and beat their heads against the wall. One maid cried: Good-bye, youth, and fainted." [11]

In 1941, a collection of twenty stories by Elsa Morante, most of which had previously appeared in newspapers, was published by Garzanti under the title *Il gioco segreto (The Secret Game)*. The stories are still slight but lengthier than her earliest ones; the subject matter is more fleshed out and certainly darker—old age, illness and death. What the characters in these stories all seem to have in common is their pathology; they all suffer or are ill in some perverse or sadistic way. Also, all are obsessed with family—questioning the institution and its social rituals: marriage, baptism and funeral rites. The women, too, have a hyperfeminine vision as they set out to explore the secrets of female vanity: jewelry, hair, clothes. In addition, since she was a great admirer of Kafka and influenced by him, Elsa Morante's method of mixing the picturesque and the squalid with the fantastic and the magical was an effort at a kind of surrealism. It was also an effort to escape from the constraints of the literature of the *Novecento* (nineteenth century), which had become identified with *verismo* (the Italian school of naturalism) whose aesthetics, as stated by Luigi Capuana and Giovanni Verga, both well-known southern Italian writers, equated realism with truth and precluded any self-consciousness in favor of presenting the story in the most objective manner possible.

In another piece Morante wrote in 1938, "Mille città in una" ("A Thousand Cities in One"), published in Curzio Malaparte's* magazine, *Prospettive*, she asks: "Is there a concrete reality of the world that exists per se, or do we have nothing but an infinity of appearances, a different one for each subjective eye?"[12] This essay introduces two other themes that will figure large in her work: travel as a mode of self-exploration and the juxtaposition between inner and outer reality; it also shows how familiar, early on, Morante was with the works of Nietzsche and Schopenhauer. And although most Italian critics were not yet particularly interested in her work, by the mid-1930s, Elsa Morante had become friends with a major critic, Giacomo Debenedetti, who was the translator of Proust and an editor at *Meridiano di Roma*. In time, too, as her stories became more polished, Alberto Savinio—his real name was Andrea De Chirico and his brother was the painter Giorgio De Chirico—who was an important magic realist writer, understood the potential power of her writing. A later critic compared Elsa Morante's early stories to the paintings of Edvard Munch[13]—to *The Scream*, more than likely.

---

* Curzio Malaparte was a well-known and controversial writer who, until the fall of Mussolini, was an active member of the Fascist Party. He is also remembered for the extraordinary modern house, Casa Malaparte, he built on a windswept cliff on the island of Capri.

three

DIARY 1938

For six months in 1938, twenty-six-year-old Elsa Morante kept a record of her dreams in a school notebook that took the form of a diary. She named the diary "Letters to Antonio" ("Lettere ad Antonio") and the "Antonio" she addresses—although there is only a single reference to him—must necessarily be her brother Mario, who died soon after he was born and who, according to Elsa, "opened his eyes and saw the light and was so disgusted that he quickly closed them again." "Letters" is a misnomer as well since none of the entries are written in the form of a letter. A quote from Dante on the opening page provided Elsa Morante with the epigraph: "Soon it will be, that to behold these things / Shall not be grievous, but delightful to thee / As much as nature fashioned thee to feel." [1] Next to it, she also wrote "Book of Dreams" ("Libro dei sogni") and "Life Is a Dream" ("La vida es sueño"), no doubt a reference to Pedro Calderón de la Barca.

The diary can be read as a quest for Elsa Morante's identity as a woman. Without following the traditional format of autobiography or memoir, it reveals her by exposing her dreams, which are filled with erotic content and desire. The significance of the diary lies in both Morante's interpretation of these dreams and her acute observations, as well as in her constant search for meaning. Not surprisingly, Elsa Morante was very interested in and conversant with the science of psychoanalysis, and with Freud's works in particular. Among the books in her very extensive library, there is a tattered French copy of *Introduction to Psychoanalysis* in which many passages that specifically deal with the interpretation of dreams have been underscored and heavily annotated. In addition, dreams were to figure often and with importance in Morante's work, and many critics have claimed that *Diario 1938* (as it was called when it was published in 1989*) was the source for and the essence of her future novels, especially *House of Liars*.

Although the entries are uneven and discontinuous—Morante wrote fairly regularly at first but less later on—she was by then too much of an accomplished author to let the writing be merely a cathartic outpouring. Instead Elsa Morante's diary is a highly self-aware exploration of both her consciousness and her physical needs—that is, her sexual desire, which is expressed, despite the heavy use of asterisks to conceal the most private or shocking sexual details, in fairly candid terms. The diary is a testimony to Elsa's lucidity, her ability to overcome her secret passions and unsatisfied longings thanks to what one critic called her "intelligent libido." [2] Yet the writing in the diary, as has also been pointed out, suggests none of the *jouissance* or delight in the experiences of the body so celebrated by feminist writers of the period, such as Anaïs Nin. Instead, Morante's investigation of her complicated and often contradictory feelings and emotions are full of anguish and

---

* The decision in 1989 by Einaudi to publish Elsa Morante's diary generated a certain amount of controversy over whether the publication was appropriate, considering that it was both a disorganized text and a private record. It was also presumed that the publication would not have been sanctioned by Morante herself.

guilt. Likewise, her depiction of femininity is, for the most part, one that is unhappy, wounded and unreconciled with itself.[3]

The diary begins:

Evidently, my dear Antonio, every day my life becomes more stupid, subject to and tormented by physical needs: material and sexual. I am aware of them in my dreams. Yesterday, a closed room facing my actual apartment, but inside a garden. I know that it is E.C.'s.* But why E.C.? Because one time on the telephone he told me that ******. These days I burn with desire for ****** for hours I think about ************. Their poses are extraordinarily lascivious or rather their ********. Nothing more than, for hours and hours, my spirit is slave to these obscene, little pastimes which give me the feeling of death. [January 19]

Nor does Morante shy away from describing intimate female experiences: "As I walk, I can feel that I have started to menstruate. A weight, liquid, soft and hot, in between my legs, everything weighs on me. Never mind, I keep walking . . . as drops of blood fall from in between my heavy legs." [January 19]

The year before Elsa began her diary, she had met Alberto Moravia. They fell in love and he appears in her diary as "A." Moravia's career as a writer had already been established with the publication of his first novel, *Gli indifferenti (The Time of Indifference)*, in 1929. One of the most influential Italian writers of the twentieth century, Moravia would go on to publish over thirty

---

* The initials E.C. have not been identified.

novels, the most famous of which are *The Woman of Rome*, *Conjugal Love*, *Two Women* and *The Conformist*. Written in stark prose, the novels' main themes are alienation, loveless sexuality and hypocrisy, especially in the institution of marriage, and the difficulty of finding happiness therein. Most of Moravia's books have been translated and many have been made into films. He also wrote for many of Italy's leading newspapers (*La Stampa*, *Il Mondo* and *Corriere della Sera*) and founded the literary magazine *Nuovi Argumenti*. He traveled a great deal, published many travel books and essays and also found the time to write film and theater reviews. In 1984, he was elected an Italian representative to the European Parliament. Moravia died in 1990.

Only a few of the other initials Elsa used in her diary are identifiable. "*S.J.C.*" probably stands for Sanctus Jesus Christus. "*G.C.*," "*G.Cap.*" or simply "*Cap.*" stands for the painter Giuseppe Capogrossi, who introduced Elsa to Alberto Moravia. And "*Giacomo D.*" must be Giacomo Debenedetti. But the rest of the first names or initials—such as "*E.C.*," "*V.*" and "*T.*"—are not identifiable. Obvious recognizable figures are her mother; her older brother, Aldo; her sister, Maria; as well as Plato (who appears in a dream as a fish), Kafka, Greta Garbo and the Marquis de Sade. Not surprisingly, given that their love affair had recently begun, Moravia figures prominently in a great many of Elsa's dreams and the dreams themselves shed an interesting light on their complicated relationship. A relationship that was categorized on her part by a feeling of social inferiority and sexual humiliation. After all, one must not forget that at the time that Elsa Morante was writing her diary, she was a young woman very much alone in the world who was constantly beset by financial worries. She lived in a tiny rented room and was filled with self-doubts about her physical appearance, her social position and her artistic vocation. A clue to how she must have felt in the company of the more urbane and well-known Moravia is provided by the dream in the second entry of her diary:

> Yesterday must have been a day filled with unacknowledged humiliations for me. It is how I explain this night's dreams. A. is a snob in fact and I myself want to satisfy his snobbism by, for example, having a high position in society or by being famous. None of this is so, and yesterday—the visit to the Exhibition, knowing that I was not an important person there, while he was talking to the Countess, and I was drunk and, on my hands, I wore these ugly little gloves, and I was not introduced to the Academics, and his stories about how he spent the last few days in this fancy villa and about this aristocratic woman who he was in love with. . . . Enough, a long list of humiliations. I thought I had overcome them with the thought that I was valuable, *that I know that I am.* . . . Mistake. [January 20]

Her subsequent feelings of loneliness are also made quite clear:

> Later that same night, I have a second dream. I was going to the cinema, and I went inside. The sumptuous and very large theater was empty. Only employees and food vendors were there, sitting like abandoned marionettes in some of the seats. I sit down and a very short film is shown, expressly for me, the only spectator. . . .
>
> *My solitude* accounts for this dream. I was no doubt, impressed by T.'s story about the woman writer who had

invitations made for her reception and nearly no one came. This impressed me because I am almost always alone. [February 20]

Often in her dreams Moravia appears unloving or, at best, merely affectionate:

Before going to sleep, he told me that I had bad breath (the result of drinking wine and liqueurs). But he said it rather crudely, turning away his face, holding his nostrils: the reason he could not love me. Just for an instant, a little repentant and tender and smiling, he caressed my cheek. In my sleep, this brief caress becomes a sign of great tenderness, love. This small comfort becomes a real and great comfort. [February 1]

Or he rejects her attempts to please him:

This night, I dreamt that I brought A. a coffee. "Must you bring me this stuff?" he remarked dissatisfied, eyeing the filter. [January 25]

They also play the games of insecure lovers:

A. loves me only when I run away, but I cannot do it, I have no money. He is famous and rich, and in a few days he is going to Paris. Also he is always unavailable, shut off. He is off to Paris, triumphant, while I? I am hurtling toward a dreadful solitude. Enough. I slept for two hours. I found myself in a sort of cottage with a lot of people. . . . Then I see A. arrive, his hat on the back of his head, very pale and as always cut off from everyone. I have to pretend not to pay attention to him so that then he will look for me, he will follow me. Desperate escape, desperate game of hide-and-seek. Why must it be like this? [February 17]

More problematic still is the fact that Moravia does not seem capable of sexually satisfying Morante. Early on, Morante mentions this with the hope that someday she will find a man who can:

But before I die I will meet a man who ********. I am afraid that then I will become his slave but what a pleasure! And what if it was A. himself? He would not have the courage *******. My life is miserable. I should satisfy these cravings only so as not to have to think about them anymore. But with whom? ***. What misery to torture oneself with such thoughts. [January 19]

Moreover there seems to be a sadistic element to Moravia's treatment of Morante. In a dream recorded on January 22 in which one of her students suddenly grabbed her naked toe, Morante remembers how a few nights earlier Moravia had violently caressed her foot. And:

Last night, before going to sleep, I wept with rage because I wanted to make love and, instead, A. came to pay me a visit with V. Continuous excitement without satisfaction, in fact, in my presence, he ********—and he does not make me come—My desire and my need, and most of all my wish for ********** is only satisfied for now in a dream.

Despite the asterisks, Morante makes the situation pretty plain
here. Nonetheless, more often than not, Morante alternates between candor and squeamishness (the use of asterisks) in her diary entries. Childishly, sex is conveyed as either scary or perverse.
Often, too, she confuses dream and reality.

> I wanted to sleep with the taste of A. in my mouth to see
> what kind of dreams I would have. [February 5]

This last entry is another indication that the sex between Moravia and Morante might have been one-sided and not particularly
fulfilling for Morante. It is also an example of how accommodating
women can be and how they tend to sustain the hope that the men
they sleep with can provide them with understanding and intimacy.

Alberto Moravia's avowed pessimism, his aloofness (perceived
often as amorality), his obsession with alienation and transgression, would hardly seem to qualify him as a sensitive and loving
partner. In fact, rumor has it that he may have been impotent or
deviant, which, considering the circumstances of Morante's own
family and her legal father's sexual issues, might appear to constitute a huge irony or at the very least a strange and bitter coincidence. On the other hand, this kind of behavioral repetition
occurs with surprising frequency in families. When I asked
Ginevra Bompiani, the daughter of Valentino Bompiani, who
was Moravia's editor, and the director of her own small publishing house, Nottetempo, about this rumor, she shrugged and made
a face to show her distaste before replying. She had known Moravia ever since she was a child, she said, and she respected him.
Although he could be quite charming they never said *tu* to each
other. There was that rumor but she did not think he really was

impotent—he was, she said, "something, something not really straight."[4] Or one might conjecture—given the authority of the writing—that the cause of Moravia's failure as a lover is not so dissimilar from that of his first-person narrator in *Conjugal Love*, who describes his attempts to love thus: "But underneath these displays of fervor, there is often an acrid and even mean shrewdness or duplicity which is not a sign of strength, but rather the expression of my egotism."[5] By the time he met Elsa Morante, however, Moravia's reputation as a womanizer was well established, along with his obsession with sexuality. He went on to have many long-term relationships—notably with of course Elsa, Dacia Maraini and his second wife, Carmen Llera—but he never had children (an early love affair with a Swiss woman ended, he claimed, with her having to have an abortion).[6]

In the spring of 1938, the relationship seems to have come to an end. In her diary, Morante asks:

> Is everything really over with A.? He has left and I don't know precisely where, perhaps it is a joke, a nightmare. . . .
> In real life, . . . he came and said: We have been lovers for a year and during that time we have had misery. Better to end it. [April 5]

But a little more than two weeks later, everything has inexplicably changed:

> It was a whole story. A. did not want to end it at all. But now I am the one who wants it to end. [April 22]

And only a month later, without explanation, Morante writes:

A. comes every day, he looks for me more and more. Me too I look for him, I don't really know why since I am no longer in love with him. [May 29]

In Morante's last recorded dream about Alberto Moravia, they seem to have switched roles. Moravia is the one who is vulnerable and helpless:

Afterward, I dreamt that A. had eaten a fish in order to die. I go to him and find him in front of the radio and I put my finger down his throat and he vomits a white substance and right away he is cured (despite his nerves he is grateful to me for having saved him). But he is tired, he wants to sleep, he is like a little child, with a white school apron. He goes to sleep on my knees, his legs are all bare and spread so far apart that I feel a bit ashamed for him. But I am happy that he is sleeping like this on my lap. [June 15]

Elsa Morante's mother, Irma, also appears in many of Elsa's dreams. In these dreams she often seems to be in danger—in a sinking boat, walking on water—and her physical appearance too keeps changing. At times she is very tall or she is "little, fat, sad and dressed in black" (February 2), her hair is in disarray, her face covered in purple bruises, her body bloated, all of which reminds Morante of death—of her own death. Elsa Morante yearns to establish a bond while her mother seems to be the withholding one, as this dream illustrates:

I was in a garden, my mother's, to be precise, in front of the house. Like a small florist's plot, the garden was cluttered with pots, with those splendid full and delicate pink flowers, the kind one puts in salons. I don't know their name. Feeling an overwhelming desire for one, I begged my mother to give me a plant. She had so many! In exchange, if she wanted it, I offered her O.'s cactus plant which did not flower. Making a little movement of regret with her mouth, my mother said that no, she could not be parted from a single plant. . . . "There"—I thought—"no one exists in the whole world who would make the smallest sacrifice for me." [January 21]

The dreams in which the rest of Morante's family—her brothers, her sister and her father—figure are fraught with anxiety and rejection. In one dream, a distraught Elsa shouts at her father to leave her apartment, which he does (he jumps out the window to his death); Maria, her sister, too, is a moody, truculent and unwelcome presence. Aldo appears bossy and unsympathetic. In several of those dreams in which her siblings appear, Elsa is naked.

There are numerous images of old women, ugly, wizened crones. In one particularly erotic dream whose psychological significance is not difficult to guess at—guilt and self-mortification—she engages in a sexual act with a nun. This dream takes place in a cathedral, which for Morante, a Catholic, must have represented an enormous sacrilege.

Among the people, there is a skinny, little, old nun, one of those who wears a little cap. Her face is lined with wrinkles, her gestures are nervous and quick. She is a hypocrite, a vicious woman, she intends to use sacred words and deeds to satisfy her degenerate and perverted senses. . . . Don't believe in this sacrilege, I cry . . . but at that very mo-

ment . . . I feel myself become a child, afraid and humiliated (attempting as I am to evade being captured by the
nun who reaches out her arms) like a school boy who tries
to escape from his stern and perverse teacher. At which
point, the nun grabs me and leads me toward a********.
[January 23]

These wizened, old crones will reappear time and time again
in Morante's fiction, in short stories (such as "Il ladro dei lumi,"
"Via dell'Angelo" and "La nonna"—where the grandmother actually murders her grandchildren) and most notably in her novel
House of Liars, where again the grandmother, instead of being a
life-affirming force, is a mad, destructive one.

But Morante also has dreams—dreams that are equally disturbing—about provocative, preadolescent young girls. These girls,
some of them prostitutes, who are usually glimpsed from afar, are
sexually uninhibited and seem to suggest a repressed eroticism. In
one dream, Morante sees a girl from a speeding train:

The protagonist of the film is a young energetic, strong
girl who is head of a band of girls whose silhouettes remain
in the shadow. Her silhouette, however, is very clear, she is
beautiful, her face is luminous and fine, her two dark braids
are tied around her temples . . . she stays seated in mid air,
keeping her balance with her feet. Tidily, she pulls her dress
over her knees (in such a way that the public cannot see on
the screen what she in her modesty hides) but I, by lowering
my eyes, can see in between her thighs, her uncovered
sex . . . which looks to me like a little gray field, shriveled a
little, with, around it, a little yellow halo. The train continues its course, the scene disappears. . . . [January 22]

In another dream, Morante watches as several young girls dance on a balcony:

> They strike shameless poses which are often obscene, they laugh and do their exercises in a disorganized manner, lifting their legs. [March 7]

It has been suggested that these two contradictory figures—the old crone and the sexy preadolescent girl—form an archetypal image of both sterility and fecundity, which might explain Morante's state of mind during this period: her ambivalence, her unreconciled sexuality, her maternal longings. It also addresses some of the difficulties inherent in her search for a feminine identity. Years later, Pier Paolo Pasolini was to find the apt phrase to describe Elsa: *"nonna bambina"* (a grandmother child).

The writing or the recording of the dreams progresses by association and in ways that are not always clear. Most of the events that occur seem to be taken from daily life. There are definite feelings of life's precariousness and a fear of death; her death and the death of others are constant themes in Elsa Morante's dreams. In a long, involved dream on February 25, Kafka is dying, unnoticed, inside a child's crib in Elsa's studio. He is wearing a flowered cretonne dress that resembles one of Morante's dresses and tied around his eyes is her black hair band. When she awakes, not surprisingly, she wonders if, in the dream, it was not she who was dying? Or was it Alberto Moravia?

The two dreams in which a baby appears are very troubling indeed, particularly as it is not clear whether they refer to a miscarriage or an abortion (the reason, it has been suggested, that Elsa could not have children). In either case, however, they appear to refer to an actual event in Elsa Morante's life.

In the first dream Morante is attending a baby's funeral; she describes the baby, whose body is not yet decomposed but gives off a bad odor.

I do my best to think but I cannot remember if this child is mine. Could it be that it was mine, the son of WILLY COPPENS? [March 16]

Who was Willy Coppens? Was he the father of her child? The reader cannot help but ask. Unfortunately, there is no answer.

In the second dream, Morante claims to be only half asleep. She is holding a baby in her arms. Feeling both anxious and happy, she squeezes him tightly so he cannot escape. The child is large, plump and blond and she thinks, Lord, now, I will no longer be alone, you are here, my love. Then, she asks God to forgive her: "How could I possibly keep him?" One had to, she goes on, it was fate, it was the will of God . . . but she has sinned.

An inspiration, I think. This child, big already, who existed and did not exist, it was him. In fact, Coppens was blond. I am afraid. But of whom? afraid of you? he is an angel, and perhaps he has forgiven me and he prays for me.

("Here is the little fetus," they said.) [April 27]

On a more positive note, she writes:

Dreams, what miracles! . . . One word, one look suffices to propel a dream toward nameless paths, adventurous voyages. It is like a thread which turns itself into fabulous lace.

Could that be the secret of art? *To remember* how one saw

the work in a dream state, to try to say again how one saw it, to try above all to remember. For to invent, no doubt, is *to remember.* [February 23]

Here her dreams are viewed as a source of inspiration:

Where do the characters in a dream come from? By that I mean not the ones who more or less represent those in our daily lives but the other unknown ones. . . . They are the veritable artistic creations. [February 25]

The last dream entry, on July 30, is very short:

Last night I dreamt about pink flowers.

Like an earlier dream on January 21 about pink flowers, which reminds her of spring and gives her a childish and sensual joy, this dream presents a hopeful image, a dream of love perhaps (it may even refer to marriage). In any case, the flowers bode well, signifying as they do the hope for salvation and lightness as opposed to Elsa Morante's dreaded state of old age and *pesanteur* or heaviness.

four

THE WAR YEARS

Elsa Morante met Alberto Moravia in 1937, the same year—Moravia was the one to point this out—that Hitler met Mussolini.[1] In fact, not too long afterward, one day in June 1938, Elsa Morante remembered how Mussolini and Hitler had paraded together in a convertible limousine underneath her apartment window and that she caught a glimpse of "the two awful heads, both shining in the sun, one round, white and greasy like a cheese, the other not so blond as I expected, glittering with brilliantine." She had prepared a pot of boiling oil on her stove and she was ready to pour it over the two heads, but at the last moment Moravia dissuaded her and convinced her of "the utter foolishness of it all."[2] At the time of her meeting Moravia, Elsa was living on via del Corso with an older man; she also had several other lovers. In fact, she invented a cockamamie story to tell Moravia, no doubt to intrigue him and which he believed, about how she had been in love with a young English lord who was a homosexual and who was murdered in front of her eyes by his lover.[3]

In his autobiography, Moravia repeatedly mentioned how poor Elsa was at the time of their first meeting. So poor that he gave her one of his old suits, "a tan chalk-stripe,"[4] which Elsa refashioned into a *tailleur* for herself. (It is difficult to imagine—no matter how good a seamstress she might have been—making his suit fit her, as Moravia was nearly a foot taller; in addition, it is a bit disturbing to think of Elsa wearing Moravia's cast-off clothes.) But, almost in the same breath, Moravia also remembered Elsa as looking elegant in a close-fitting black dress with a beautiful blue fox fur. These disparate descriptions of her clothes, however, serve to reaffirm the sort of hand-to-mouth existence that Elsa Morante must have led during those years.

Soon they became a recognized couple, Morante-Moravia, and they had dinner every evening at one of several local, inexpensive trattorias with their friends—the artists Giuseppe Capogrossi, Toti Scialoja, Renato Guttuso, and the writers Mario Pannunzio, Vitaliano Brancati, Sandro De Feo. All ardent anti-Fascists, they spent most of their meals vociferously denouncing the regime and the anti-Semitic racial laws that Italy adopted in 1938. These, the most striking step in the Fascist radicalization, affected a lot of intellectuals—one out of twelve university professors had to abandon their chairs.[5] But as if paralyzed, these anti-Fascists did nothing. Moravia recalled how he and his friends waited for something awful to happen, none of them capable of foreseeing the specific horrors to come in the German occupation of Europe. However, by 1939, Moravia believed that everyone must have known about the camps and the extermination of the Jews as he claimed to: "I knew also about the Russian concentration camps," he said. "I went often to Paris and received all possible information: I bought books, I met Russian and German exiles. I remember that in 1940 Alberto Mondadori, returning from Poland, told me, 'horrible things are happening.' 'What?' (I asked.) The Germans had invited him to witness a massacre of Jews, like a performance. He didn't accept, naturally, but he went around Milan telling about it."[6]

At the time, too, Moravia—despite the success of his first

novel, *The Time of Indifference*—had very little money. He was living at home with his parents, which actually was not an unusual situation for a thirty-year-old bachelor in Italy. However, it was also the incidental and not particularly flattering reason that Moravia gave for marrying Elsa, since Rome, he said, was unusually cold the winter of 1940–41 and he could hardly bear walking home every night from her place. Years later, in a series of conversations with Alain Elkann that formed the basis of his autobiography, Alberto Moravia also claimed never to have been in love with Elsa Morante. Instead, he said, "I loved her, yes, but I never managed to lose my head: I never fell, in other words. She always knew this, and it was perhaps also the chief reason for the difficulties of our life together. I wasn't in love, but I was fascinated by an extreme, heart-rending, passionate quality in her character. It was as if every day of her life were the last, just before her death. So in an atmosphere of impassioned aggressiveness on her part and defensive affection on mine, we lived together for twenty-five years." Nor did he ever feel a violent physical desire for Morante.[7]

On Easter Monday, April 14, 1941, a day known in Italy as the Monday of the Angel, Elsa Morante and Alberto Moravia were married in Chiesa del Gesù, the Jesuit church whose gorgeously lavish baroque interior houses the remains of St. Ignatius Loyola. Father Tacchi-Venturi, a Jesuit priest who was also Mussolini's confessor, married them. Elsa Morante had insisted on being married in church for, although not a practicing Catholic, she was a devout one. Too poor to buy her a ring, Alberto Moravia brought her a bouquet of lilies of the valley. Moravia's family did not attend the wedding, but, afterward, they invited the newlyweds to dinner. At this dinner, Moravia's mother tried to give Elsa some domestic advice and Elsa responded rudely to her.

According to Moravia, Elsa believed that there were two sorts of people—those who had a soul and those who didn't. His mother, she said, did not have a soul. The two women never saw each other again.[8]

The same year Elsa Morante translated Katherine Mansfield's posthumous short story collection *Scrapbook* into Italian. No doubt the work was motivated by both financial necessity and a shared aesthetic sensibility. Morante and Mansfield each believed in the importance of mood and atmosphere, rather than plot or action, as the driving force in the short story, which ideally would culminate in "one blazing moment" (Mansfield's words)[9] or in an epiphany. Also, both writers were admirers of and influenced by Chekhov. And, at a time when experimental writing was in vogue, and even though they experimented with narrative techniques, neither writer trespassed far beyond the barriers of the classical prose style. More specifically, it is interesting to take a look at the similarities, which also includes a similarity in the choice of story titles: Katherine Mansfield's "The Man without a Temperament," written in 1920, and Morante's "Un uomo senza carattere" ("A Man without Character"), written in 1941, the same year of her translation. In both stories, the self-sacrificing, overly sensitive male protagonists are intent on trying to support and help a woman who in one case is a pathetic invalid and in the other a ludicrous and self-deluded fool. Robert Salesby, in the Mansfield story, gives up his life in London in order to look after his sick wife while, in Morante's story, the artless and naïve hero, Poeta—in what turns out to be a misguided attempt to be chivalrous and honest—tells silly, stupid Candida that the men in the village are making fun of her, a bit of truth that causes her to become mortally sick. And although Poeta fantasizes that he might marry her (the ultimate self-sacrifice to save Candida's dignity), Candida dies, thus perhaps illustrating Elsa Morante's own feelings of unworthiness. The outcome, in both stories, subverts the males' traditional roles as well as exposes the females' feelings of dependence and unworthiness. In the case of Katherine Mansfield, the autobiographical elements in the story are obvious, since like her female character she was ill with tuberculosis and hospitalized, and she had written the story in part to show that she understood the difficulties her illness was causing her marriage. In Elsa Morante's case, it has been pointed out that the year she wrote the story coincided with the year of her marriage to Alberto Moravia, to whom she always felt inferior and whose social and intellectual stature intimidated her.[10]

The next year, 1942, Elsa Morante's book of children's stories *The Marvelous Adventures of Cathy with the Long Tresses and Other Stories (Le bellissime avventure di Caterì dalla trecciolina e altre storie)* was published exactly as she had written and illustrated it years earlier in school. A letter from publisher Giulio Einaudi offering his most cordial salutations and the copy of a check stub confirm that the balance of 2000 lire was paid to Elsa Morante for the rights to this book. The money must have been most welcome.

In Rome, Alberto and Elsa lived in a two-room attic apartment on via Sgambati; the apartment had a marvelous view of the Borghese Gardens but was too small to allow them to work separately. As a result, they spent quite a lot of time on Capri during the early years of their marriage. Capri was cheap and the beauty of both the island and the sea around it provided them, especially in wartime, with a consolation of sorts. The many months the two spent there in the village of Anacapri, in large rented rooms in a villa owned by the former mayor, remained one of the most beautiful memories of Moravia's life:

> Anacapri was a genuine village, very likable, with hos-
> pitable, simple people. . . . They never locked the doors
> of their houses because nobody would think of stealing.
> We ate sandwiches on the beach, or we ate in a trattoria,
> Maria's, at the Piccola Marina, four tables under an arbor.
> We ate eggplant, octopus, things like that. Then around
> four we would go back up to Anacapri where we would
> have tea. I'd buy the newspapers in town, writing paper,
> cigarettes. . . . At five we would take a walk in the interior
> of the island. The war was on, and in Anacapri there were
> only some Swedish families. . . . We went to see the can-
> nons that were supposed to defend the Bay of Naples. . . .
> They never fired a shot. Elsa walked around with a Siamese
> cat on a leash and I had an owl on my shoulder.[11]

Because they had so little money, they went everywhere on foot—climbing up the steep, winding road from the village of Capri to Anacapri—often quarreling the whole time. Moravia was working on his coming-of-age novella, *Agostino*, and Elsa Morante had begun writing her eight-hundred-page first novel, *House of Liars (Menzogna e sortilegio)*.

Alberto Moravia's 1952 story, "Bitter Honeymoon" (in Ital-ian, "Luna di miele, sole di fiele," which translated literally means Moon of Honey, Sun of Bile) is set in Capri. The story contains so many recognizable biographical details that the reader cannot help but try to draw certain parallels between the relationship of Moravia and Morante and that of the protagonists. The story

begins with a description of Anacapri, to which the newly married Giacomo has just returned, bringing his wife, Simona, for
their honeymoon:

> But this time, immediately upon their arrival, every-
> thing seemed very different. The sultry dog-days of mid-
> August were upon them and steaming humidity overclouded
> the sky. Even on the heights of Anacapri, there was no trace
> of the crisp air, of flowers or the violet sea whose praises
> Giacomo had sung. The paths winding through the fields
> were covered with a layer of yellow dust. . . . Long before
> autumn was due, the leaves had begun to turn red and
> brown, and occasional trees had withered away from lack
> of water. Dust particles filled the motionless air . . . and the
> odours of meadows and sea had given way to those of
> scorched stones and dried dung.[12]

Even Simona's looks have lost their romantic appeal, although
the description of her—except for the color of her hair—
certainly brings to mind Elsa Morante:

> Although Simona was not tall, she had childishly long
> legs with slender thighs, rising to an indentation, almost a
> cleft at either side, visible under her shorts, where they were
> joined to the body. The whiteness of her legs was chaste,
> shiny and cold, she had a narrow waist and hips, and her
> only womanly feature, revealed when she turned around to
> speak to him, was the fullness of her low-swung breasts,
> which seemed like extraneous and burdensome weights,
> unsuited to her delicate frame. Similarly her thick, blonde

hair, although it was cut short, hung heavily over her neck.[13]

Clearly, Moravia's descriptions are designed to show Giacomo's disillusionment and fear that his marriage is a failure—Simona had refused to make love the night before, on their wedding night. Giacomo's unease is further enhanced by his own feeling of impotence and frigidity:

> It was really hot—there was no doubt about that—and in the heavy air all round there seemed to Giacomo to reside the same obstacle, the same impossibility that bogged down his relationship with his wife: the impossibility of a rainfall that would clear the air, the impossibility of love. He had a sensation of something like panic, when looking at her again he felt that his will to love was purely intellectual and did not involve his senses.[14]

Toward the end of the story, when again Simona refuses to sleep with him, Giacomo cuts his finger to pretend there is blood on the sheets and finally—after he does consummate his marriage (during a fierce thunderstorm)—he reflects: "Nothing was settled." [15] Like many of Moravia's male protagonists, Giacomo is both filled with sexual desire and frightened by the object of his desire. This ambiguity is often dramatized by an act of violence.

This violence is not just imagined violence but based on Moravia's own actions or reactions. The events in another story, "The Unfortunate Lover" ("L'amante infelice"), he admitted, were "ready made" for him. Not only did he transcribe them exactly how they had occurred, he claimed that although he had lost his head over the woman, he was *not* in love with her: "We spent a magnificent day. We went out in a boat to swim at the Grotta Verde. Then we ate at the Piccola Marina: a perfect day. We took a carriage and went up to my room. She fell asleep. But I tried to make love. . . . She rejected me crossly and—as if seized by a temporary homicidal insanity—I grabbed her by the neck and tried to strangle her." [16]

People, Elsa Morante always claimed, were essentially divided into three categories: there was Achilles, the man who lived out his passions; there was Don Quixote, the man who lived out his dreams; and, finally, there was Hamlet, the man who questioned everything. Moravia, in her opinion, was part Hamlet and part Achilles; she herself was all Don Quixote. In addition, she complained of Moravia's "incurable detachment." [17]

Although he had declared himself an anti-Fascist as early as 1935 and stated that his sympathies lay with the Communist Party, Moravia did not actively participate in the war effort. Certainly his pronounced limp—Moravia had had coxitis (tuberculosis of the bone) as a child, which left him with one leg several inches shorter than the other—rendered him unfit for active service. Another reason was his detached temperament. Nevertheless, he has been criticized for pursuing his literary career and writing fiction on the island of Capri during the early years of the conflict.

One other factor that should be noted—although in no way offered as an excuse—is that the position of the majority of Italians evolved during the course of the war: in 1939, as World War II broke out in Europe, most Italians did not want to take part in the war; in 1941, most Italians hoped they would win; by 1942, they hoped the Germans would win; by 1943, most Italians hoped they would get out of the war without too much injury; and, by 1944, they hoped the Allies would win. Moravia's attitude, which was shared by many of his compatriots, is reflected in his statement "Everyone thought that Fascism could, and should, collapse, but since the outcome of the war was uncertain almost to the end, its fall wasn't a certainty; depending on the person, it was a hope or a fear. The anti-Fascists, of course, hoped; but those who feared weren't only the Fascists but also a part of the population who had got used to Fascism. In any case, everyone was waiting." [18] This wait-and-see attitude, however, would change for Alberto Moravia, as well as for Elsa Morante.

In July 1943, Benito Mussolini was arrested and Pietro Badoglio became prime minister. The uneasy period that followed, known as the Forty-Five Days, ended on September 3 with the signing of a secret treaty between Italy and the Allies calling for Italy's unconditional surrender. Nevertheless, Badoglio's evasiveness during this period resulted in still more confusion: Italy was cut in two between the north and the south, the Italian royal family fled, the Germans occupied Rome where the Fascists, wearing their black shirts, were back in full force, marching everywhere in the streets, armed, and waving banners that carried their slogan "*Viva la morte!*" (Long live death!)

That summer instead of following the advice of his friend Curzio Malaparte to return to Capri, Alberto Moravia and Elsa Morante decided to stay in the capital. But not for long. Moravia learned he was on the wanted list of the Fascist police and that he would be arrested; in addition, Moravia was half Jewish.* He and Elsa went into hiding at the home of Moravia's Swedish translator. After two days, realizing that they could not jeopardize him, they moved on to the house of Carlo Ludovico Bragaglia, a friend

---

* Moravia's father, Carlo Pincherle, was Jewish only, according to Moravia, his Judaism was invisible.

of Elsa, for another two days. Moravia tried to seek refuge at the Belgian embassy and Elsa Morante appealed to Father Tacchi-Venturi, begging him to hide them in the vast cellars of his church, but both efforts proved futile. Packing a single suitcase with toilet articles and summer clothes—it was a warm September day and the British army, they assumed, would be arriving to liberate the city within the next ten days—they decided to take the train to Naples.

Alberto Moravia remembered that he was wearing a light sharkskin suit and Elsa had on a flowered cretonne dress. He also remembered that the train did not go to Naples. All of a sudden it stopped at a deserted-looking station and the conductor told them to get off. There were no more train tracks. "We got off and found ourselves in the station parking lot, with the sun beating down, hot but beautiful, the Italian summer sun. The countryside was filled with the rasp of cicadas. An atmosphere of extreme peace, nothing to suggest war. We set off along a dusty road between hedges of blackberries."[19] Alberto Moravia and Elsa Morante spent a few days in the village of Fondi, until the Germans began to round up people in the village and they had to leave.

So one fine morning, I in my gray double-breasted suit, Elsa in her flowered cretonne, we loaded the suitcase on a donkey and began to climb. . . . We climbed and climbed, and finally we arrived at a little house. Nearby we saw a peasant who was working his field. His name was Davide Marrocco; he was young, but he had one walleye, and this had saved him from the draft. The other men of the area had been sent to Russia, where they all died. So I had happened onto a community all of women. . . . These were mountain peasants, very poor, absolutely without anything.

They tilled the slopes with a system of terraces and steps . . . patches of arable land, sustained by little walls of stone, homemade: the women bring the stones in baskets, and the men lay them. On these . . . they grow everything: wheat, flax, corn, potatoes, tomatoes, and so on. Not only what they need for food, but also for their clothes, because with the flax and the wool they weave their own cloth. It was a *ciociaro* community, or rather, since the men were absent, *ciociara*."*[20]

As a political prisoner, Carlo Levi was another Italian writer who was forced to live in a remote hill village during the Ethiopian war. About his time there, he wrote: "Christ never came this far, nor did time, nor did the individual soul, nor hope, nor the relation of cause to effect, nor reason, nor history. Christ never came."[21] And although Levi described the people in the village as decent, he also said how "their life was a continuous renewal of old resentments," how they had been "held back by ineptness or poverty or premature marriage or family interests or some other fateful necessity from emigrating" and how "they had funneled their disappointment and their mortal boredom into a generic rage, a ceaseless hate."[22] Nonetheless, the villagers accepted their fate with patience and in silence. "Of what use are words?" Levi asked. "And what can a man do? Nothing."[23]

It was not so surprising then that when Alberto Moravia and Elsa Morante arrived at the village of Sant'Agata, the people there were hardly curious about them. For the villagers, Moravia

---

* Instead of shoes, the peasants of this mountainous area traditionally wear *cioce*, a kind of slipper with long laces that crisscross the leg and are tied at the calf. The region is called Ciociaria. In the original Italian, Moravia's *Two Women* is *La ciociara*.

and Morante's presence reinforced the notion that they, like everyone else, were the victims of fate. And nothing could be done about that or—for that matter—done for them.

Alberto Moravia and Elsa Morante lived for nine months in a one-room hut built against the side of a rock. The hut had a metal roof and was furnished with a bed and a loom (a woman sat at the loom all day weaving and making a deafening racket). The bed was a plank with a sack of corn husks for a mattress, rough linen sheets and no blankets (since the room was so small, however, Moravia claimed that they were never cold); the floor of the room was packed earth and when it rained heavily, they had to stand ankle-deep in water. There were no pens or paper; the only books they had brought along were the Bible and *The Brothers Karam-aζον* (the pages of the latter were used for toilet paper). They got water to wash from a well and shared one meal a day with the peasants—bread, beans, a glass of acidic local wine—inside a smoke-filled hut that was reserved for meals. Each day, however, the food got scarcer (by springtime, they were reduced to looking for any kind of edible herbs).

They did nothing during those nine months. They stared at the rocky landscape and waited for the Allies to come. From time to time they could hear bombs dropping in Fondi and they watched dogfights between the German and British up in the sky. Twice Moravia and Morante were targets of an attack and strafed by planes while they were out walking: once by an English Spitfire, the other by a squadron of American Flying Fortresses. Each time they managed to save themselves by throwing themselves into a nearby ditch.

As Moravia pointed out in his autobiography, he was the one wanted by the police and Elsa chose to stay with him out of her own free will. She suffered all the discomforts and privations, never once complaining. Also, she did a courageous thing. In October, when it began to get cold, Elsa Morante went back to Rome alone to get some warm clothes. She went to their apartment, packed a suitcase—ironically enough, a German soldier helped her carry the heavy suitcase at the train station—and she returned to Sant'Agata. She also had a chance to stop and check on the manuscript of *House of Liars*, which she had left behind with Carlo Ludovico Bragaglia. It was safe. That and Moravia were all she cared about.[24]

Forty years later, Moravia went back to visit the village; the hut where he and Elsa had stayed remained unchanged. Davide Marrocco, the walleyed peasant who had given them shelter, was living there still and was very pleased to see Moravia again. He kissed him and recalled how he used to call Moravia "Albé." Marrocco also remembered how they had to hide in the mountains to avoid the Germans, how they all ate their meals together and how his mother and his wife, in the dead of winter, drew cold water from the well so that Elsa could bathe.[25]

La ciociara (Two Women), considered by some Moravia's masterpiece, was, as he described in a letter to his publisher, his "war novel," written "ten years later, with sufficient perspective to mix fantasy with reality and not find myself too close to the events."[26] When Elsa Morante read *Two Women*, she told Moravia that of all the books she had read about the war, it was the one that held up best.[27] It has also been said that of all of Moravia's novels, *Two Women* is the most elemental: the protagonist, Cesira *is* Moravia.[28]

The novel begins with two women, Cesira and her daughter, Rosetta, leaving Rome in September 1943; food has become scarce and the atmosphere dangerous, and they head back to the village where Cesira is originally from. Since it is still warm, they pack two small suitcases with only summer clothes. They plan to take the train to Fondi but are forced to get off before they reach their destination because the train line has been cut. "There was no one on the station platform. We went through the waiting room: no one there; and out into the open space outside; no one there either. A straight road lay in front of us, a real country road, white, covered with fine dust, blinding in the sunlight between hedges veiled in dust and a few dusty trees." [29] The two women start to climb, following a mule track, and when they finally reach the little village of Sant'Eufemia, they are shown to a hut that Moravia, in the novel, describes almost exactly like the hut he and Morante had lived in: the noisy, wooden loom occupying most of the room, the bed made out of a plank resting on two iron trestles with a sack filled with corn husks for a mattress and the bare-packed earth floor.

Moravia was able to write convincingly about the makeshift, arduous lives of the peasants barely surviving in their rude stone huts, the scarcity of food, water, clothing, and their ruthless and often savage behavior, prey as they were to the constant menacing and outlaw presence of German and former Fascist soldiers. The women's story, too, is a bleak allegory of the cost of historical consciousness: war, suffering, sacrifice and deprivation—the women are raped by Moroccan soldiers (part of the Free French Forces).

One of Elsa Morante's stories, "The Sicilian Soldier" ("Il soldato siciliano"), written in 1946 and later a part of her collection *Lo scialle andaluso (The Andalusian Shawl)*, was also influenced by the nine months she and Moravia spent in the mountains. A haunting tale about a soldier who wanders the countryside with a miner's lamp on his head looking for death, it begins, "At the time when the Allied armies blocked by the winter were forced to halt at the Garigliano River, I was living as a refugee in the mountains on the other side of that river. One day, for the sake of the safety of the people whom I loved, I was obliged to make a quick trip to Rome. The trip filled me with bitterness because Rome, the city where I was born and where I have always lived, was for me, at that time, an enemy city." [30]

This passage recalls Elsa Morante's brave journey back to Rome to check on her manuscript and to fill a suitcase with winter clothes, which took place soon after Italy's surrender to the Allied forces. The surrender was followed by Pietro Badoglio and Pope Pius XII's futile attempt to try to keep the city safe from destruction by calling Rome an "open city." Instead of being "open," however, Rome remained brutally besieged by the ferocious and hated German occupying forces while the Allied attempts to capture the city proved in vain (their repeated bombing made them almost equally unpopular). To make matters worse, the Vatican and Pope Pius XII maintained a rigid and un-Christian-like neutrality (their excuse was to save the world from communism and the city from ruin) at the same time that small courageous bands of partisans were desperately trying to salvage Italy's reputation and honor (and, in the process, harass and obstruct the occupying forces)[31] often with tragic consequences and horrendous reprisals. The most gruesome of these was the execution of 320 innocent men by the Germans in Rome's Ardeatine Caves. Meanwhile the population of the city was slowly starving to death.

Many years later, in her third and most famous novel, *History*, Elsa Morante vividly captured that period of misery and desperation:

During the last months of the German occupation, Rome took on the appearance of certain Indian metropolises where

only the vultures get enough to eat and there is no census of
the living and the dead. A multitude of beggars and refu-
gees . . . camped on the steps of the churches or below the
Pope's palaces; and in the great public parks starving sheep
and cows grazed, having escaped the bombs and the confis-
cations in the countryside. Despite the declaration of open
city, the Germans were encamped around the inhabited
areas . . . and the disastrous cloud of the air raids . . . spread
over the city a great tarpaulin of pestilence and earth-
quake. . . . The populace had fallen silent. The daily news
of roundups, torture, and slaughter circulated through the
neighborhoods like death-rattle echoes without any possible response. It was known that just outside the city's girdle
of walls, ineptly buried in mined ditches and caves, num-
berless bodies were thrown to decompose. . . . And even
the exalted mirage of the Liberation was being reduced to a
fatuous dot, subject of sarcasm and mockery. For that matter, it was said that the Germans, before abandoning the
city, would blow it up completely. . . . But finally, inside
the isolated city, sacked and besieged, the true master was
hunger.[32]

On May 23, 1944, Alfred de Grazia, an American lieutenant,
was trying to make his way to Rome from the battlefronts of
Cassino and the Anzio beachhead in his jeep, with his driver, an
Italian-American named Alfredo Segre, when he stumbled upon
Alberto Moravia and Elsa Morante. Apparently, Segre had heard
a rumor about two writers hiding in the mountains and both he
and de Grazia drove up to investigate. "We're Americans," Segre
shouted in Italian, as he pounded on the hut door in an attempt to
allay the couple's fears while de Grazia, who was armed to the

teeth, worried that the couple inside might be Fascist sympathizers. Once face-to-face the American soldiers studied Moravia and Morante carefully. Elsa, Alfred de Grazia later wrote, was "wearing a shapeless dress and old shoes; her hair was a curly light-brown, uncombed, with intimations of grey, though she was young. She had a smooth round sweet face, a soft buxom figure. Her smile, now that she smiled with even teeth that parted in the middle, could hardly convey but a mild and generous soul." His impression of her husband, however, was quite different: "Alberto Moravia . . . was a head taller than she, well put together, save for a gimpy leg, a bit slumped of shoulder, of a satanic countenance that refused to transform itself pleasantly. His lips were tight, his jaw clenched, his attitude grim. When he smiled, he might be sincere, but you would never be sure. He appeared to be retaining secrets." [33] After Moravia and Morante were able to reassure Lieutenant de Grazia that they were not Fascist sympathizers, he wrote a letter authorizing them to travel on military conveyances to Naples, which they did, while he continued on his way to Rome.

Although politics always took second place to literature for Elsa Morante, she, like Moravia, sympathized with the Communist Party and with the left. She was also not afraid to express her opinions or her outrage. On May 1, 1945, three days after Benito Mussolini and his mistress, Clara Petacci, were arrested and shot, their bodies strung upside down for all to see, Elsa Morante wrote a long piece in her diary excoriating Il Duce. Interestingly enough, she begins the piece by blaming the Italian people: "All of Mussolini's faults were either tolerated or encouraged even, and applauded. Thus a people who tolerate the faults of their head of state are *complicit* with these faults. But if they encourage and applaud them as well, it is worse than being an accomplice, it makes them an accessory to these faults." She describes Mussolini as a mediocre man, a crude man, a man outside the culture, a vulgarly eloquent man with a simple kind of effectiveness, which is the reason he appealed so well to the people. She called him "Venal," "Corruptible," a "Flatterer," a "Catholic who did not believe in God," a "Pervert," "Conceited," "Vain," "Superficial," and much more. She compared him to the *cocotte* who sells herself to the old lover then betrays him by speaking ill of him, and to the *cocotte* who deludes herself into thinking that she is loved by the younger lover who will soon abandon her when she is no longer useful to him. She also accused Mussolini of having vulgar taste: reading inferior books, listening to sentimental music (Puccini), not caring about poetry, moved as he was by the mediocre (Ada Negri). Furthermore, in Italy, she wrote angrily, it would be difficult to find a better or more perfect example of an Italian than Il Duce himself. The Italian people, in her opinion, were made in such a way that they would rather give their vote to the strong man than to the just man, and if they had to choose between their duty and their profit—even if they knew what their duty was—they would choose their profit.[34]

five

HOUSE OF LIARS

The war over, Elsa Morante and Alberto Moravia returned to Rome. They settled back into their small
apartment on via Sgambati with the beautiful view of the Borghese Gardens and Elsa resumed work on her novel. She—unlike Moravia who was very disciplined in his work habits and
wrote every morning for a prescribed number of hours—was the
sort of writer who could go days, months even, without writing a
single word but once she began, she wrote day and night, hardly
stopping. "At a time like this," she said in a magazine interview,
"to have a little bit of peace and a little table all of my own is a
great privilege." She was particularly grateful, she also said, that
she was allowed to finish a book that she had been yearning to
write ever since she was a child, the novel *House of Liars* (a more
literal translation of the Italian title *Menzogna e sortilegio* is A Lie
and a Spell), and she thanked the year 1946 for having forgotten
about her and for having left her in peace so that she was able to
spend an entire year of *real* time.[1]

Morante had first conceived and developed the idea for *House
of Liars* in an unpublished novella called *Vita di mia nonna* (My
Grandmother's Life), which she began before World War II. The
novella was a tale with two narrative threads: the first, about the
narrator's grandmother, introduces the theme of the malevolent
old crone; the second, about a young man befriending another in

his search for his real father, introduces the theme of the double father. After the war, when Morante was able to return to writing, she incorporated those two threads and reused some of the material from *Vita di mia nonna* in a much larger structure that became *House of Liars*. Before settling on the title, she had toyed with several others, filling page after page with all sorts of possible choices: *Diamante e rubino* (Diamond and Ruby), *Il cugino* (The Cousin), *La fenice* (The Phoenix), *Il corvo* (The Raven), *Ricordi immaginari* (Imaginary Memories) and *La morte del padre* (The Death of the Father)—this last was accompanied with the dedication "To the memory of F.L.," who clearly must have been Francesco Lo Monaco, Elsa Morante's biological father.[2]

House of Liars was inspired by a story Elsa Morante had heard about an old blind woman whose son was killed in the war in Ethiopia. Her relatives did not want to tell her he was dead and they read her made-up letters from him. The models for the novel, she claimed, were *Don Quixote* and Ariosto's *Orlando Furioso*. Morante also claimed, in an interview in 1968 with the French literary critic Michel David, that with *House of Liars*, she had wanted to write the last possible novel on earth. She wanted to "kill" the novel genre, she told him, as well as put in it everything that had ever occurred in her life, everything that had ever tormented her. And although still young then, she said, she had had a very dramatic, full life, and she wanted to include in the novel everything that was in the nineteenth-century novel: parents who are rich, parents who are poor, orphans, good-hearted prostitutes, etc.[3]

Elsa Morante always denied that the novel was autobiographical. (However, it is difficult to ignore the similarities between the names of the novel's protagonist, Elisa, and the author's own as well as that of the protagonist's father, Francesco Monaco, and the author's own father.) She said that she was incapable of reporting on "real" events, she could only write about them symbolically. Reality, she went on to tell Michel David in the same interview, was much closer or "truer" in childhood. Adults distanced themselves from reality: they were interested in careers, in money, in absolutely absurd things. The only way to try to look at reality was through the eyes of children. In fact, all her real friends—Pier Paolo Pasolini, the poet Sandro Penna, even Moravia—had remained children or were childlike. Her goal was to try to understand the truth and to express it.[4]

On the subject of reality, however, Moravia tended to disagree. He claimed that he was the one who loved reality with all its warts and problems, but that he invented the characters in his novels based on his experience and observations, while in Morante's case, it was just the opposite. She disliked reality—she regarded reality, he said, with as much fondness as her many cats regarded water—but in her novels, one could find Elsa herself and the people in her life without their having undergone much transformation.[5]

Many of the characters in *House of Liars* bear out Moravia's claim and have recognizable and familiar traits: one character is blond and robust and has a beautiful singing voice; another, like Elsa's own maternal grandmother, is prone to fits: "Her crises had become more violent. She was seized with a furious hatred for her own person and abused herself, beating her head and fists against the wall."[6] Still another is a hunchback of whom the family is deeply ashamed.

House of Liars is a sprawling and confusing novel of over eight hundred pages. Any attempt to summarize the plot is likely to lead to more confusion. Suffice it to say that it is the story of three generations of women in an eccentric Sicilian family—Cesira, the grandmother; Anna, the mother; and the granddaughter Elisa. At the outset, Elisa, who narrates the novel, claims that she is merely obeying "the insistent whispers of many voices" in an attempt to write and come to terms with her childhood and her legacy, a "poison of lying and deception [that] creeps through the branches of my family."[7] A family she describes thus: "My mother was a saint, my father a grand duke in disguise my cousin Edoardo was a desert sheik, my Aunt Concetta a prophetess and queen."[8] She too admits to having fallen victim to their make-believe: "To make oneself a worshiper, a disciple of illusion! Deliberately to make falsehood the substance of one's thought and one's wisdom—to reject all experience. . . . And while you must expect to meet in the course of my story more than one person contaminated by our family disease of illusion, you must real-ize that you have already met the sickest of all. And that is of course the person who writes this book: I, Elisa."[9] Thus, imme-diately, the narrator establishes—or, to put it more accurately, stresses—the fact that she is unreliable.

A Gothic tale peopled with narcissistic and deceitful charac-ters, *House of Liars* begins by describing how Cesira, a dreadfully deluded and angry woman, marries an impoverished and weak aristocrat, Teodoro. Their beautiful daughter, Anna, also de-luded and angry, falls in love with her cousin Edoardo; when he rejects her, she marries Francesco Monaco, whom she grows to despise and whom she tries to humiliate. Victims of their roman-ticism and imaginations, both Cesira and Anna are incapable of living in the real world or accepting it. Most of their illusions are the result of their misguided and inappropriate idea of love—mother love in particular, which is either improperly sexual and incestuous or withholding. Here is a scene between the imperious young aristocrat, Edoardo, and his mother, Concetta: "While he laughed at his mother, he held her tight in his arms and covered her faded face with kisses and then playfully he began to remove the hairpins one by one. This childish game had once made her angry but as her beautiful gray hair fell about her shoulders now, she sighed with pleasure." [10] There is a similar scene between Francesco Monaco and his mother, Alessandra: "in the morning when his mother dipped her comb in the basin and combed her long, shining black hair, he watched her with wide eyes. What particularly attracted him to his mother was her beauty." [11] In the case of the narrator, Elisa's love for Anna is more of an affliction: "My mother was the first and the most serious of my unhappy loves. Thanks to her, I knew from early childhood the bitterest agonies of the unaccepted lover." [12]

Most of the novel's characters are either from the working classes or from the aristocracy—at the end of the nineteenth century in Sicily, there was no substantial middle class and society was arbitrarily divided between the elegant lords and ladies and the vulgar poor people. Also, many of Morante's characters tend to suffer from some disease or are sick—the men are deformed, blind or ugly (Francesco Monaco, for instance, is pockmarked) and the poor women tend to be prostitutes. As in the novels of Émile Zola—a writer Elsa Morante greatly admired—there is a connection between the characters' psychology and their social status. She represented this dichotomy stylistically: on the one hand, there is the picturesque and the squalid (the poor, struggling, starving peasants) and on the other, the realistic and fantastic (the aristocrats and their dazzling palaces and clothes). The fact that the language in the novel is baroque and full of archaisms, mannered phrases and words that evoke romantic stereotypes is, by her own admission, done consciously in order to hide what is going on beneath the surface. It is also an attempt at literary parody, a tactic that Elsa Morante would use again and again and that would evolve into what she called an "alibi."

Despite these subterfuges, Elsa Morante was a close observer of human nature. Describing Francesco's disfigurement, she wrote: "And in spite of his deep need for sympathy, Francesco fled from companionship for two motives which, although they are opposed in nature are often joined in ferocious league: pride and shyness." [13] Or recounting Concetta's excessively righteous anger: "We may observe at this point how women passionate in virtue feel one of two conflicting emotions toward women passionate in sin: either a great love which makes them long to convert their erring sisters, or hatred, the blind and uncontrollable hatred of a rival." [14] Some of Elsa Morante's images are no less haunting: "All my thoughts, like flags beating against the wind, turned back to the burning season behind me which had cut short my childhood and transformed my destiny. Even today, in a sense, I live in that childhood summer around which my spirit wheels and beats ceaselessly, like an insect around a dazzling lamp." [15]

The book's central and most significant episode, however, does not occur until nearly the end and it returns the reader to the original inspiration for the novel: the letters. Anna, the narrator's mother, writes herself letters from the now dead Edoardo (the lover she had as an adolescent and with whom she has been all along obsessed). Not only does she read these letters out loud to Donna Concetta, Edoardo's mother, who is equally obsessed with her son, but writing them becomes the principal cause of Anna's joy and her sexual pleasure: "Her eyes shone with an extraordinary splendor, her lips parted softly and flushed a fresh pink, and an ardent color lighted her face and even spread over her bared shoulders," [16] or again, "When finally she came to bed, she did not stretch out but slipping the letter she had just written under her pillow, she lay half uncovered, her head resting against the head of the bed. She would lie like that for several minutes with her eyes closed; she was not asleep, I could tell, because her face was not in repose but was filled with a bright ecstasy." [17] Edoardo is a phantom, a ghost, a product of Anna's overwrought imagination and yet the effect he has on Anna is that of a flesh-and-blood lover: "Anna's imaginary adultery had brought about a great change in her body and face, no less than a real transgression would have done. . . . [S] he had the ambiguous air of involuntary suggestiveness and remembered pleasures that loose women have after a rendezvous. Her face was soft and relaxed, her full, half-parted lips preserved the traces of imagined kisses, and her elusive, languid, glowing glance seemed dazzled by recent visions of love." [18]

These made-up letters are the crux of the novel and are largely responsible for its ambiguity and complexity. They address the theme of powerlessness or impotence, which manifests itself through silence, omission and lies. Not revealing the content of these letters, which presumably is erotic (another form of self-censorship), was the way that Elsa Morante chose to express the difficulty of writing about the female experience, both sexual and psychological. The self-censorship too can be said to echo the use of asterisks in the 1938 diary where, again, erotic content is implicit, not explicit.

In the end, notwithstanding the admiration one might feel for the ambitious enterprise, *House of Liars* remains a strangely anachronistic and lugubrious novel. The reader is not drawn to any of the characters, nor does he or she care much what happens to any of them. No matter that it was willed, the writing is irritatingly precious, the plot is too convoluted and contrived to be credible. The result is a kind of artificial airlessness. Michel

David, the critic who interviewed Morante, made the same sort of observation about *House of Liars*, saying that fresh air seemed to be lacking in this Sicilian hothouse, although he was ready to bite into lemons and discover that they taste of oranges.[19]

Curiously and inexplicably, *House of Liars* ends with an ode to a cat. The cat's name is Alvaro and Elisa claims that, although she has concealed him until the end, he is "one of the most endearing and important of characters."[20] The last stanza goes:

> *The simple joy of having you as a friend*
> *Fills my heart to the brim; my agonies and fancies*
> *Die in your kisses and your sweet laments,*
> *So deeply you console me,*
> *O cat of mine!*[21]

At the time of the publication of *House of Liars*, the Hungarian critic Georg Lukács said that it was the greatest modern Italian novel and he praised the writer for both her style and her ability to move huge blocks of narrative with ease. Most contemporary critics, however, greeted the novel with incomprehension: they accused it of being retrograde and romantic, a nineteenth-century novel written in the twentieth century and severely out of step with the realism or neorealism of the day. Others interpreted *House of Liars* in popularized and imprecise Freudian terms, or simply as a popular romance. Critics often asked what sort of relationship the writer had to the women in the novel—where they are depicted as either crazy or evil and where love for them is a *via dolorosa* and suffering is joy. All love, the novel seems to say, is a game of force and violence; the female dream of love is masochistic (an embrace of suffering, delusion and eventual death) and the male one is sadistic (men prefer the pain of others)—which would lead one to believe that the answer might be that Morante did not like women. Instead, I would argue that Morante disliked a certain type of woman: a petty, deceitful, manipulative, falsely powerful woman who gave women in general a bad name. Ultimately, too, Elsa Morante understood that it was a man's world and to be a woman was more difficult.[22]

There has, however, always been a very strong tradition of women writers in Italy, and Elsa Morante must have been well aware of it. If one looks only at the literary scene dating from the unification of Italy (after 1861), there is no lack of female writers (not to mention poets). Enrichetta Caracciolo, a nun, wrote a widely read and translated memoir called *Misteri del chiostro napoletano (Mysteries of the Neapolitan Convents)*; Neera, a pseudonym for Anna Radius Zuccari, wrote twenty-two novels; La Marchesa Colombi (her real name was Maria Antonietta Torriani) wrote a little jewel called *Un matrimonio in provincia (A Small-Town Marriage)*, which is said to have influenced Natalia Ginzburg and whose style is both ironic and quite modern (this novel ends with the surprising line "The fact is I am gaining weight" to summarize a life filled with disappointment). Other writers include Contessa Lara, Bruno Sperani (a pseudonym for Beatrice Speraz), Maria Messina, Matilde Serao and Grazia Deledda, the latter nearly forgotten now even though in 1926 she won the Nobel Prize for literature. These women writers wrote what today would probably be considered popular literature and at the time they were widely read.

In the twentieth century, the writer Sibilla Aleramo particularly stands out for her autobiographical novel *Una donna (A Woman)*, which tells the story of a young woman who, after being raped, is forced into a loveless marriage in order to hush up her disgrace. She manages to escape to Rome, leaving her husband and young son, and goes on to lead a scandalous life and to have many heterosexual and homosexual affairs. *Una donna* can be considered the first truly Italian feminist novel because it introduces a protagonist who is self-aware of her plight and her lack of freedom. (Interestingly, when male scholars speak of this work, they mostly stress Aleramo's erotic and scandalous life.) More contemporary writers are Rosa Benedetta, Fausta Cialente, Paola Masino, Gianna Manzini, Anna Banti (who was married to the well-known art critic Roberto Longhi) and Anna Maria Ortese.

What most of these women writers have in common is their social class; they were all well connected and well educated. Unlike Elsa Morante, they did not have to earn a living. Also, in their novels, they showed a tendency to move away from the popular *verismo* (realism) of the day and write more surreal and mythical stories. No doubt Elsa Morante had read many of these women writers and no doubt, too, she was influenced by their presence. Whether she was influenced by their work is less certain.

Fifty years after the novel's original publication and on the occasion of a new edition, when writing about *House of Liars*—a sort of retrospective summation—Cesare Garboli, Elsa Morante's great friend and one of the executors of her estate, who wrote extensively about her and her oeuvre, compared Morante's work to Natalia Ginzburg's. Both writers, he said, expressed the provocative force of sex and wrote about the fragility and vulnerability of the female experience. Garboli claimed that Natalia Ginzburg was a more forgiving and wiser writer—she often rendered the female experience as a sort of flat dialogue—and looked at the nature of women with compassion, while Elsa Morante's relationship to sex was terrible and savage; she wrote about the nature of women with such mocking animosity that Garboli had to wonder whether *House of Liars* was in fact a misogynist novel.[23]

As it turned out, however, Elsa Morante was the writer of her generation whom Natalia Ginzburg admired most.[24] Natalia Ginzburg was also Elsa Morante's first editor and, years later, she recalled the experience of receiving the novel and working with Elsa:

> In '48, I think it was in winter, a letter came to me from Elsa Morante. In it, she told me that she had just finished a novel and she wanted to know if she could send it to me. I lived in Turin and I was working at the publishing house Einaudi. I had met Elsa Morante in Rome, I don't remember anymore where we met; we did not exchange very many words. It seems to me that I told her how much I loved one of her short stories, which had come out in a magazine several years before, during the war. In any case, our meetings, according to what I remember, were few and brief. But I was the person she knew best in that publishing house. That's how I got the manuscript of *House of Liars*: I received it in the mail. There were corrections on it in red ink. I remember with what surprise I read the chapter titles, because it seemed like a novel from another time, and I was intrigued when glancing through the pages I found here and there words capitalized: the Pockmarked, the Cousin. . . . I read *House of Liars* straight through and I liked it immensely: although I can't say that then I clearly understood its importance and greatness. I knew only that I loved it and it had been a long time since I had read anything that gave me such life and joy. It was an extraordinary adventure for me to discover, among the chapter titles I perceived still like

those of the nineteenth century, the time and cities that
were our own, and that had the painful and shattered inten-
sity of our daily life; for me, it was a great emotion to discover the possibility even in our time, when books were
miserly and tangled, of giving our fellow human beings a
work of art so luminous and generous. Perhaps, in a way, I
understood the greatness. I had not worked very long at
this publishing house and I did not have the authority to
decide alone to publish a book; I sought the advice of Pavese; I don't think that he read it then in manuscript but he
thought it was a good idea to publish it.

In the spring, *House of Liars* was ready in page proofs
and Elsa came to Turin to correct them. She stayed in an inn
near the railroad station; an inn not far from the one where
a few years later Cesare Pavese died. I had a copy of the
proofs and she had another; I remember that because of the
tremendous effort and the emotion and because of the fear
she had of printed errors, she got a fever.* When she was
cured of this fever, she used to come out in the evenings and
sit in a café on the street, waiting for Pavese, myself, Felice
Balbo and Italo Calvino to leave the office and come sit
with her. She and Pavese discussed many things but without great anger; they did not agree on anything yet in these
discussions there was never any sign of animosity.[25]

In 1948, *House of Liars* won the Viareggio Prize, a prestigious
Italian literary award. Elsa Morante shared the prize with Aldo
Palazzeschi, one of the most prolific Italian writers, for his novel

---

* Elsa Morante attributed the fever to bacteria from the rubble. Turin was
still in ruins after the war.

The Cuccoli Brothers (I fratelli Cuccoli). As a result, the fortunes of Alberto Moravia, who had just published *The Woman of Rome (La romana)*, and Elsa Morante were very much improved. To celebrate they rented an elegant house on Capri and briefly spent money extravagantly—mainly, according to Moravia, to chase away the nightmare of the miseries they had endured. They traveled together, and Elsa went to France and England for the first time. (In London, apparently, food was still so scarce that when they went to an elegant restaurant, which Moravia described as decorated "with Doric columns, red plush, that sort of thing," and he ordered a shrimp cocktail, he was brought a single shrimp on a dish.[26]) Moravia sold the small apartment on via Sgambati and purchased a larger, more elegant one at via dell'Oca 27, near the Piazza del Popolo. He also bought a small apartment on via Archimede as a studio for Elsa and he bought Elsa a beaver coat. After that, Moravia said, he was broke.[27]

The American edition of *House of Liars* came out in 1951, three years after its original publication in Italian. The novel was much abridged—from the original 800 pages, more than 200 pages were cut. These cuts were made without consulting the author, and as a result Elsa Morante wrote a letter complaining bitterly about the abridged American version, threatening to take legal action. Natalia Ginzburg, her editor, answered with an apology, saying how she too was angry and sorry. However Sanford Greenburger, the American agent for the book, claimed that if the cuts had not been made, the book would have been too long and too costly and would not have been published in America. Elsa Morante wrote another letter in which she said that the cuts had caused her great sorrow and more suffering than she had the whole year.

Yet more suffering must have been caused by the description

on the front jacket flap of *House of Liars*: "This long and distinguished novel, winner of Rome's literary prize—the Viareggio—is the first work of Elsa Morante, who in private life is Mrs. Alberto Moravia." Elsa did not want to be known by Alberto Moravia's name, and many stories have evolved around people committing this error. Moravia himself described how once finding the weather unexpectedly cold in Egypt, he sent a telegram to Elsa, who was to join him shortly, asking her to bring him his overcoat. He addressed it to "Elsa Moravia," with this result: "Elsa received the telegram, took the overcoat, came to Cairo, and the moment she arrived began a scene that lasted three days, because I should have written Elsa Morante. Practically speaking, this scene, so cruel and unjust, cast a pall on our whole journey. . . ." [28] When Elsa's favorite nephew, Daniele Morante, was nine or ten, he made the same mistake, addressing a letter to Elsa Moravia. She replied, in an affectionate but firm manner, saying that her name was Morante and would always be Morante. [29] Another error—this time on the back jacket flap of the same American edition of *House of Liars*—was the claim that "she [was] a native of Sicily." Elsa Morante was a native of Rome; she had spent *three days* in Sicily prior to writing the novel.

In a review of *House of Liars* that appeared in *The New Yorker*, Maeve Brennan praised the fine translation and hailed Elsa Morante (mercifully, not Mrs. Alberto Moravia) as "a young Italian writer of extraordinary emotional power." She was able to appreciate the novel despite the fact that there was "no development . . . , no plot, no solution," and despite the often melodramatic exaggerated tone of the prose and the overly passionate nature of the characters—"operatic in their transports of fury and despair" was how she described them. Mostly, Brennan understood that Elsa Morante was a writer of enormous talent and that she was quite fearless. "Miss Morante, it is clear, is not afraid of romantic dénouements. Neither is she afraid of passion or of melodrama or of the extravagant, elegant phrases she handles so superbly. She seems afraid of nothing, except, possibly, the dullness and resignation of a sensible solution." [30]

Behind or along with Elsa Morante's fierceness, willfulness and unpredictable sense of humor there was also a sweet and disingenuous side to her nature. William Weaver, the translator, recalled how as he gave Elsa Morante his copy of *House of Liars* to sign, afraid that she would quiz him on the book, he quickly confessed that he had not yet read it. Instead of chiding him, Elsa was full of genuine and quite childish enthusiasm: "Oh, how I envy you!" she told Weaver. "How I wish I could read my book with a fresh mind! What a wonderful experience you have in store for you! You're really lucky!" [31]

six

ROME

"Ialways tell everyone, when I have the chance, that Rome is the most beautiful city in the world," wrote Pier Paolo Pasolini, the filmmaker, writer and poet. "Of all the cities I know, it's the one where I'd rather live; in fact, I can't imagine living anywhere else. In my worst nightmares, I dream that I am forced to leave Rome and return to Northern Italy. Its beauty is a natural mystery. We can attribute it to the baroque, the atmosphere, the composition of the terrain, with its elevations and depressions, a landscape that continually offers new perspective, to the Tiber that runs through it, opening glorious airy spaces in its heart, and most of all the stratification of styles which at every angle offers up a new, surprising cross section. The excessive beauty produced by this superposition of styles is a veritable shock to the system. But would Rome be the most beautiful city in the world if it were not at the same time, the ugliest?" [1]

William Weaver, the preeminent translator of Italian literature—he translated not only Elsa Morante and Pier Paolo Pasolini but also such writers as Giorgio Bassani, Roberto Calasso, Italo Calvino, Umberto Eco, Carlo Emilio Gadda, Primo Levi, Italo Svevo and Alberto Moravia—would have agreed with Pasolini. For Weaver, Rome represented "the fabled, the perfect, the ideal answer to every dream." He had first come to Italy during World War II as an ambulance driver for the American Field

Service, and since both the Germans and his duties kept him between Naples and Monte Cassino, Rome seemed "unattainable, [and] became legend, the stuff of my constant frustrated daydreams. . . . Rome—the imagined Rome of my obsession—was tidy, clean, brightly-lighted, sunny; there were bookshops with books in English, newspapers, theater, music. There were dinner-parties and smart cafés—there was the Europe I had yearned all my brief life to visit."[2] Weaver, a near penniless student at the time who was hoping to write a novel, finally realized his dream when he arrived in Rome in 1947. And despite the fact that, for an entire generation, most artistic creation had come to a halt in Italy, Weaver's naïve enthusiasm proved prescient. It was not long before he saw what he called a "creative explosion," with films like Roberto Rossellini's *Germany Year Zero*, and Vittorio De Sica's *Bicycle Thief*, and books like Carlo Levi's *Christ Stopped at Eboli* and Alberto Moravia's *The Woman of Rome*. Exhibitions, too, he noted, presented new painters and sculptors as well as the innovative industrial designers who produced the sleek and elegant Olivetti Lettera 22 typewriter. All this, according to Weaver, was proof of the Italian spirit and the country's creative vitality, which indeed had revived and was flourishing.

Another writer, Sybille Bedford, herself recently arrived in Rome, echoed these sentiments: "Early post-war Italy was glorious. One embraced the people for whom the springs of life were flowing again; they were at one with the staggering beauty of what there was to see, *everywhere*, dawdling in the sun, the sweet air, the new near quiet. Petrol was scarce, the Vespas and rattling trams were joyful toys, their noise another attribute to being alive."[3] Certainly, there seemed to be much to look forward to. In a 1946 referendum, the majority of Italian voters preferred a republic over a monarchy; the change represented hope for the

reconstruction and modernization of a war-torn country, the possibility of a democratic debate between political parties and an
opportunity for a more egalitarian and prosperous society, especially in the country's very poor south.[4]

Nonetheless, in the late forties and early fifties, despite all the
new activity in business and in the arts, Rome—all of Italy, in
fact—was far from being an ideal or easy place to live. The country was still in political turmoil and suffering from the aftershocks
of the war, which included shortages of food, fuel, housing. Re-
acting to the general poverty and popular unrest as well as to the
recent horrors of the Fascist regime, hundreds of political parties
sprang up, taking part in what Norman Lewis, a British intelligence agent stationed in Naples, called "the wild democratic free-
for-all."[5]

Most intellectuals were either Communists or Socialists but
the majority party was the church-sanctioned Christian Democrats. To ensure victory, the Roman Catholic Church threatened
anyone voting for the Communist Party with excommunication,
local priests exhorted their parishioners to vote for the Christian
Democrats, armies of nuns were sent out to preach to housewives.
Posters showed Communist wolves trying to devour Italian children. When the Christian Democrats, whom Weaver called "the
party of film censorship, of reaction, of former Fascists slightly
whitewashed over," won the election of April 1948, "[s]omething
went out of Roman life . . . ; a kind of dull resignation set in."[6]
Alberto Moravia was more pragmatic: "I was sure the Christian
Democrats would win, because Italy is a pendulum: many Italians voted for the Communists, but they didn't want communism
to take over."[7] Moravia believed his fellow intellectuals felt the
same way as their countrymen. "To understand the situation of
the intellectuals, and of the Italians in general, you have to realize

that they had hated Fascism because it was a dictatorship of the bourgeoisie: a contradiction, in other words. The bourgeoisie is either liberal or it's nothing. But from that to go to communism, to Stalin, is a great step, too big for the Italians at that moment in history."[8]

The Christian Democrats, with Alcide De Gasperi at their head, managed to gather support from many different sectors of Italian society and become the leading political party in all postwar Italian governments (of which there were many). Nonetheless, the average Italian citizen never identified with the government, which he viewed with cynicism and as fundamentally oppressive and corrupt. Also, a large minority of Italians, made up primarily of the working class, embraced a counterideology and remained profoundly opposed to the government. Still more controversial were many of the government's policies which reflected the need to maintain the support of the United States. From 1948 to 1951, the Marshall Plan poured money into Italian redevelopment and industrialization, with the implicit caveat that the Christian Democrats eradicate the Communist Party. The end result was that the governments led by the Christian Democrats were inherently unstable, founded as they were on weak leadership and a bare majority of unenthusiastic popular support. And finally, the fact that Christian Democratic rule was based on Catholicism, Americanism and anticommunism gave critics good reason to compare it to an autocratic regime, a regime that, according to many, lasted until the death of Aldo Moro in 1978.

As it turned out, William Weaver's pensione in Rome was located not far from via dell'Oca, and, as a result, he saw a great deal of Elsa Morante and Alberto Moravia. He recalled how, for the first time in their lives, thanks to their combined royalties and the film reviews Moravia had begun writing, they were able to furnish their apartment comfortably with sofas and chairs, put up paintings on the walls and populate it with Elsa's numerous Siamese cats. Elsa, who had grown up in semipoverty, was particularly pleased to be able to afford the luxury of a cook. For the first time in her life, she gave dinner parties. Otherwise, she, Moravia and their group of friends, which included Weaver, would gather at the last minute to dine—after a heated discussion on the merits and faults of the various restaurants—at one of the local trattorias.

Weaver quickly learned the protocol to adopt with Elsa when inviting her and Alberto Moravia for dinner, as she was extremely sensitive to slights—no doubt that feeling was exacerbated by having always to defer in public to her more famous husband. When calling to make a date, Weaver cautioned: "You were never to say, 'Could you and Alberto come——?' Even the use of the plural *voi* was a grave infraction. . . . The proper course was to invite Elsa: Can you—*tu*—come for dinner on Thursday? . . . Then when all was agreed, you could venture, in as offhand a tone as possible: 'If Alberto's free, tell him to join us.' 'I'll tell him,' she would reply, audibly dubious."[9]

Alberto Moravia and Elsa Morante were well-known (famous, in fact) for their terrible arguments. Some arguments grew so loud that they could be heard all the way from their apartment to the Bolognese, the restaurant below them on Piazza del Popolo. According to Moravia, the fights were never personal but the result of their two very different views of the world.[10] Nonetheless, Elsa tended to say hurtful and outrageous things. She liked to quarrel, she liked to cast blame. In public, too—because Moravia acted so cold and indifferent—Morante tried to provoke him by insulting him, humiliating him, accusing him of sexual impotence. Often, according to the filmmaker Bernardo Bertolucci, a friend, Moravia had to get up from the table, leave the restaurant and walk around the block several times in order to cool off. One particularly memorable quarrel occurred in a restaurant called Romolo, and was over the habits of the Italian peasants. During it, Elsa shouted, "Don't talk nonsense, Alberto, in the south peasant mothers masturbate their children to put them to sleep at night." The crucial verb was uttered in such a shrill, loud cry, William Weaver reported, that it seemed to echo interminably beneath the low vaults of the restaurant ceiling. All the diners stopped talking and ate their meals in shocked silence; no one, not even the waiters, dared to speak. Only Elsa remained oblivious and unaffected.[11]

But William Weaver also recalled more congenial times. One of the pleasures he described was the popular weekly Sunday ritual—not mass but a trip to the Cinema Barberini, closed to the public on that day and reserved for the Rome Cineclub. This predominantly leftist group—most were students hoping to become directors, actors or screenwriters—showed avant-garde films each week. Older film buffs like Elsa Morante and Moravia often attended, as well as professionals like Luchino Visconti, surrounded by his court of good-looking young men, and Vittorio De Sica, looking like a distinguished ambassador from a small country.[12]

My father, Rodolphe Solmsen, was a regular member of the Cineclub and here I will digress from Elsa Morante's story and perhaps also suggest a reason for my telling it. A German and a Jew—albeit an assimilated one, he was baptized a Lutheran—my father settled in Rome after the war to make movies along with William Wyler, Carlo Ponti, Dino De Laurentiis and, of course, Roberto Rossellini. Two of the films he produced were set in

Rome. *Le ragazze di Piazza di Spagna (Three Girls from Rome)*, far and away my favorite, was directed by Luciano Emmer and was shot on location. I remember how I watched mesmerized as Lucia Bosé, Cosetta Greco and Liliana Bonfatti sat together on a parapet on the Spanish Steps, their shapely legs dangling in the air while the makeup lady ran back and forth in between takes to comb their hair, apply more lipstick or rearrange the fold of their clothes. In fairly straightforward and predictable fashion, the movie followed the troubled romances of the three young women, seamstresses in a fashion house located on Piazza di Spagna. Made in 1952, the film (whose cast also included Marcello Mastroianni and Eduardo De Filippo) was basically a romantic comedy and followed the new trend in filmmaking, a more humorous, rose-colored look at life called *neorealismo rosa*. But, mostly, I think, I loved the movie because of Lucia Bosé. I was enchanted by her grace and beauty. (A few years later, Lucia Bosé was to give up her movie career to marry the Spanish bullfighter Luis-Miguel Dominguín.) *Villa Borghese* (in English, *It Happened in the Park*), the second of my father's films set in Rome, was likewise a comedy of sorts. It was written by Sergio Amidei and co-directed by Vittorio De Sica and it had a distinguished cast that included De Sica himself, Gérard Philipe, Micheline Presle, Terence Hill (then known as Mario Girotti) and Anna-Maria Ferrero. The film consisted of a series of interconnected vignettes, a kind of *la ronde* that took place during a single day—beginning in the morning with a nanny and her charge and ending late at night with a prostitute—all set in historic Villa Borghese park. An earlier film produced by my father, *Donne senza nome (Women without Names)*, which starred Simone Simon and was set in a displaced persons camp (shot at Cinecittà as well as in Alberobello, a town famous for the curiously shaped roofs of its houses), had the gritty, unflinching realism the two later films lacked. In 1950, it won the Golden Laurel Award at the Venice Film Festival, the citation reading, "A tribute to the motion picture produced in Europe by Europeans in the Italian language that has made the greatest contribution to mutual understanding and goodwill between the peoples of the free and democratic world."

Most nights, if they were not otherwise occupied, my father and Sergio Amidei, who wrote the screenplays for most of my father's films (he also cowrote the screenplay for Rossellini's *Open City*), dined together in a restaurant called Nino. Then there were two Ninos in Rome—one was expensive and fashionable and owned by a man named Nino; the other, less fashionable, and the one my father and Sergio Amidei went to, was near Piazza Barberini and owned by Nino's brother, Mario. Mario had been given a small part (as a restaurant owner) in *Le ragazze di Piazza di Spagna* and he was eager to please my father and, by extension, me, by cooking us special dishes. Sergio Amidei always brought his bulldog, Cesare, to Nino; Cesare, although a gentle-tempered dog, wore a leather collar with spikes on it and every night he was fed a sumptuous dish of pasta in the kitchen. The atmosphere at Nino was cordial and lively, people shouted to one another across the tables, they joked about the quality of the food and the slowness of the service, calling the waiters by name. Most evenings one or more friends of my father or of Sergio Amidei joined us at our table. One evening Anna Magnani dined with us and I recall how shocked I was when I saw that she chewed her food with her mouth open. I also remember dining with Roberto Rossellini and Ingrid Bergman. While Rossellini and my father talked business, Ingrid Bergman asked me a lot of questions: What was I studying in school? What was my favorite subject? Did I like boys yet?

I was the same age as the daughter she had had to leave with her first husband and no doubt I reminded Ingrid Bergman of her.

Since I began writing about Elsa Morante, I have gone back to Rome several times—trips that have brought back vivid memories of driving to the beach in my father's silver Lancia "Spider"; of cantering along the via Cassia, then bordered by fields, on a spirited gray mare named Magali; of eating late at night in trattorias with Mario Alberto, my first boyfriend; of buying impractical but beautiful high-heeled shoes; and of the luxury of being carefree, young and naïve. I also met a lot of people whom I might never have met otherwise, friends and associates of my father who worked in the film industry, actors struggling to be discovered and now almost forgotten: Francine, my father's Jamaican girlfriend, who had the role of a slave in *Ben-Hur* and took me shopping for a bikini; the man whose name I have forgotten, more like a magician, who arrived on the set with just a small attaché case from which he unpacked a few ordinary items with which he managed to fill the film's sound track; and handsome Lex Barker, who played Tarzan and also played high-stakes gin rummy with my father. Mostly, I remember how fortunate I was. And, fortunate, too, because although I never met Elsa Morante, who lived in Rome all her life, I can picture her there—vividly.

The success of *House of Liars* gave Elsa Morante more confidence, especially since she had always felt that Moravia took her for granted. At the same time she valued his good opinion. Fortunately for her and for him, he liked the novel—according to Moravia, Morante was "something of a totalitarian: either you were with her or against her." Moravia claimed that he had always been "with her" while she, in turn, had not always been "with" him. Unlike Moravia, who said that he had little pride and did not take offense from adverse criticism, Morante did, so that with her one had to be careful.[13] As for the writers they admired, Moravia's favorite was Dostoevsky while Elsa's was Kafka. They both loved Rimbaud. Later on, Elsa gave up Kafka in favor of Stendhal, who was less "heavy." "Stendhal, along with Mozart in music and Rimbaud in poetry," Moravia said, "represented for her that ideal of lightness to which she aspired all her life."[14] Otherwise, they rarely discussed books or the virtues of the authors they were reading or, if they did talk about books now and then, they did so in the way any couple might. Interesting to note, too, that Morante and Moravia rarely played the role of the professional writing couple as did Simone de Beauvoir and Jean-Paul Sartre, Mary McCarthy and Edmund Wilson or Sylvia Plath and Ted Hughes. They did not read each other's works in progress, nor did they criticize each other's manuscripts. In fact, Elsa, according to the poet Patrizia Cavalli, was the sort of person who never talked about what she was writing; she was superstitious that if she did, the writing would be destroyed. The one time Elsa showed Moravia a story, he did not like it and she tore it up. Later she regretted her decision and resented being influenced by him. She thought the story was good and she had been wrong to destroy it. This, in Cavalli's opinion, showed that there must have been a very subtle kind of interior competition between the two writers, a competition that rarely surfaced. In any case, Morante never wrote "against" Moravia. She had her own very distinctive style and although she admired him as a writer, she could never write like him. Finally, their working methods were totally opposite: Moravia wrote every morning and he produced a novel a year, more or less (later, when Moravia had left Elsa and was living with the writer Dacia Maraini, both were very disciplined and even on a summer holiday in Ischia, they could be heard typing away all morning); Elsa, on the other hand, worked sporadically but when she was writing, she wrote obsessively.

Elsa and Alberto Moravia, according again to Patrizia Cavalli, were like people who belonged to two different worlds. They did not understand each other, although Elsa understood Alberto better than he did her. On the most basic level they could not hear each other and they were constantly saying, "What did he say?" "What did she say?" The sensation this produced was that someone should be in the middle to interpret—not only physically since Moravia was slightly deaf, but also psychologically as one felt each was made of a totally different matter. Nevertheless, Elsa had a great affection for Moravia. She admired him at the same time that she wanted to protect him. Also, still according to Patrizia Cavalli, the fact that Elsa must have known that Alberto was never in love with her must have been terribly hurtful, because she could not have what she really wanted. This would explain her often bitter and aggressive behavior toward him. Elsa was always testing people and hoping that by sort of "breaking them" something strong would emerge. She would say funny things too about Moravia—for instance, how he was stingy while she was not. She liked splendor, luxury; she liked staying in fancy hotels like the Danieli in Venice, while Moravia preferred staying in a pensione so he could save the money.[15]

In 1951, Elsa Morante went to work for RAI, the Italian public radio station, where she had a weekly show called *Cronache del cinema (Chronicle of the Cinema)*, reviewing films. The job came to an abrupt end when Elsa refused to bow to pressure from the station and give the film *Senza bandiera*, produced by Luigi Freddi, a favorable review and she was fired. She wrote a letter of protest complaining that "it was clear that from now on it was impossible to express one's honest and free opinion on the Radio." The letter was published in the weekly *Il Mondo*, where she had begun writing for a column called "Rosso e Bianco" ("Red and White").[16] The dozen or so very short pieces she collaborated on over a period of less than three months (November 4, 1950, to January 27, 1951) range from a piece on the fickleness of glory to another on the pleasure derived from women's fashion as opposed to men's which are dreary, except for the necktie—itself the subject of an essay. The necktie, Morante writes, should be made from "brocade, lace, satin, ermine or painted with flowers and all sorts of surprises, composed out of feathers, woven from silver and gold. [The tie] is the last bridge between man and fantasy." [17] Two pieces discussed Tolstoy's Prince Andrei and Goncharov's Oblomov, and how they both share the same characteristics: pride and indolence. There is an essay on the devoted nonjudgmental friendship of animals; animals, Elsa Morante writes, are special because unlike human beings they were not expelled from Paradise and therefore they still live in it. Another essay, "The Real King of the Animals" ("Il vero re degli animali"), is, not surprisingly, about the cat, the Siamese cat. In this piece, in order to do justice to the cat, Morante writes that one must adopt the precious language of Diderot and "dip one's pen in a rainbow, and dry one's writing with the powder from butterfly wings." [18] She also tells the story of a Siamese princess who, whenever she washed her hands, was in the habit of slipping her rings around her cat's tail, then, in order not to lose them, of tying the cat's tail in a knot; this apparently is the origin of this graceful deformity one sees in the Siamese cat's tail.

Elsa Morante's love of cats was legendary. Her favorite cat was called Caruso, named not for the Neopolitan singer but because, in Sicilian dialect, the word *caruso* means "child." Caruso lived to be nineteen years old. He was not castrated and together, with the pretty little Siamese wife Elsa provided for him, they produced 150 kittens—or so Elsa claimed. She baptized each kitten with a different name (both a Christian name and a surname) and expended a great deal of time and effort placing it in a proper home, making certain that the prospective owner was worthy enough. On account of the cats, the furniture in her apartment on via dell'Oca was said to be in ruin. The upholstery was torn and shredded by Caruso's claws—worse, the furniture was stained with his scent, which Morante called "the benedictions" of Caruso.

Bernardo Bertolucci, who met Elsa Morante for the first time in the mid-1950s when he was fifteen or sixteen years old, talked admiringly of Elsa's determination to embrace the truth, her rigor, and her refusal to accept half measures or any bullshit. No one, he said, was allowed to lie in her presence—if one did, Elsa immediately saw through it and called the person on it. Bertolucci talked about the difficulty of leading a life governed by such high, self-imposed standards and the invincible tension it created. Elsa always faced the absolute in the eye, and this was an inspiration to others. He praised Elsa's courage and said he had never known anyone quite like her. Bertolucci also recalled how during those formative years, his father, the poet Attilio Bertolucci, had very much wanted him to go to university but he refused to go. "My university," Bertolucci told his father, "is having dinner every night with Elsa Morante, Alberto Moravia and Pier Paolo Pasolini."

Bertolucci spoke with great fondness of Elsa and also with regret since, as time went by, they grew farther apart. Not without reason. Several years later in 1972, soon after Bertolucci made *Last Tango in Paris* and it was a great success although it was also, he said, a time of personal anxiety for him, he ran into Elsa in the street near Piazza di Spagna and she told him, "Oh, I have seen you on the cover of *Time* magazine and you have become just like Moravia and Adolf Hitler."* Understandably, notwithstanding his great affection for her, Bertolucci was very hurt by Elsa's remark, even though he understood that she had this idea that if someone was to suddenly become popular or famous, it would lead to a vulgarization.[19]

But despite her high moral standards and her harsh judgments, Elsa Morante had a tremendous sense of fun. She loved to play games, guessing games and the tower game—in this last, the player imagined him- or herself in a high tower with two other people, one of whom he or she had to push off: Elsa or Alberto? Elsa particularly liked a game called Asassino (Murder in the Dark), which Pier Paolo Pasolini, another avid player, had complicated somewhat by adding psychological motives (before they began to play, each person had to give a reason why he or she would want to commit murder). One of the players, Ginevra Bompiani, laughingly remembered how Elsa always said she wanted to murder *her* because that way she could get her hands on the beautiful necklace Ginevra wore.[20]

Still another well-known figure who loved playing games was the charismatic, aristocratic director Luchino Visconti. His friend the filmmaker Michelangelo Antonioni recalled how "[s]ome of the games . . . were naughty. We played murder in the dark, the light went off and the 'detective' stayed away for a long time: in the darkness everything would happen."[21] Visconti owned a beautiful house on Ischia called La Colombaia (The Dovecote) with a garden planted with blue hydrangeas that grew all the way down to the sea, and a villa in Rome, on via Salaria,

* In another version of this story, Morante accused Bertolucci of being like Mao.

which was filled with his mastiff dogs and an eclectic assortment of splendid antiques (he was an avid collector and had wonderful taste). He entertained a great deal and both houses were always open to his friends and guests—even if no one was expected, his chef was told to prepare dinner every night for fourteen (so he would not get out of practice). Visconti's regular guests, who became known as his "group," included the actors Walter Chiari, Paolo Stoppa, Rina Morelli and Massimo Girotti, as well as Suso Cecchi d'Amico (his screenwriter), Franco Zeffirelli (his assistant, later a director as well), Antonioni and, for a time, Elsa Morante, who fell in love with her handsome host.

Openly bisexual, Visconti, in his youth, had had a long affair with Coco Chanel and was engaged to marry an Austrian princess, Irma Windisch-Graetz, when he fell in love with the German photographer Horst Horst. His affair with Elsa began in the early 1950s and lasted two years—years during which Visconti staged Tennessee Williams's *A Streetcar Named Desire*, with Marcello Mastroianni, and *Death of a Salesman*, the first play by Arthur Miller to be performed in Italy. Visconti was also directing *Bellissima*, a film set in the crass and vulgar movie world at Cinecittà that starred Anna Magnani. In the course of shooting the film, Magnani was said to have fallen in love with Visconti, as well, and it is not difficult to imagine how these two strong, outspoken women, Anna and Elsa, might have competed hotly for Visconti's affection.

Accounts, however, differ as to what sort of an affair Elsa and he actually had. In his recent autobiography, Franco Zeffirelli, also Visconti's lover, writes that he knew everything about Visconti's love stories but that his private life was full of "mystery." There were actors and several women, including Elsa Morante, who lost her head over him. Elsa, he writes, dedicated her poems to Visconti and filled his house with beautiful Persian cats.[22] Zeffirelli also quotes Visconti's jaded observation about his women lovers: "The problem is when you satisfy them once, they don't ever leave you in peace," to which Zeffirelli himself adds, "as the dear Elsa Morante knew very well."[23] Yet neither Bertolucci nor the actress Adriana Asti, who lived with Bertolucci for ten years and who knew Visconti very well herself, believes that Elsa Morante and Luchino Visconti had a "real" affair. Adriana Asti said that "everyone" fell in love with Visconti: he was so fascinating, so handsome, yet so distant and no one could have him—not even Marlene Dietrich, who also was in love with him.[24] Visconti's biographer, Gaia Servadio, too, supports this theory. She wrote that although Visconti adored Morante and was flattered by her attention, his involvement with women never really made a dent in his sentimental makeup. It did not keep him awake at night, while his involvement with young men often did.[25]

According to Moravia, during those years when Elsa was in love with Visconti, she would spend the entire day at his house on via Salaria, taking part in his life. She only returned home late at night and since Moravia was usually still awake, she would sit at the foot of the bed and tell him in great detail all that had transpired between her and Visconti that day. And Moravia would listen, he said, "Like an affectionate friend." Elsa described how, for instance, when Visconti looked at her, he was so moved that his legs trembled. Although Moravia admitted to being embarrassed by these intimate confessions, he also said that he and Elsa had not had physical relations for years and this proved to him that everything between them was over. Still he insisted on what he called an "existential symbiosis" that existed between them, which made everything comprehensible, even infidelity. At the end of the two years, Elsa told Moravia that she was leaving him

to live with Visconti. On the actual day when they were supposed
to meet and go off together, Visconti did not show up and Elsa
Morante stayed on with Moravia. Soon after, Moravia and Morante went to Venice to a music festival, and Moravia recalled
how Elsa dramatized and flaunted her grief and suffering over
losing Visconti. Her grief, however, he said, eventually turned
into rancor.[26]

By the mid-1950s, Moravia had become a well-known public
figure in Italy and he increasingly distanced himself from Elsa by
his busy schedule as a film critic, a travel writer and the founder,
in 1953, along with Alberto Carocci, of *Nuovi Argomenti*. This
left-wing magazine was financed by Adriano Olivetti and modeled on Sartre's *Les Temps Modernes*; its goal was to publish works
that represented the new Italian culture such as painting and an-
thropology, as well as literature. But Moravia also complained of
boredom. He admitted that his feelings for Elsa were cooling and
he attributed this to Elsa's preference for "the exceptional" and
for the "impassioned moments" in life. He said that during the
war and while they were in hiding "[a]t Sant'Agata she had found
herself in her element: danger, devotion, sacrifice, contempt for
life. In Rome, on the other hand, daily life made her lose patience
and become difficult, intolerant and even cruel." As an example
of Elsa's cruelty, he described how once when they were in Paris,
staying at the Hotel Pont-Royal, she began to moan and then
pretended to faint, lying motionless on the floor of their room,
seemingly unconscious—perhaps to punish Moravia for some
perceived misdeed—as Moravia tried to revive her. He even
called several doctors, but it was Sunday and just as he was beginning to despair and not know what to do next, Elsa opened her
eyes and started to laugh—not a joking laugh but a mean laugh.
Her eyes too, he said, looked mean.[27]

Also, and without actually laying the blame on Elsa, Moravia began to complain of various inexplicable and often very strange ailments. He could not move his arm to the right for a while. Stranger still, one day he wanted to walk to the right but instead his legs took him left. The worst was another terrifying time when he felt as if his legs were being attracted toward the ceiling by some dire magnet. (These were all symptoms of a neurological disorder known as locomotor ataxia, which is associated with syphilitic spinal sclerosis.) On several occasions, he developed the skin infection impetigo—no doubt for psychosomatic reasons. In sum, Moravia was always sick with illnesses that came and went for no evident organic cause. Finally, since Moravia also suffered from all sorts of allergies (including one to cat hairs), he did nothing, he said, but sneeze and weep.[28]

Beginning in 1957, Adriana Asti, whose bright eyes and expressive smile have not changed much over the years, saw Elsa Morante every day—she and her first husband lived in the same building as Elsa and Alberto Moravia. At first, Adriana told me, she was more a friend of Alberto and she remembered how he used to say to her about Elsa, "Look at what small hands she has—people who have small hands are very choleric." This was true, Adriana said, laughing. They were always arguing but it was also part of their charm. Adriana and I were having lunch at the Hotel Excelsior in Naples, the sort of quietly elegant hotel I am sure Elsa Morante would have loved, on a very stormy day. From where I sat, I could look out at the bay and at a tumultuous sea of crashing waves and white caps. At one point, it even began to hail. Adriana went on to say how Elsa could be harsh at times but that she had very good instincts. She was always ahead of her time and was the first to speak to Adriana about eastern religions. Adriana also recalled how she and Elsa were always classifying

everything: "the most delicious fruit, the most wonderful painting," and so on; once, Elsa inscribed a book of poetry to Adriana:
"To one of the most beautiful women in the world." Elsa encouraged Adriana in her acting career and told her how talented she
was, but when Adriana asked Elsa to write something for her in
the theater, she refused. She hated the petit bourgeois side of the
Italian theater, she hated Pirandello. Instead Natalia Ginzburg
wrote a play for Adriana Asti called *I Married You for Happiness
(Ti ho sposato per allegria)*. While the play was a great success,
Elsa criticized it, saying it was dreadful. Only, Adriana said, Elsa
did not say this out of jealousy because Elsa was not someone who
was ever envious. If she criticized you at all, she criticized you for
your soul. Another thing that Adriana remembered was how
when Elsa telephoned her, instead of speaking right away into the
receiver, she would play music. Mozart. Adriana was living with
Bertolucci then and, together, they had dinner with Elsa and
Alberto and Pier Paolo Pasolini nearly every night. Adriana also
recalled that Elsa had a little car, a yellow Morris Minor, that she
loved. Only she drove very badly and, to make matters worse,
Elsa did not see well. Again, Adriana began to laugh, an infectious laugh of pure pleasure at the memory of Elsa and at perhaps
the power of recollection.[29]

seven

ARTURO'S ISLAND

"*A*rturo, *c'est moi!*" Elsa Morante told Jean-Noël Schifano, her French translator, echoing Flaubert's famous remark about Madame Bovary in an interview in November 1984, a year before her death. Arturo, the young protagonist of her novel *Arturo's Island (L'isola di Arturo)*, was so much her that she quickly added, "I, who prefer cats, once I began writing this book, began then to love dogs!" [1] Elsa Morante's identification with Arturo also stemmed from a feeling—more like an instinct—that, perhaps in a previous life, she had been a boy. She felt that she had to tell the story of what she recalled of her past as that boy, a boy who still expected much out of life and looked at the world with innocence before he suffered the hardships of maturity and before she, Elsa Morante, suffered the aridity of old age. [2] In the same interview (a revealing one, since Elsa Morante was already gravely ill and rarely granted interviews), she also talked about her love of children, of babies, and her love of mothers: simple mothers, real mothers (mothers like Nunziatella, Arturo's stepmother in *Arturo's Island*), not feminists or intellectuals or society women. She even spoke of how she too had wanted to be a mother—only illness and the war had prevented her. [3]

Elsa Morante began *Arturo's Island* in the spring of 1952. At first she thought to publish two novellas and call them *Due amori impossibili* (Two Impossible Loves). She described one as the story of a young man in prison in Africa who recalls his home on the beautiful island of Procida and the impossible love he had there; the other, a fable titled *Nerida*, was to be about the daughter of a miner who passionately loves to dance and dies trying to realize her dream. Early that summer, ostensibly in order to write, she went to Sils Maria in the Engadine. Sils Maria is where Nietzsche spent his summers and, thanks to the cautious ministrations of the tourist office, the Swiss village has not changed much since his day, nor have the surrounding mountains and lakes for which Sils is famous. Famous, too, is the wind around these lakes, which comes up suddenly and unpredictably and is strong and dangerous. It may have acted as a reminder for Nietzsche of man's place in the universe in relation to the force of nature.[4]

Whether this was true or not for Elsa Morante is unclear. In a new diary that she began on August 6—she had just destroyed an old one, which she felt was too passionate and subjective—she sounded disgruntled and unhappy. She wrote that since she disliked planning far ahead, all the places she tried to go to for the summer were booked up and she had no choice but to return to the mountains. She also complained that since she was staying at the same hotel and in the same room where she had stayed the summer before, she was beginning to feel like the ghost of herself. The table she wrote on was too low, the chair she sat in too high and she no longer much liked the shape of the trees outside. She blamed the weather: it rained a great deal and she could not go out and sunbathe. The electricity was out that day—due probably to the dangerous winds—and as she sat writing in the dark, she did some soul-searching. Was her desire to lie in the sun and show off her body a sign of narcissism? She had always, she wrote, cared tremendously about her body, its youth and perfection. At first she thought the reason for this was that she was wait-ing for love but now she realized that no one could truly love her. Her body's decline and aging (she would turn forty in twelve days) and the loss of her beauty made her sadder, she wrote, than even the thought of her own death. Then trying to cheer herself up, she asked: Was Elsa Morante ever really beautiful anyway? No, never. Her teeth were set too far apart; her forehead was too high; her nails were not perfectly shaped. In addition, she wanted to be a great poet. And what for? To be loved. But no one had ever loved her. And even if she was not a *great poet*, was she a poet at all? She doubted it. The electricity came back on then, but it continued to rain. Enough for today, she wrote.[5]

Elsa Morante spent the rest of the summer on the island of Procida—which was smaller than she remembered but no less beautiful and where, from afar, the fishermen called out to her playfully, Maria? Antonia? Concertina? and laughed at her reserve—and then in Capri, where her room was like an aviary, suspended over the sea. Despite scornfully referring to Canzone del Mare, the popular swimming club owned by the comedienne Gracie Fields, as an "odious" and "bourgeois" establishment, she nevertheless joined the other women who, as she put it, "flaunted themselves" and sunbathed with them. She loved the sea but was afraid of it and if only she could swim, she noted in her diary, her fear might disappear. She appreciated the happiness and good-ness of A. (Alberto Moravia), the delicious simple seaside meals of fish soup and baby octopus and that a friend said to her, "Oh, but how beautiful you are!"[6]

And she was beautiful, as photographs of that time show. In one taken presumably in Capri, she is standing in the street, wear-ing a long striped summer skirt, sandals and a little cotton top knotted under her bosom that shows off her flat midriff. Under one arm she holds a large straw hat. She is frowning ever so slightly—perhaps at the photographer or at having her picture taken—but one can see her finely molded features: her straight nose, small chin, straight, thick eyebrows and full, curly hair. She also appeared to have had several romances or flirtations that summer—with M., for instance, who was "young and handsome" and who took a boyish pride in protecting her while she, in turn, helped get his poetry published. She also mentioned L. (no doubt Luchino Visconti), whom she referred to as her last and impossible love to whom she had to say good-bye—and say good-bye to her youth as well.

Back in Rome, after what, she described, had turned out to be an "idle summer," she again wrote in her diary about how she felt torn by conflicting sentiments. On the one hand, she felt that she must love everyone and how words like "condemn," "scorn" and "forgive" seemed more and more presumptuous; on the other hand, she was aware that apathy had become part of her nature, as had an increasing intolerance for other people. This was not a moral judgment and not the fault of others but hers alone. She found it increasingly difficult to communicate; in certain cases it had even become physically impossible. Most people hurt her feelings and it was she who was vulnerable. It was her fault, too, that she had never been loved, that she had no friends and that she was not happy. All this she wrote from her studio on via Archimede, with only her kitten Useppe Mandulino for company. Useppe Mandulino was the last offspring of her beloved Giuseppe, a cat who she claimed was the other half of her soul as, not long before, she had come to understand this one absolute truth: "animals are angels and Siamese cats are archangels." It was also time, Elsa Morante wrote in her diary, for her to start work again on *Arturo's Island*; and who knew, she asked herself, if

she could recover that youthful passion she had had for writing it
when she had left off.[7]

A few months later, Elsa described a wonderful dream:

> I was in a sort of vast, green hollow, between the sea and
> high hills; on the summit there was a small fort like the one
> on the island of Procida. I was in the company of someone
> dear but I could not say precisely who it was. It was the day
> of my birthday and I was feeling sad because no one present
> remembered it and no one was wishing me well. At that
> very moment, mysteriously, from high up, two pink roses
> fell into my lap. . . .
>
> I have noted that in the last fifteen years or so, every time
> I dream about pink roses, a confused and gloomy period of
> my life will come to an end and a new one will begin.[8]

Morante always wrote in longhand in large, black, unlined
notebooks that she bought at Zampini, a stationer on via Frattina
not far from her apartment. She wrote on every other page, leaving the intervening pages blank for notes and corrections. The
notes she wrote to herself remain as guidelines to how she worked
and many of her edits show that she was striving to achieve more
simplicity in the text: "Important! Get rid of these expressed sentiments and thoughts, let the facts speak for themselves." Several
of the pages have large passages crosshatched and crossed out.
She used different colored pens and she often doodled or drew
pictures of cats and stars on the side of the page.

Her handwriting is functional and spontaneous—a sign, according to a graphologist who analyzed it, that the writer presents herself to the world without pretension or embellishments.
At first glance, it was difficult for the graphologist to tell whether

the handwriting was that of a man or a woman. However, it was clearly the handwriting of someone whose intellect transcended gender and background. It was also the handwriting of someone with a sharp and sensitive mind and of concentrated purpose who was not easily distracted from her task. The writer was able to form her own opinions, independent of public trends and conventions. While she was an extroverted thinker, she was a private person in other ways as well, and it was through her imagination that she could best express her true self. The graphologist also noted that Elsa Morante was too independent to be accommodating and that she must have been a difficult person to understand. Her high standards, her personal sensitivity, combined with an often intolerant attitude to others, could have created friction and irritation. In addition, her response was not always predictable. Her imagination and her wit, nonetheless, made her a stimulating person to be with. Finally, it was Elsa Morante's signature, the graphologist said, that most revealed her feminine sensibility as well as her emotional insecurity.[9]

Procida is a volcanic island in the warm, blue waters of the Bay of Naples. Its beauty has been much extolled and admired and Elsa Morante's protagonist, Arturo Gerace, describes it thus: "On my particular island, up on the hills outside the town, there are small lonely roads shut in between old walls, and beyond them orchards and vineyards that look like imperial gardens. There are beaches of fine white sand, and smaller beaches covered with pebbles and shells, hidden between great cliffs that overhang the water. Seagulls nest in the rocks there, and wild tortoises, and in the early morning you can hear the birds' cries, sometimes gloomy, sometimes gay. On calm days the sea there is gentle and cool and touches the shore like dew." [10] Much smaller—the island is one and a half miles square—than either Ischia or Capri, Procida was never a popular tourist resort. The main reason for this was that until 1988 it was home to a national prison. The prison was situated on the highest and most scenic promontory of the island, which was also the site of the original sixteenth-century walled town known as the Terra Murata.

Not so long ago, on a warm, sunny day in April, I took the boat from Naples and spent a day on Procida. In the harbor, I hired a taxi and, after I explained the reason for my visit, the driver was most solicitous and helpful. First we went up to Terra Murata and walked around the old town, where a jumble of pink, blue and white houses had been built in such a way as to form a defensive block against the invasion of the Saracens in the Middle Ages. Then we visited the eleventh-century Abbey of the Archangel Michael, the patron saint of Procida. There, according to the story I was told, one of the paintings of Saint Michael was restored by a prison inmate who, in his zeal, substituted his own face for the one in the portrait. From the church terrace, there is a splendid view of the rest of the island as well as of the Bay of Naples.

Close by, one can also see the grim four-story façade of the abandoned prison, dotted with small, barred windows that offered the prisoners a spectacular view of the sea and of tantalizing but unattainable freedom. Apparently the prisoners were housed according to the gravity of their crime: the worst criminals, the murderers and assassins, were put on the lowest floor where the cells were the dampest and narrowest. From the Terra Murata, we drove down to a black, volcanic sand beach (the setting for a scene in *Il Postino* in which the movie's Pablo Neruda explains what a metaphor is), then down narrow, winding roads past pretty villas. A particularly pretty one, where Elsa was said to have stayed, is named in her honor. The trees in the garden were loaded down with lemons—twenty or thirty to a branch—and my driver picked a few. Before catching the boat back to Naples, I had lunch in a small trattoria on the harbor. Off season, although it was warm enough to eat outside, the trattoria was nearly empty—at the only other occupied table, a few locals were drinking coffee. Along with my meal of spaghetti *con vongole*, a veal cutlet, salad and cheese, I ordered a half liter of the local white wine known as Falanghina. For once, I did not mind eating in a restaurant alone. The island felt peaceful and quiet and it was easy to imagine Arturo there and how Procida must have seemed like his own private paradise.

"First of all, I was proud of my name" is how *Arturo's Island* begins. (The name Arturo is an homage to Elsa Morante's favorite poet, Arthur Rimbaud—Jean-Noël Schifano recalled seeing a portrait of Rimbaud on the wall of Elsa Morante's studio and how, with her usual offbeat sense of fun, she had written on it, "To Elsa, Arthur." [11]) "I'd found out early on . . . that Arturo is the name of a star—the fastest and brightest in the figure of the herdsman, in the northern sky. And ages ago there was some king called Arturo as well, who had a group of loyal followers; and, as they were all heroes like himself, he treated them as brothers and equals. The pity of it was, as I later discovered, this famous old king of Britain wasn't proper history, at all, but just a legend," [12] which leads the reader to wonder about Arturo's own destiny. Will it be predicted by the stars or will it follow the course of a heroic tale? [13]

Ostensibly, *Arturo's Island* is the first-person story of a motherless young boy, who grows up feral and free on the island of Procida:

Although we were fairly well off, we lived like savages. When I was two months old my father left the island and was away for nearly six months; and he left me in the care of our first boy servant who . . . brought me up on goat's milk. It was he who taught me to talk, and to read and write, and afterward I taught myself, out of books I found in the house. My father never bothered to send me to school; I was always on holiday, and my vagabond days, especially when he was away, had no rules or fixed hours at all. When I was hungry or sleepy I knew it was time to go home. No one ever thought of giving me money, and I never asked for it; anyway I didn't need it. I don't remember ever possessing a penny during my whole childhood.[14]

Arturo's only companion, who also doubles as a kind of nurse-maid, is his beloved dog, Immacolatella, whom he describes thus:

What a lot of fuss about a dog, you'll say. But when I was a boy I'd no other friend, and you can't deny she was extraordinary. We'd invented a kind of deaf-and-dumb language between us: tail, eyes, movements, the pitch of her voice—all of them told me every thought of hers, and I understood. Although she was female, she loved daring and adventure. She'd go swimming with me, and act as my pilot in the boat, barking when some obstacle loomed up. As I wandered about the island, she'd always follow me; and every day, as we came back through the alleys we'd used and the fields we'd crossed a hundred times, she'd get as excited as if we were two explorers in uncharted country.[15]

The only female presence in the boy's life, Immacolatella will die giving birth to her pups.

Arturo's father, Wilhelm, a bastard by birth and half German, is an outcast on the island, yet Arturo worships him. "The main reason for his supremacy was his difference from everyone else; this was the most wonderful, the most mysterious thing about him. He was different from all the men on Procida, which was like saying from everyone I knew in the world, and even—which made it so galling—from me." Not only is the father different, he is handsome. "In summer his body seemed to drink in the sun like oil, and glowed, darkly, caressingly; in winter it grew as pale as a pearl again. . . . His soft straight hair was blond—of a dense fairness that gleamed and glowed in particular lights; and at the nape of his neck where it was shorter, almost shaven, it was actually golden. And his eyes were a violet blue like the sea at moments, darkened by clouds" while, Arturo, his son, "is dark in every season." [16] And, more difficult still, no matter what Arturo does, Wilhelm remains coldly indifferent and emotionally unavailable to his son:

> In the meantime, when we were together, I took every opportunity to show him my courage and fearlessness. Barefoot, almost flying from point to point, I'd cross the burning rocks and dive into the sea from the highest of them. In the water I did the most astounding acrobatics and showed I was expert at every sort of swimming. . . . He'd sit on the shore without taking the smallest notice of me; and as soon as I ran up and flung myself on the sand beside him . . . he'd get up, with a kind of capricious indolence, looking absent, frowning, as if listening to some mysterious invitation murmured in his ear. He'd raise his lazy arms and float away on his side, and slowly, slowly swim away, in the arms of his bride, the sea. [17]

A moody, unpredictable yet romantic loner, Wilhelm's comings and goings remain a mystery to his son: "He always got ready to leave at the last minute" and "He might come back in two or three days, or he might stay away for months, until the winter or longer." Each time, "[t]he very minute he left Procida, my father would turn into a legend again." [18]

Women are scorned and ignored by the Geraces. Their house has been nicknamed the House of the Guaglioni (in Neopolitan dialect *guaglione* means "boy" or "young man"), and, under the auspices of the previous owner, the house had been the site of wild parties exclusively for men. Rumor had it that the house was fatal to the women who lived there—Arturo's eighteen-year-old mother died in the house giving birth to him. As a result, Arturo is disdainfully ignorant: "Although I knew nothing about real women, the glimpses I got of them were quite enough to make me conclude that they had absolutely nothing in common with the women in books. Real women, I thought, weren't splendid or magnificent. They were little creatures who could never grow as big as men, and they spent their whole life shut up indoors; that's why they were so pale. All bundled up in the aprons, skirts, and petticoats that had to hide those mysterious bodies of theirs, they seemed to me misshapen, almost deformed." And again: "Sometimes, though not very often, some foreign woman would come to the island and go down to the beach and get undressed to bathe, without the slightest modesty, just like a man. . . . My father seemed to consider them ridiculous and hateful. . . . And as for the women, no one even looked at them. As far as Procidans were concerned, as far as I was concerned, they weren't women at all, but crazy beasts come down from the moon. It never entered my head that their shameless bodies might be beautiful." [19]

On a winter afternoon when "a cold squall of rain was clouding Procida," this near idyllic isolation changes with the arrival of Wilhelm's young bride, Nunziatella, an uneducated, simple girl not much older than Arturo himself. Not surprisingly, Arturo does not know what to make of Nunziatella; he is both attracted to and repulsed by her, and his sexual feelings for her are confused: "I saw her rise bewilderedly from the blankets, showing her small bare shoulders and the shape of her bosom; and I hated her more furiously than ever. I suddenly wished that she was really a boy like me, that I could punch her until my anger was satiated." Arturo is also jealous of her as she has drastically altered the relationship between him and his father, which leads him to complain, "I was enduring the trials more bitter than Othello's. In his tragedy the unhappy Moor at least knew what he was up against, and why he was fighting: the woman he loved on one side, the enemy on the other. While Arturo Gerace's battlefield was one great confused dilemma, without the relief of hope or of revenge." He avoids Wilhelm and Nunziatella and spends the days by himself; at night, in bed, rather than listen to their lovemaking, Arturo covers his ears with his hands "for fear of hearing that shriek again from their room. . . . I'd sooner have seen a wild beast rise up before me than have heard it again." [20]

Arturo's feelings are further complicated by the fact that Wilhelm Gerace does not love his wife; instead he takes pleasure in humiliating and abusing her. "[W]omen," he tells her, "are like leprosy—when they get hold of you they want to eat you up completely, bit by bit, and isolate you from the rest of the world. Women's love brings bad luck; they don't know how to love." Arturo, who is listening, shares his father's ill will toward Nunziatella: "I was glad he was ill-treating her, and, what's more, hoped he'd vent his rage on her physically, fling her on the floor, even, stamp on her. I almost felt I'd find peace in an outrage like that."

Once Wilhelm leaves the island, Arturo takes his own revenge by being cruel and insulting to Nunziatella while she is naïvely and sweetly oblivious and continues to try to please him and to act like his mother—which only succeeds in further infuriating and confusing Arturo. "My rage, with nothing to vent itself on, became such a torment that I began to moan furiously, as if I'd been wounded . . . [P]erhaps I was unconsciously suffering for my heart's impossible longings and for the interwoven, contradictory jealousies and complex passions that were to be mine." [21]

After Nunziatella gives birth to Arturo's half brother, Carmine, the tone of the novel changes, as do Arturo's feelings for Nunziatella. Although still jealous, the object of his jealousy has shifted and his thoughts are tinged with melancholy and longing. Here Arturo is watching Nunziatella kiss her little son: "I didn't know there were so many kisses in the world, and just to think that I had never had any or ever given any! I watched those two kissing each other as, from a solitary ship out at sea, I might watch an unapproachable, mysterious, enchanted country, full of flowers and foliage." He becomes obsessed with her and with kisses: "it would seem to me that everything in all the world was kissing. The boats tied together along the beach were kissing each other; the movement of the sea was a kiss as it ran in to the island; the sheep as they cropped the grass were kissing the ground; the wind in the leaves and the grass was all a lament of kisses. . . . There was no one about in the street who didn't know the taste of kisses: the women, the fishermen, the beggars, the boys—I was the only one who didn't. And I had such a longing to know them that I thought of scarcely anything else night and day." [22]

Arturo gets to satisfy his longing; he kisses his stepmother and the novel heads toward its inevitable conclusion. Along with his loss of innocence, Arturo's life on the island starts to unravel: he is introduced to sex (but not love) by a young widow who is a cripple and he finally understands that his love for Nunziatella—although reciprocated—can never be consummated. But far more traumatic for Arturo is his discovery that his father, whom he has idolized, is perversely infatuated with a common criminal incarcerated in Procida's prison. He witnesses the mortification and self-abasement his father endures when the convict rejects him with the rude epithet *"Vattene, parodia!"* (the phrase is translated as "Beat it, you grotesque," but a more accurate meaning is "Go away, you pervert!").[23] The novel ends with Arturo leaving the island of Procida, leaving behind his childhood, his dreams and the tales of heroism that, in the past, sustained him. Ahead, in Arturo's future, looms the tragic specter of World War II. He had dreamt about sailing away and now the reader knows that he is probably going to war. He has lost the paradise of his childhood. Happiness was that moment, that place, that point in space and time.[24] The opening lines of the poem that serves as an epigraph for the novel predict the end: "That which you thought was a small point of earth / was everything," as does the last line: "there is no paradise except in limbo." The island was limbo and that limbo was the only true paradise.

When *Arturo's Island* was first published it was compared to Alain-Fournier's *Le Grand Meaulnes*, but it turned out that Elsa Morante had never heard of either the book or the author. Both *House of Liars* and *Arturo's Island*, as the critic Cesare Garboli pointed out, were written in a sort of intellectual vacuum. For ten years, Elsa Morante wrote nearly in secret with, for company, only her pen, paper, ink and a bunch of cats. She escaped all models and influences or what Harold Bloom, many years later, was to call "the anxiety of influence."[25] (Except for Mozart. Mozart, Elsa Morante always claimed, was her greatest influence and the greatest master in her life. While she was writing *Arturo's Island*, she listened obsessively to *The Magic Flute*.) But "anxiety of influence" or not, the inspiration for *Arturo's Island* must certainly have been Luchino Visconti. Readers have gone so far as to say that the novel was written "under the sign of Visconti" and the relationship between Arturo and his father, Wilhelm, certainly appears to bear this out by mirroring and translating fictionally Elsa's own story with Visconti. It would seem as if, consciously and deliberately, she chose an alter ego in the character of Arturo to tell her own story and to describe her infatuation with Visconti and her eventual deception (like Wilhelm, he was homosexual). A bit childishly, Elsa tended to idolize the men she loved and Visconti always represented someone mythical to her, perhaps precisely because of his very otherness, his unavailability—like a distant star.

For me, *Arturo's Island* will always be Elsa Morante's most lyrical and luminous work. Despite its persistent themes of loss, rejection, adult betrayal and even sadism, the novel manages to celebrate childhood, the power of magic and myth, and the redemptive goodness of nature and animals. It is clear that Elsa Morante loved children and that she believed that the only way to look at reality was through their eyes. Children are the wise custodians of fables and the innocents with paradisal fantasies—both qualities lost to adults. Children always play a central role in Morante's work and, to depict them, she depended on her own personal biography and memories, often intruding or inserting herself in the narrative. As a result, her characters have often been accused of being narcissistic. In *Arturo's Island*, Arturo himself admits, "Maybe while I thought I was in love with this or that person, or with two or three people at the same time, I really didn't love anyone. The fact was that, on the whole, I was too much in love with love; this has always been my real passion." Love, in Elsa Morante's work, always consumes and usually turns into hate; it is rarely joyful or peaceful. Yet, even while Arturo, at the end of the novel, wonders whether he in fact ever really loved his father, he allows a ray of light to fall on this dark tale and a promise of some happiness (however narcissistic) as he pictures Carmine, his half brother. "She [Nunziatella] preferred calling him by his second name, Arturo. And I like to think that there is another Arturo Gerace on the island, a fair boy who now, perhaps, races along the beaches happy and free. . . ."[26] Not so surprising then that the other epigraph for the novel, a line from Umberto Saba, reads, " If I see myself in him, I am content. . . ."

Arturo's Island won the prestigious Strega Prize in 1957. That same year Blanche Knopf acquired the American rights to it for $1500 and triumphantly wrote a colleague that "I have just bought the one great book in Italy that by all accounts is worth having."[27] Soon after, Blanche Knopf received a lovely letter in French from Elsa Morante expressing her pleasure at being published by the prestigious house founded by Blanche's husband, Alfred A. Knopf as well as her personal happiness at having recently met Blanche in Rome. She wrote that she was convinced that "books, like people, flourished most in sympathetic circumstances and such circumstances brought good luck." In addition, she told Blanche Knopf that she hoped to visit the United States the following year and was looking forward to seeing her.[28] Over the next year and a half, their correspondence grew more affectionate, Blanche Knopf writing that she had begun taking Italian lessons and addressing Elsa Morante in her letters as "dearest Elsa," while Elsa reciprocated with "dear Madame Blanche." A large part of their correspondence concerned translation issues. Knopf had decided to share the translator, Isabel Quigly, with the British publisher, William Collins Sons. Although an adequate enough translator, Quigly fell ill and fell far behind schedule; worse, her translation turned out to be too anglicized and Herbert Weinstock, another Knopf editor, had to do a lot of editing. Judith B. Jones, Blanche Knopf's assistant, also mailed several memos querying errors in the translation, specifically about the word "parody," arguing that "grotesque" was not a good substitute and suggesting instead the words "poseur," "buffoon" and "imposter"—even "charlatan," for, at the risk of sounding "fussy" (her word), Jones understood that "parody" was a key word in the novel.[29] Unfortunately, her advice was not taken.

Inexplicably, both Collins and Knopf wanted to change the title. "The House of Dreams," "A King and a Star," "The Golden Island" "The Golden Spider" were proposed and fortunately discarded.[30] Two American writers, both of whom had spent a great deal of time in Italy and were well acquainted with Elsa Morante, contributed blurbs for the novel's jacket. Robert Penn Warren wrote, "To miss the fiction of Elsa Morante is to miss one of the beautiful and important things the literature of our time has to offer," and Francis Steegmuller added his praise, "The most beautiful novel I've read in years." Published in England in May, *Arturo's Island* was a great success and jumped up to the best-seller list. Meantime, Erich Linder, Elsa's agent and friend, sold foreign rights to the novel in Germany, Sweden, France, Norway and Finland.

In the United States, *Arturo's Island* finally came out on August 17, 1959, which nearly coincided with the date of Elsa Morante's birthday—this, as Elsa wrote to Blanche Knopf, "was the best possible omen for the occasion."[31] This turned out to be true as *Arturo's Island* received two rave reviews in *The New York Times*.

A day after publication, Gilbert Millstein began his review by saying: "From time to time there appear works for which the only possible description is sublime." Afraid that his praise might appear excessive, he went on to write, "I also want the book to be as widely read as is possible for a fine contemporary novel. . . . Whatever uplift is to be found in the book derives from watching the growth of a fourteen-year-old boy into a sixteen-year-old man on an exotic island in the Bay of Naples two years before the opening of the World War II. Whatever its sonorities, they are the cadenced, functional ones of excellent prose." [32] Frederic Morton also glowingly reviewed the novel in the Sunday *Times Book Review*, comparing the language of the novel to the "melody of legend." He continued, "Miss Morante possesses the Italian gift of distilling universality out of the primitive. But, she also has a fine feminine instinct for the singing detail. The combination enables her to create a poetic, princely savage of a hero, half freebooter, half Huckleberry Finn. She catches the echo and iridescence of a tragedy from which lucky old Huck was spared: growing up." [33]

In September, Elsa Morante was finally able to fulfill her wish and come to New York for a month. During her stay she was invited to Sunday lunch in Purchase, New York, by Blanche's husband, Alfred—the Knopfs famously did not get along and Blanche was away in Europe at the time. As Elsa later wrote in a thank-you letter, she enjoyed her day in the country very much. [34] Also, during her visit to America, Frederic Morton interviewed her over lunch for the *Times*. He described her as looking like "a small, delicately molded dark blonde, with the cheeks and eyes of a melancholy cherub . . . and with a tiny gap between front teeth that would do the prettiest gamine honor." He also said that she looked younger than someone in her early forties and that she was shy. The shyness, he soon came to realize, was not due to Elsa Morante's lack of self-confidence but due to insecurity about speaking English (as they talked she often switched to French). In the interview, Elsa Morante again said how she believed that there were three kinds of heroes: Achilles who accepts reality, Hamlet who refuses it and Don Quixote who invents his own, and that her characters were like Don Quixote. Arturo was like that too. She then told Morton: "I've always wanted to be a boy, a boy like Arturo, who can hunt and fish and climb big rocks, and go about dressed badly, and have the dreams and illusions of a boy. And I've always wanted to swim, but . . . I never learn [*sic*]. Maybe that is why Arturo is so much in the ocean. So you see, through writing I am like Don Quixote." Morton concluded the interview by asking Elsa Morante whether she and Moravia influenced each other's writing—as he put it in "an attempt to foist some American togetherness on a superbly Continental couple," and a question that Italian interviewers no doubt knew better than to ask. Putting her coffee cup down firmly, Elsa replied, "No. He has an identity. I have an identity. *Basta*."[35]

eight

WITHOUT THE COMFORT
OF RELIGION

In 1959, on her first visit to New York City, Elsa
Morante fell in love with Bill Morrow, a twenty-three-
year-old painter from Madisonville, Kentucky. Bill Morrow
was tall, blond and very handsome. Bill was introduced to Elsa by
a mutual friend. As it turned out—a strange coincidence—
the friend was Sergio, the same young Chilean I knew in Rome,
who took me to Fregene to have lunch with Moravia. (Later I
learned that Sergio had committed suicide. His death, I imagine,
must have been due in part to the times. Times that were spent
recklessly—drinking, doing drugs, sleeping around—and that
became known as *la dolce vita*.)

Apparently Bill Morrow was the sort of person everyone—
men, women, children—fell in love with (in retrospect, this
may have been part of his problem). Not only was he very, very
handsome—he had once been a model and his looks were a cross
between James Dean's and Alain Delon's—but too many people
loved him. The actor Allen Midgette, a friend of Bill and later a
friend of Elsa Morante as well, remembers how a package once
arrived in New York for Bill. The package was from Elsa in Italy
and it contained a mirror with a note that said, "Dear Bill, This is
for you to look at your beautiful face." Allen also recalls how surprised he was that anyone could speak so frankly and right away

he thought Elsa must be an interesting woman. According still to Allen, Bill Morrow was incredibly alive and colorful and completely without prejudice or guile—in a word, "dynamite." He also inspired truth in people, which is probably why Elsa was so attracted to him.

Bernardo Bertolucci, too, was curious about Bill. One day, he asked Allen (who had gone to Rome to pursue his acting career), "Can you tell me about this Bill Morrow because all these people speak about him as if he were Jesus Christ?" Allen, who must have been a bit in love with Bill himself, replied that Bill was a holy man but not in the way Bertolucci might think. Later, in Bertolucci's film *Before the Revolution*, Allen Midgette played the part of a disaffected young Calabrian man who kills himself. Just before he does so, there is a poignant scene in which Midgette acrobatically rides his bicycle—sometimes standing on the seat—in a sort of dance where he repeatedly crashes and gets up again, seemingly unfazed, as if to prove his infallibility. Allen told me that, during that scene, he was thinking of Bill. Later, Pasolini made a film called *Teorema (Theorem)* in which Terence Stamp plays a stranger who is either Christ, God, the devil or simply a hustler and who manages to have sex with everyone in a family—husband, wife, son, daughter—as well as their maid, forever changing each of them. However, except for the maid, all the family members live the experience but do not understand it because, according to Pasolini's theory, the bourgeoisie has lost the sense of the sacred. Only the servant, who is a peasant, has not. It has been suggested that the character played by Terence Stamp was based on Bill Morrow. Alberto Moravia, of all people, once said that he never understood how a man could love another man until he met Bill Morrow. The poet Sandro Penna, Pier Paolo Pasolini, Natalia

Ginzburg, all loved Bill Morrow. They thought he was the reincarnation of Rimbaud.[1]

According to everyone who saw them together, Elsa and Bill had a very intense, dramatic love affair. Elsa was almost fifty and Bill was less than half her age, although it was he who had sought her out. Elsa rented an apartment for them both on via del Babuino, but Bill spent most of his days painting in Elsa's via Archimede studio, with his cat, Kumquat, that he had brought with him from New York, and listening to his favorite music, Buddy Holly, Bessie Smith, John Coltrane. Apparently, he never learned much Italian—he and Elsa spoke English together, Bill talking in his Kentucky accent. All the while, however, Elsa worried a great deal about Bill. She understood his problems and wanted to both protect him and make him strong. She often acted more like a mother to him than a lover. An epileptic, Bill was prone to seizures; also, he drank too much and was addicted to Seconal. He had already been hospitalized in New York after a suicide attempt. Allen Midgette remembers another incident when both young men were out on the terrace at via Archimede. "I could feel he was up to something," Allen told me, "and I sat down next to his legs as he was standing there looking over and I knew I had to grab them and sure enough, it happened, and I grabbed his legs and would not let go and he just laughed and said, that, anyway, he would have fallen on the terrace below, which was just a couple of floors down. Bill was not the kind of person you talked with about things like that, you couldn't say: 'Hey, what was that about?' because he would tell you not to come around anymore."[2]

Together Elsa and Bill went to Ischia, Switzerland and Venice; Elsa also went to New York several times with Bill. At the time, she was very attracted to the burgeoning American counterculture and to the beat poets Allen Ginsberg and Gregory Corso and the novelist Jack Kerouac. She also loved New York City, as a letter she wrote to Pasolini in 1960 illustrates: "This is not *a* city, but *the* city, it is the universe, the firmament, the viscera of the earth. You would love it! Millions of Anglo-Saxons, Italians, Spaniards, Chinese, Negroes, Puerto Ricans, running around on the streets. Everyone returns your greeting, as if they knew you. They ask your [first] name and right away start calling you by it. And all around, buildings like immense rocks, and cars like shooting stars."[3]

Elsa Morante traveled a great deal during the late fifties and early sixties. She went to the Soviet Union with Giacomo Debenedetti; to China as part of a cultural delegation; to Brazil on a PEN conference with Moravia; and, finally, in 1961, to India with Pasolini and Moravia. Happy at the time and in love and, as a result, perhaps more forthcoming, she gave an interview to Francine Virduzzo, a reporter for the magazine *Afrique-Action*. The piece begins by describing Elsa: "Elsa Morante is a strange woman who has a catlike face and, who, like a cat, has that deceptive lethargy, that 'farniente' aspect which allows her to relentlessly observe quotidian reality. Like a cat, Elsa Morante gives herself over to the pitiless dissection of life so as to be able to act slowly and seldom, but with absolute certainty."

The interview's most interesting section covered contemporary literature and other writers:

Francine Virduzzo: Do you think one can speak of an influence of the French *nouveau roman* on modern Italian literature?

Elsa Morante: No, thank goodness. The French phenomenon of the *nouveau roman* is not a cultural one. It has to do with eccentricities, which are not susceptible to any developments. . . .

F.V.: Who then, according to you, are the principal young Italian writers?

E.M.: Pasolini, naturally, and then [Carlo] Cassola, [Italo] Calvino, and also Natalia Ginzburg, who is an extremely interesting writer.

F.V.: What book are you actually working on now?

E.M.: I have already written about half of it. Its title? *Without the Comfort of Religion.* It is the story of a young man after the war who dies of a terrible disease.

F.V.: And now the classic question: who has influenced you the most?

E.M.: I can't really say that I have been influenced by any writer—by a musician, yes: Mozart is my master. He is the only artist whom I can recognize as a master. From him, I learned a lot of things that I was never able to understand. No, no single writer has really influenced me, but I can tell you who my favorite authors are: Saba. I very much like Saba and Penna. They are two very important poets and I always quote them. As for novelists? Verga, and then, if we are speaking of foreign literature . . . Cervantes, Stendhal, Tchekhov [*sic*], Melville.[4]

A few years earlier, in the spring of 1959, Morante participated in a survey, consisting of nine questions, conducted by *Nuovi Argomenti*, the magazine cofounded by Moravia. The first question in the survey asked whether there was a crisis in the novel as a literary genre. Morante did not think so: wonderful novels, she said, had been written and she named their authors: Proust, James, Svevo and Saba (she dismissed Joyce but admitted that she might be mistaken). She maintained that, every day, the word was constantly being renewed with life, like a fresh rose. Another question asked whether the novel had turned its back on psychology (Michel Butor, Alain Robbe-Grillet and

Nathalie Sarraute were the examples given), Morante answered in the negative: every novel, she claimed, is a psychological drama because it represents the relation of man to reality and each writer, she continued, has a predominant sentiment that stimulates or colors his or her discovery of the world. The penultimate question was about the difficulties of writing a historical novel and it seemed to already address those that would later be raised by her novel *History*, which she would not begin writing for at least another decade. She answered with examples of historical works that have captured certain truths: "In a most psychologically intimate poem, Petrarch describes his secret love for a married woman and yet the Sonnets give one of the perfect images of fourteenth-century Italy; Manzoni's *The Betrothed* tells the story at the time of the Lansquenets* yet it presents a perfect picture of nineteenth-century Italy; Kafka writes surreal fables yet no photographic or documentary work expresses certain atrocious verities of this present century as do those surreal fables." To the last question, "Who are your favorite novelists and why?" Morante's answer was consistent with the one she gave Francine Virduzzo: Homer, Cervantes, Stendhal, Melville, Chekhov, and Verga; the reason she chose these writers, she said, is that they elicited from her "an extraordinary surge of vitality." [5]

The novel Elsa Morante was working on, *Senza i comforti della religione* (Without the Comfort of Religion), was going to be totally autobiographical—not in the sense of reality (the characters were invented), but in the sense that the main character, Giuseppe, would represent a part of her soul and be the opposite of Arturo in *Arturo's Island*. It is the story of two brothers—one a

---

* German mercenary soldiers in the fifteenth and sixteenth centuries.

bastard, the other legitimate; one dark, the other light; one a poet, the other a filmmaker; one shy and sensitive, the other brash and ambitious; etc.—that, in Morante's hands, would have turned into a tragedy, the tale of a fallen idol. Morante had not yet decided whether to write the novel in the first or third person but, according to her notes, the problem that interested her was one not of style but of religion. A Catholic, Elsa Morante was religious, although not in a conventional or orthodox sense. She had studied a lot of Indian philosophy—Hinduism, Buddhism and Sufism—and she did not believe in a divinity who was a single entity and was outside the universe. Instead, she believed in an incarnate god who manifested himself in the forces of nature. Her religiosity was more mystical and a bit idolatrous—for instance, she thought of Christ as a sort of rebellious youth, an idea that also greatly influenced Pasolini. Basically, she embraced all religions.

Later, Elsa was very influenced by Simone Weil. One could not, she felt, live without religion—the kind of religion that was altruistic and a help to others. Art, too, that was born from this desire to be useful was a form of religion. In *Without the Comfort of Religion*, her work in progress, she planned for the main character to solve the religion problem by becoming a poet. Italy, she also added in her notes for the novel, was the country that was the least religious in the world; the Italians could be a great people in moments of misery, but when they became fortunate they lost their direction.[6]

At the opening of an exhibition of Bill Morrow's paintings at the Nuova Pesta gallery in Rome, in March 1962, Enzo Siciliano, the critic and writer, saw Bill for the first time and described him as "thin, graceful and looking like certain well-bred Anglo-Saxons; wrapped in a single-breasted, beige raincoat, the color of which seemed to match his body. . . . His smooth, blond hair fell on his forehead, his features were sharp and animated, his eyes were the color of water." Siciliano also wrote that rumor had it that Morrow's sexual orientation was ambiguous and that he had a taste for "the honey-sweet perfume of hashish." He compared the bright, pure colors of Morrow's paintings to the collages of Matisse, then, taking into account his nationality, compared them to the paintings of Stuart Davis, "a Stuart Davis who had gone back to the roots of figurative art."[7] The year before, at the Galerie Lambert in Paris, Alberto Moravia wrote a brief introduction to another of Bill Morrow's exhibits. He repeatedly mentioned the violence inherent in the paintings at the same time that they evoked "the silence, the suspension, the fluctuation, the depth, the light and its reflection that are inherent in the states of mind arrived at by contemplation."[8]

Now, Carlo Cecchi, Elsa Morante's executor,* owns all of Bill Morrow's paintings. (Anna Magnani owned one once, a painting of a horse, but after Bill Morrow died, Elsa Morante bought it back from Magnani.) On a cold winter morning I drove thirty or forty kilometers north of Rome to Carlo Cecchi's eighteenth-century house, built on the side of a cliff, to see them. Cecchi had taken a lot of trouble—his house was being renovated—and he had spread the unframed paintings on the floor against the walls of his living room for me to see. I am afraid he was disappointed by my reaction. For the most part, while they are quite vibrant and colorful, the paintings seem fairly naïve and a little childish. A lot of them are of animals: horses, pigeons, cats—the reason Elsa may have liked them.

---

* Carlo Cecchi and the critic Cesare Garboli were appointed Morante's co-executors. Garboli passed away in 2004.

Above: Elsa Morante and her nurse

Right: Elsa Morante as a little girl

Elsa Morante with Aldo, Marcello and Maria at the beach

One of the drawings for a children's book that Elsa Morante did
when she was thirteen years old

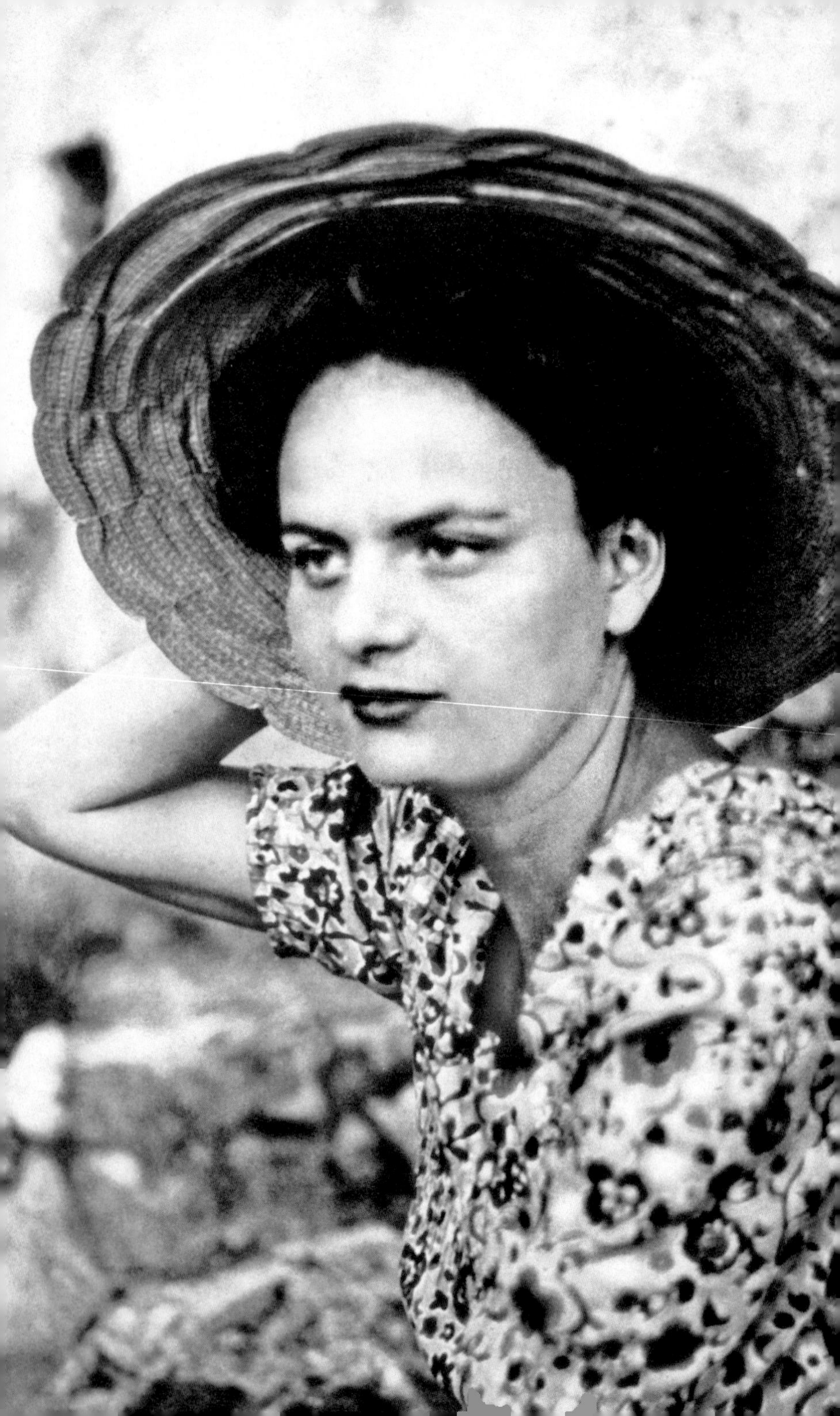

Elsa Morante with Alberto Moravia in Capri

facing page: Elsa Morante wearing a hat

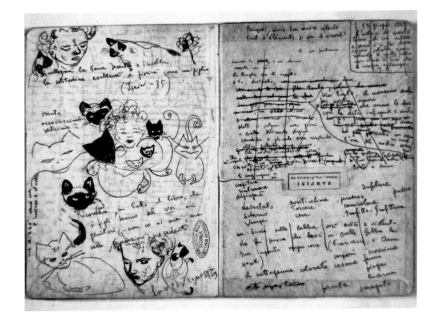

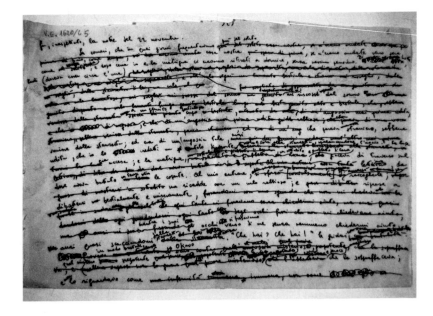

Manuscript pages from *House of Liars (Menzogna e sortilegio)* and
Arturo's Island (L'isola di Arturo)

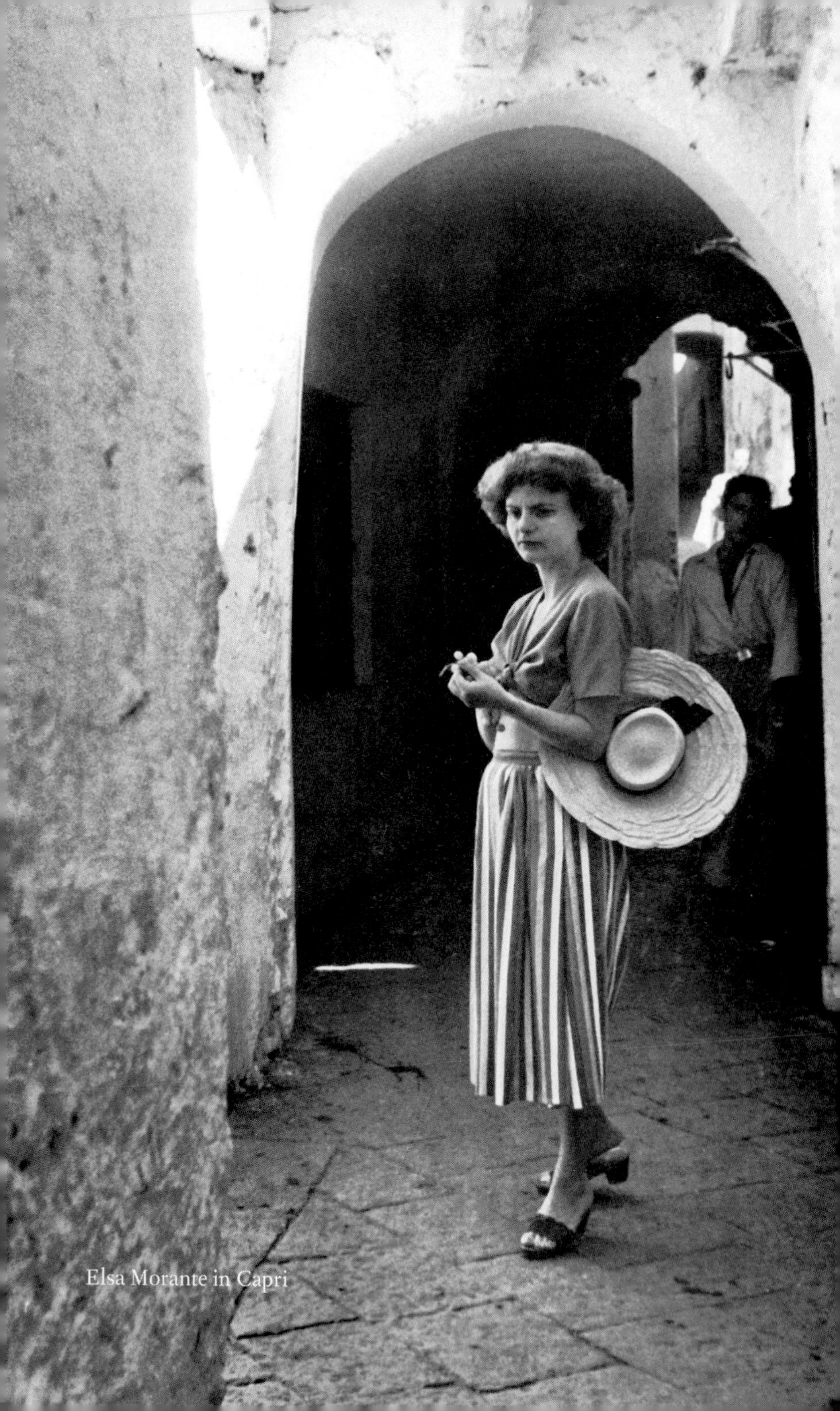

Elsa Morante in Capri

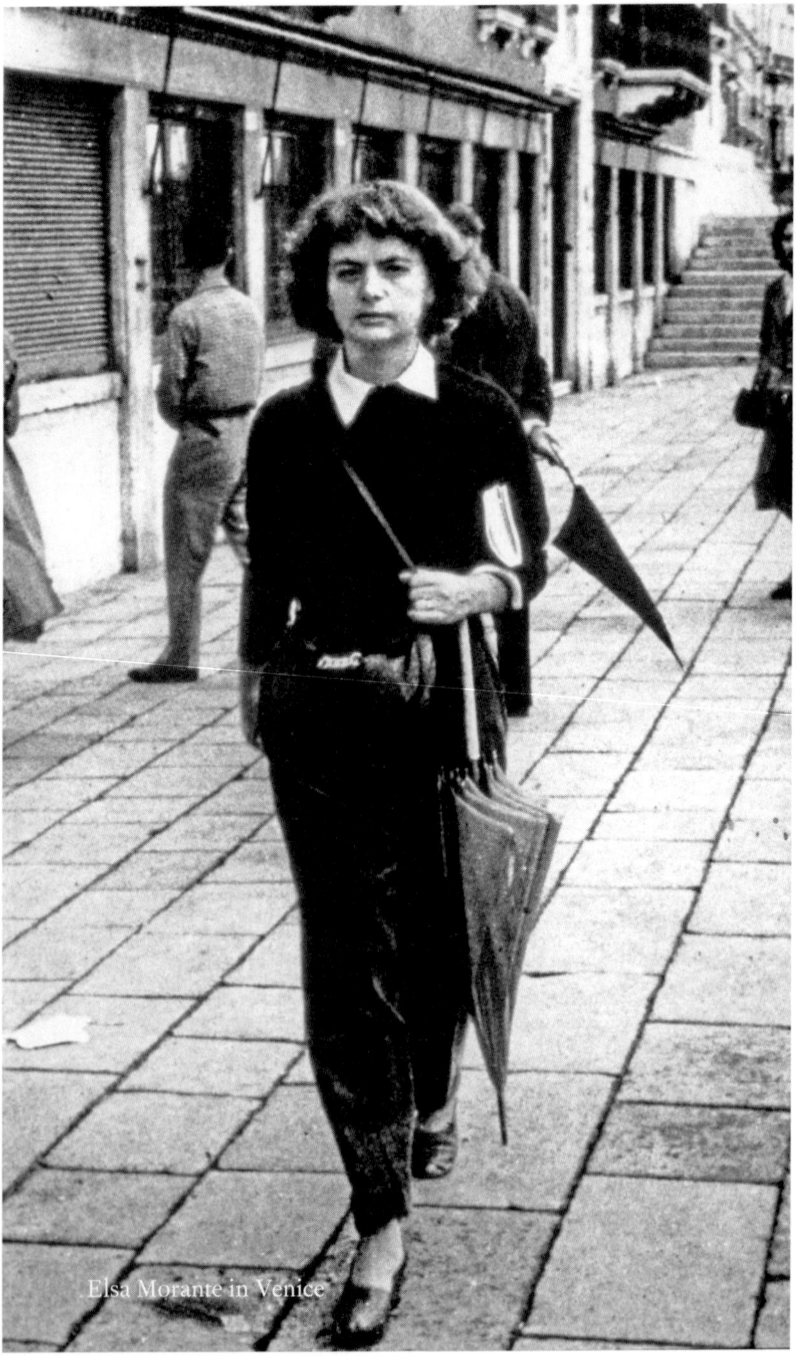
Elsa Morante in Venice

Elsa Morante with Luchino Visconti (he is wearing a mask) on New Year's Eve, 1950 or 1951

Elsa Morante during the judging of *Arturo's Island (L'isola di Arturo)* for the Strega Prize

Elsa Morante on a trip to Turkey with Alberto Moravia

Elsa Morante with Bill Morrow and Allen Midgette

Elsa Morante with Anna Magnani at the exhibition of Bill Morrow's paintings

Elsa Morante with Pier Paolo Pasolini

Elsa Morante and Cesare Garboli at the Einaudi bookstore on via Veneto for the publication of Morante's collection of stories, *The Andalusian Shawl (Lo scialle andaluso)*, December 1963

Congratulatory telegram from Italo Calvino on the publication of Morante's *The Andalusian Shawl*

Elsa Morante with Sandro Penna, Giacomo Debenedetti and Carlo
Levi

Elsa with Carlo Cecchi

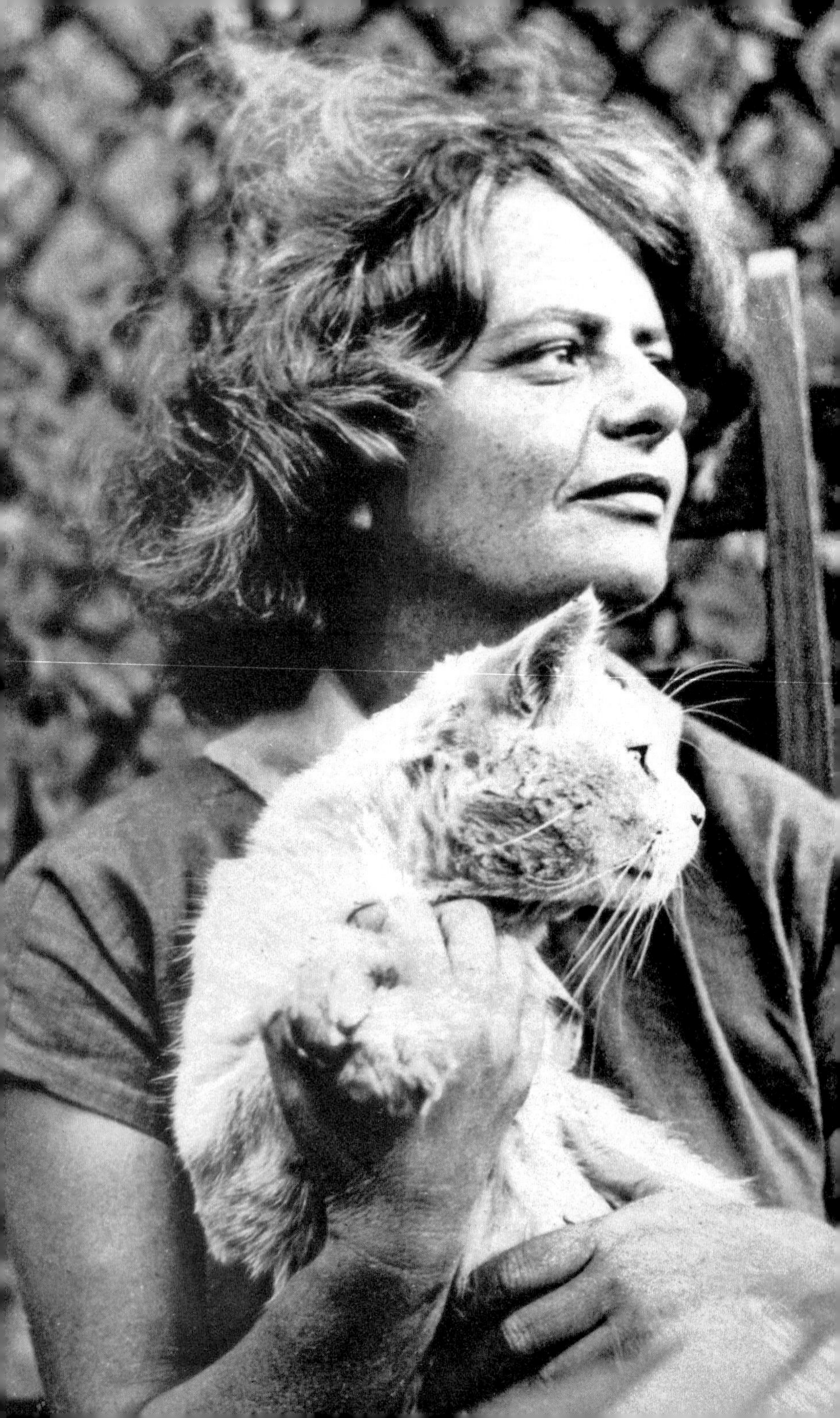

Elsa Morante at work in her studio

facing page: Elsa Morante with her cat

Elsa Morante at home after she broke her leg

In April 1962, while Bill Morrow was in New York for a brief visit—he was planning to return to Italy and live there permanently with Elsa—he was killed. It was presumed (although never confirmed) that, hallucinating on LSD, he had thought he could fly and he jumped off a Manhattan skyscraper. It has also been said that that day was particularly windy. When Elsa Morante heard the news of Bill's death, she was devastated. She locked herself up in her bedroom and, for two months, never left it. Prescient perhaps, Moravia had ended his introduction to Bill Morrow's show at the Galerie Lambert in Paris with the words "And although these paintings appear so immediate, so pure, so calm and limpid, they are born of the rage of a youth spent in the anguish and strangeness of a world profoundly alienated which is that of the United States. Thus, once again, art will have been paid for by life." [9]

That year and those that immediately followed must, most certainly, have been among the unhappiest in Elsa Morante's life. She turned fifty and, added to the remorse and sorrow she felt for the tragic and premature death of Bill Morrow, there might have been another even deeper and crueler reason for her unhappiness. Her marriage to Alberto Moravia, always difficult under the best of circumstances, had come to an end. Moravia left Elsa to live with Dacia Maraini, a younger woman who was a poet, playwright, novelist and journalist. His feelings on leaving Elsa—he and Dacia were on their way to Africa together—Moravia described thus: "During the night, as we were flying out, I was awake and was trying to look down at the shadows of the Sahara. And then all of a sudden I felt a sense of absolute physical liberation. As if I had rid myself of something heavy, like a plaster cast." Elsa Morante and Alberto Moravia never divorced or got a legal separation. Moravia simply moved out and went to live with Dacia. They remained on cordial terms, seeing each other from time to time, for as Moravia also said, "the separation was never entirely complete."[10] To support Elsa, he opened a bank account in her name—one she could draw on whenever she needed money. Elsa's needs were modest and she did not often make use of this account; also her books, especially *History*, brought her income.

After Bill Morrow's death, Elsa Morante no longer had the desire to write. She abandoned *Without the Comfort of Religion*, the novel she had been working on. If someone asked what she was doing, she answered that she was "writing very little." Consumed by grief, idle and restless, Elsa appeared to be living one day at a time. On the spur of the moment, she traveled to Spain, to Greece, to islands in the Mediterranean, sometimes alone or sometimes with a friend or someone she had met by chance. One day, for instance, she called Allen Midgette at his hotel and asked him to go to Spain with her for a few weeks, which he did. In a diary entry written in September 1963, she described her peripatetic way of life: "I travel at random, from island to island, without a specific plan. I stop where I like and for however long I like. I travel alone and go from one island to the other on old steam liners and on fishing boats."

Six months later, she wrote:

Two years since April 30 [the date of Bill Morrow's death]. And I continue to live as if I were still alive. At certain moments, I forget the horror. Some bit of consolation arrives, as if I had found you in something else. But then the pain returns unexpectedly. Also, now the other dead are *death* itself. Before you, it was not like this.

How many more years must I still linger: twenty, thirty? The only humanly possible way to reach the end is not to be myself, but to be all the others, all those who remain. Not to be *separate*. To be all who are past, present and future, all who are alive and are dead. That way I can also be you. . . .

The only possible happiness: not to be *one* but to be *everyone*. . . .

A sort of parody of the gestures I made when I lived. Putting notebooks in order, moving around, putting on records in between the times that I was writing novels.

This terrible feeling—like a siren—Sleep sleep sleep— Fall fly—

To keep a diary?!?! He used to say: yes, to put in all the shit [*sic*; in English] —rubbish, the dregs—[11]

Meanwhile, Blanche Knopf wrote to Elsa, "It is so long since I have heard from you that what I really expect is a new novel on my desk tomorrow morning. What has happened and where have you been and have you been writing?" [12] Several months later, Blanche sent another letter complaining that Elsa had not answered her and that too much time had elapsed since she had heard from Elsa and since Elsa had written a novel.[13] In a third letter, she was persistent but optimistic: "I hear, and am very interested in the news, that you are finishing a novel. It is high time. . . . Tell me how it is coming along and when I will be likely to see [*sic*]. It has been too long since I have heard anything from you so I long to have an answer to this. I hope you are well and having a lovely time and getting on fast with this new book." [14] Blanche Knopf also wrote to Elsa's agent and to her Italian publisher in the hope of having more definite news. Both men put her off politely. Erich Linder wrote: "I am also sorry to disappoint you over the Morante novel: I have heard absolutely nothing about it, and as far as I know there is no sign of it . . . [w]hich may not mean much, as she may produce it any day all the same." [15] Giulio Einaudi reinforced these uncertainties: "But I have the impression that the work goes on very irregularly, with long pauses, and I cannot foresee when it will be finished." [16] Clearly, Elsa was not in touch with either her publisher or her agent.

However, earlier, in 1963, Einaudi had published *Lo scialle andaluso (The Andalusian Shawl)* a collection of twelve short stories. Except for the title story, which was written in 1951 and published in *Botteghe Oscure*, the literary review founded by the American-born Princess Marguerite Caetani (née Chapin), and two other stories, "Donna Amalia" (1950) and "Il soldato siciliano" (1945), the other nine stories were all written well before World War II. Most of them had appeared in the 1941 collection *Il gioco segreto*.

The title story tells of a son's obsessive love for his mother, an old ballerina whose lack of talent has driven her from the corps de ballet of the Opera of Rome to a provincial theater where she is booed offstage, and the mother's love for the son. Morante deftly depicts the mother through the adolescent, jealous eyes of the son and the son through the besotted eyes of the mother and how both live in a fabulous world of make-believe. As in *House of Liars*, it is this world of make-believe and how they will remain trapped in their fantasies—not their obsessive, inappropriate love—that is the subject of the story. For the critic Cesare Garboli, "The Andalusian Shawl" was a little jewel, a perfect short story that also had the "contour" of a novel. He wrote that the story maintained a perfect balance between hilarity and tragedy and that the style stood halfway between what he called the "shadow" of *House of Liars* and the "smile" of *Arturo's Island*. [17]

The stories "The Thief of Light" ("Il ladro dei lumi") and "Donna Amalia" represent two apposite aspects of Morante's belief: in the first story, the protagonist becomes the symbol of

modern man by robbing the world of light and plunging human-
ity into darkness; in the second, the eponymous character represents the splendor of art and of life. The story "The Sicilian
Soldier" ("Il soldato siciliano") stands in between the two and
perhaps expresses Elsa Morante's true message: the solitary wan-
derings of the soldier with a miner's lamp on his head looking for
death. The strongest of the other stories in the collection, "The
Secret Game" ("Il gioco segreto"), which was discussed earlier
and has been compared to Henry James's *The Turn of the Screw*, is
a fable of infancy and death where literature becomes the salvation for the three unhappy children who are unable to establish a
healthy relationship with reality.[18] Here again, the underlying pathology is not sex but an obsessive fascination with make-believe.
The deliberately formal and old-fashioned style and language
in these short stories was also intended to take the reader back to
the past, to an older literary period. This is grammatically true as
well. (Instead of using the conditional past, the accepted and
mandatory tense to denote the future in Italian, Morante deliberately chose to use the conditional present, no longer a commonly
used tense, to denote such a future action.)

The novel Morante had set aside when Bill Morrow died,
Without the Comfort of Religion, would never be completed. It belonged to a period when Elsa Morante was happy. It was also a
time when Rome, according to Cesare Garboli, was beautiful and
there was an immense hunger for life, the desire for pleasure and
celebration. A time, too, when he described Elsa as being full of
life. He talked about her gaiety, her puerile naïveté, her pleasure
at giving joy to others, her laughter, her engaging way of talking
and her moodiness, which he compared to the smallest cloud in a
blue sky that could herald more clouds, a storm.[19] With the death
of Bill Morrow, the beautiful magic boy, the angel made of flesh

and blood, all this changed for Elsa Morante. She had to face the awareness of herself as an older woman without fantasies, without a foreseeable future. This sudden and unwelcome self-knowledge may have driven her selection of stories: revisiting old stories and rewriting them may have been a way of surviving.

nine

POETRY AND PASOLINI

Elsa Morante had a distinctive style of dressing that was all her own—she did not follow any fashion. She was, for instance, one of the first women in Italy to wear trousers. She also loved the color blue, electric blue, which is a difficult color to wear. Patrizia Cavalli, who became one of Elsa's closest friends, has kept some of Morante's clothes and one day while we were talking, she opened two large cupboards in her apartment and showed me some of them. She held up several tight-waisted taffeta evening dresses with voluminous skirts—an especially elegant one had a black velvet top and an iridescent pleated silk skirt, made by the French designer Jacques Fath—and a satin evening coat with dolman sleeves. All the clothes were very "sixties" and made up a much less austere and more youthful-looking wardrobe than I had imagined. Patrizia also showed me some bright cotton blouses that had large cuffs and high romantic collars. I particularly liked a purple one and held it up to myself for size. It was obvious, from looking at her clothes, that Elsa was quite small and slender—and she had no hips. In today's sizes, she might have been a four or a six—except for her bust, which Patrizia, gesturing with her hands, suggested was ample.

Lighting a cigarette, Patrizia Cavalli recounted how she first met Elsa Morante in either 1971 or 1972—the way she remembers is that Elsa gave her a cat who died when he was five years old in 1977. Patrizia Cavalli was a young student then (lazy and feckless is how she described herself), and a new life opened up for her as a result of this meeting. She described Elsa Morante as a kind of magnet for people, people Patrizia got to meet and who, to this day, have remained her friends.

She also described a day—a day she would never forget—when, walking back to Piazza Navona after lunch, Elsa suddenly turned to her and asked, "And you, Patrizia, what do you do?" Quickly taking stock and coming up with something, Cavalli told Morante that she wrote poems—something she had never admitted to anyone before because she was afraid of both committing herself and of risking judgment. Elsa Morante said, "Ah, why don't you let me read your poems? I want to know how you are made." This, naturally, posed an even greater threat for Patrizia. She kept making up excuses and putting Elsa off, hoping she would forget but of course she didn't. At the same time, Patrizia was forced to reevaluate her poems—some of them, she realized, were awful. She began to write new poems, she developed an ear and she figured out what her relationship to language was. Finally, after six months, Patrizia Cavalli chose some older poems that she thought were not too bad and some new ones and gave them to Elsa. Most of her poems were very, very short:

> *Mi darà la mano mi dirà:*
> *"Ciao bella ci vediamo."*[1]

> You will give me your hand and you will say to me;
> "Good-bye beauty we will see one another again."

Afterward she went home, had lunch and worried. Half an hour later the telephone rang, and it was Elsa, who said, "Oh,

Patrizia, I am happy! You are a poet." From that moment on, Patrizia Cavalli's life was changed forever. She felt accepted by Elsa, who had given her confidence and allowed her to become a poet. Elsa was also generous. She introduced Patrizia to her publisher and, in turn, Einaudi took the poems. But the funny thing, Patrizia Cavalli said, was that she herself was so naïve that she was not even surprised or excited by this—she thought that was how it always was. She was so indifferent, she said, because the important thing for her was that Elsa had liked her poems. Elsa Morante chose the order of the poems in the collection and even chose its title: *Le mie poesie non cambieranno il mondo (My Poems Will Not Change the World)*. In appreciation, Patrizia Cavalli dedicated her book of poems to Elsa.[2]

The poet Sandro Penna was also a great friend of Elsa Morante and Alberto Moravia. Known as a protégé of Umberto Saba, Penna wrote exclusively about love—his love for young boys. Like Patrizia Cavalli's, all his poems are very short and record an equally short and fleeting encounter, a moment of intense feeling or obsessive desire:

> *Tu morirai fanciullo ed io ugualmente*
> *ma più belli di te ragazzi ancora*
> *dormiranno nel sole in riva al mare.*

> You're going to die, kid.
> And so am I.
> But kids more beautiful
> than you already
> sleep in the sun
> at the seashore.[3]

For Penna the adolescent boy, *ragazzo* or *fanciullo*, was both the inspiration and the personification of love. Not surprisingly, Sandro Penna and Pier Paolo Pasolini were good friends as well. Rumor had it that Penna and Pasolini were in competition to see who could seduce the greater number of young boys—the famous *ragazzi di vita** (the literal meaning is "boys of life")—along the banks of the Tiber or, for that matter, anywhere in Rome.

Pier Paolo Pasolini was, for many years, Elsa Morante's greatest friend. He was also the most talked about, the most discussed and insulted man in all of Italy and, probably, the most misunderstood. For many people of that era, Pasolini was the "emblem of scandal," "the personification of provocative transgression" and "the prototype of indecency."[4] Anticonformist, difficult, private, extreme, he was attacked equally by right-wing conservatives, Fascists and Communists. Writers were made uncomfortable by the way he flaunted his homosexuality, filmmakers were jealous of his vast success, politicians mocked his meddling. He constantly took controversial positions—against student demonstrators and in support of the police, against divorce, against abortion—some of which, like his appeals to abolish schools and television and his obsession with preserving the Friulian dialect, seemed downright contrarian. Finally, his "cult of youth," his boyish clothes (tight jeans and boots), his obsession with staying fit, his habit of playing pickup soccer with local boys, his fast cars, his vanity, were all derided.

Pier Paolo was extremely affectionate. He loved Elsa and they saw each other nearly daily. If not, they corresponded to each

---

* *Ragazzi di vita* was also the title of Pasolini's first novel, the first two parts of a projected trilogy, which was published in 1955.

other in verse—Pasolini once sent Elsa a poem in the shape of a rose *(poesia in forma di rosa)* and she wrote back a calligram in the shape of a cat *(madrigale in forma di gatto)*. They told each other their dreams and tried to interpret them. Pasolini made his deep attachment to Elsa clear: "What a pleasure; we meet almost every day, and to meet her gives me a feeling of celebration, as though each time we were returning from long journeys. We don't think about it, but deep down it's always a miracle to see one another." Describing her with his keen filmmaker's eye, he wrote, "Elsa is sitting on the edge of the divan, upright, swathed in one of her undersea colors, with those eyes whose nearsightedness spreads a film of light haze around the pupils, the eyelids, and the stormy face." [5]

They shared their obsessive truth-telling as well as their love of games. More important, however, they were interested in Eastern religions and philosophies; they both had a similar theory of reality, which they loved to discuss. For Morante and Pasolini, the opposition between the real and the unreal was more significant than the opposition between life and death. They believed that only the authentic—the concrete, however painful or unhappy—mattered. Both ranted against the establishment, against power, illusion and the idea of possession. Morante's concept of reality, which was influenced by her reading of Simone Weil, especially Weil's *Cahiers* (a book she had read so often the pages were in tatters), was based on the imaginary—not necessarily a contradiction—and on how fables, fantasies, mystery and magic serve to illuminate the "real" world. For Morante, the "real," which could be as ephemeral as happiness or a song, is the world transformed by the imagination and is invisible. It is the "dream of the thing," an expression attributed to Karl Marx that Pasolini planned to use as a title for a novel and which conveyed reality to him in its entirety.[6] Pasolini was also influenced (as to some extent was Morante) by the writer Carlo Levi, who believed in an art where naming things for the first time made them exist. He also believed in a reality that was easier to find among the simple, southern Italian peasantry than among the corrupted bourgeoisie.

In 1955, Elsa Morante did Pasolini a large service. She persuaded Moravia to publish Pasolini's great verse epic, *The Ashes of Gramsci (Le ceneri di Gramsci)*, in *Nuovi Argomenti*, which, until then, did not publish poetry. The eleven poems in this work were based on the notebooks of Antonio Gramsci, the cofounder of the Italian Communist Party who, for ten years and until his death, was a political prisoner of the Fascists. *The Ashes of Gramsci*, which is often compared to Allen Ginsberg's *Howl* (while the poet himself is often compared to Che Guevara), is Pasolini's best-known literary work. It is an angry lament for lost hopes and, in the words of a Pasolini biographer, "the betrayal of the dream for which Guido [Pasolini, Pier Paolo's brother*] died: the failure of the left, and of all Italians, to hold together and realize the vision of a more-just postwar society."[7]

> *tra le vecchie muraglie l'autunnale*
> *maggio. In esso c'è il grigiore del mondo*
> *la fine del decennio in cui ci appare*
>
> *tra le macerie finito il profondo*
> *e ingenuo sforzo di rifare la vita;*

---

* A partisan in a Republican guerrilla band during World War II, nineteen-year-old Guido Pasolini was shot by the Communists in February 1945.

Inside the ancient walls
the autumnal May diffuses a deadly

peace, disquieting like our destinies,
and holds the whole world's dismay
the finish of the decade that saw

the profound, naïve struggle to make
life over collapse in ruins.[8]

In his verses, Pasolini managed to integrate his personal anguish with Italian history in a tone that was a remarkable combination of confessional poetry and public rhetoric. When it was subsequently published in book form, *The Ashes of Gramsci* was an instant success and sold out. It won the Viareggio Prize for poetry in 1957.

The next year, there was additional cause for celebration. Longanesi Editions published the collected poems of the three friends: Elsa Morante's *Alibi (Alibi)*, Sandro Penna's *Croce e delizia (A Cross and a Delight)* and Pier Paolo Pasolini's *L'usignolo della Chiesa Cattolica (The Nightingale of the Catholic Church)*. Of the three, Morante's collection received the least attention from the critics and the public. She was accused of being a beginner and her poems were thought to strain too hard to be experimental and modern. Even Cesare Garboli, her ardent supporter, admitted that he preferred poems with rhymes and rhythms and liked only old-fashioned, traditional verse.[9] Hard as it is to judge poetry, harder still when it is written in another language, it may nevertheless be interesting to look at how her poems illumine her prose, keeping in mind what she wrote in the preface to *Alibi*. Perhaps anticipating the criticism, Elsa Morante asked the reader to forgive the little worth and importance of the pages that were to follow. She wrote that she was by nature and by destiny a writer of prose stories. Her few verses were no more than an echo of her novels and no more than a pastime—a game, to which she sometimes liked to abandon herself without too much commitment for the simple pleasure of the music. And if she had decided to publish these verses (some of which dated back to her youth), she had done so only in the hope that they might offer the reader the same bit of repose and pleasure she received from composing them.[10]

The main theme of the sixteen poems in Morante's collection is love, a love that ranges from a sort of glorified love to one that is idolatrous and addictive. In the poem "Avventura" ("Adventure"), which is addressed to Luchino Visconti and begins:"Do you have a heart? Legend has it that you don't have one," the love described is not mutual. Instead, it becomes a mirror of the speaker's own self and is a narcissistic and masochistic love. Every love, according to Morante, is a lost love and she, in particular, has a vocation for unhappy loves. Certainly, in Visconti's case, it was an impossible love. "Alibi," the title poem, has been read as a metaphor and the key to Morante's universe and how she understands the creative process and the writing of fiction. As the meaning of the word suggests, an alibi is an absence or an excuse, and it was how Morante saw fiction or poetry as providing a way of creating an alternate reality, a reality that does not necessarily replace present reality but becomes a part of it, and changes it. Morante also claimed, "Only the one who loves knows. Unfortunate the one who does not love!" Only through love, Morante is saying, can one break through the barrier of conventional knowledge and truly know reality (implicit, too, in the poem is the concept that one cannot know a person unless one loves him).

The German composer Hans Werner Henze, who was living

in Italy (and still is) and was a friend of Elsa, set "Alibi" to music in his *Cantata della fiaba estrema*. The piece was first played in Zurich on February 26, 1965, and Elsa attended the performance. According to Henze, she was not particularly pleased and felt that the music was not sufficiently impassioned while he felt that he had captured the gentle and childlike quality of the poem. Wisely, he did not try to justify his interpretation or explain his intentions to Elsa.[11]

Elsa Morante's extensive library contained a volume of Coleridge's complete poems and, as an exercise, it is interesting to see which verses she earmarked and made notations beside, as they may shed a light on her private feelings. Among those she underlined were "Alone, alone, all, all alone, / Alone on a wide, wide, sea! / And never a saint took pity on / My soul in agony" from *The Rime of the Ancient Mariner*; "I know 'tis but a dream, yet feel more anguish / Than if 'twere truth" and "Will no one hear these stifled groans and wake me?" from "The Night-mare Death in Life"; and "By woman wailing for her demon-lover!" from *Kubla Khan*. Morante also penciled in crosses beside: "Composed on a journey Homeward; the Author having received Intelligence of the Birth of a Son," and "To a Friend who asked how I felt when the Nurse first presented my Infant to me." Both sonnets have to do with the birth of a child and the writer's rather ambivalent reaction and could very well be indications of Elsa Morante's own feelings of loneliness and loss.[12]

"To a Fable" ("Alla favola"), written in 1947 and dedicated to Anna in *House of Liars*, despite its difficulties, is regarded by most critics and readers of her work as Morante's most successful poem.

> *Di te, Finzione, mi cingo,*
> *fatua veste.*

Ti lavoro con l'auree piume
che vestí prima d'esser fuoco
la mia grande stagione defunta
per mutarmi in fenice lucente!

L'ago è rovente, la tela è fumo.
Consunta fra i suoi cerchi d'oro
giace la vanesia mano
pur se al gioco di m'ama non m'ama
la risposta celeste
mi fingo.

     O Fiction, I draw about me
     your concealing garment
     and adorn it with golden plumage
     that was mine in the great lost season
     before I grew all fire
     and rose a radiant phoenix!

     But the needle is flame, the cloth is smoke,
     and the vain hand lies withered away
     under the golden rings—
     even if in the game of "loves me, loves me not"
     I invent a consoling reply:
     an illusory voice from heaven.[13]

Again, the poem posits that fiction is not just an external quality added to reality but a quality of reality, and that there is no real conflict or dialectic between what is real and what is imaginary. It also implies that the duty of the artist or writer is to penetrate more deeply into this reality.

The language of Elsa Morante's poetry is often artificial, theatrical and difficult to respond to. She makes a point of using outmoded words and the poems appear self-conscious. Often, she seems to be writing with magic formulas. There is a strong sense of destiny in the poems and many references to Greek mythological figures, but fortunately this high-mindedness is undercut by Morante's never taking herself too seriously. She is aware that there are bigger tragedies in the world than her unhappy loves, and there is always a strong sense of irony in the poems. She deliberately sets out to act the part of the *pazzeriella* or fool (in the Shakespearean sense). "Oh, crazy one" (*"Ah, pazza"*) is how she addresses herself in "Avventura," which is a way of establishing empathy with the reader and of keeping the poem from becoming too heavy-handed. And, of the sixteen poems in *Alibi*, three of them are addressed to Elsa Morante's beloved cats.

Alberto Moravia's friendship with Pasolini was based more on their mutual interest in political and cultural matters, although they did not always agree on them. In addition, they traveled a great deal together, to Africa and to India. Both men wrote books about the 1961 trip to India that Elsa also went on. It is indicative of the difference in their personalities that Pasolini's is called *The Scent of India* while Moravia's book is called *An Idea of India*. In his account Pasolini often mentions that he and Moravia took long, contemplative evening walks through the streets of Calcutta, Delhi, Agra and Benares, but he does not always make it clear whether Elsa Morante was with them or not. She does not appear until he describes a visit to Sister (not yet Mother) Teresa, who was administering a leper colony. According to Pasolini there were sixty thousand lepers in Calcutta. Clearly he was very impressed with Sister Teresa and used his poetic and cinematographer's sensibility to describe her: "Sister Teresa is an old woman, brown of skin, because she is Albanian, tall, dry, with two almost masculine cheek-bones, and a gentle eye which 'sees' wherever it looks. In an impressive way she resembles a famous Saint Anna of Michelangelo: and on her features is impressed true goodness, of the type described by Proust in his old maid Françoise: goodness without sentimental additions, without expectations, both tranquil and tranquillising, powerful and practical." [14]

The second time Elsa is acknowledged concerned a young beggar named Revi, whom Pasolini befriended. With the hope of bettering the boy's prospects, Pasolini took him to the home of a Dutch priest where, with very mixed feelings, he left him. "That evening at supper in the hotel I tormented Moravia and Elsa with my scruples: we were getting towards the end of our voyage in India, and were practically drained by the pressure of its suffering and by pity. Every time one leaves someone in India one has the impression that one is leaving a dying person who is about to drown in the midst of the flotsam of a shipwreck." [15] (It has been pointed out that the two times Pasolini mentioned Morante on that trip to India, the circumstances had to do with acts of charity.[16]) Later, Elsa was to describe to a friend a more lighthearted moment in India with Pasolini: "There was this little waiter serving us, and after a few words in broken English, off goes the boy and off goes the poet after him. Six minutes later the poet comes back and says: 'I made love to him.' 'Love?!' said I, 'what love? Six minutes' love!? Call it a little spasm of evacuation, that's all.' " [17]

It was Pasolini who was finally able to rescue Elsa Morante from her solitary grieving over Bill Morrow's untimely death. He asked her to choose the music for the sound track of his new film, *The Gospel According to St. Matthew.* Elsa selected Bach, Mozart and the recently released Congolese Mass *Missa Luba*; although not credited, she also assisted him directing. The cast included Elsa's brother Marcello Morante as Saint Joseph, her nephew Giacomo Morante as one of the apostles, Pasolini's good friends Enzo Siciliano and Giorgio Agamben as two other apostles, Natalia Ginzburg as Mary of Bethany and her second husband, Gabriele Baldini, as Mary's husband. (Pasolini's first feature, *Accatone*, caused an uproar at the 1961 Venice Film Festival for its sympathetic portrayal of amoral characters, pimps and prostitutes. In it, Elsa Morante appears briefly as a prisoner sitting on the floor of her cell, looking dejected.) The work seemed to revive Elsa. She moved back to the apartment on via dell'Oca from the one she had rented for herself and Bill Morrow on via del Babuino, and she busied herself redecorating it. She bought new wallpaper and new furniture—rattan sofas and chairs covered in pale, linen fabrics—and she hung Morrow's colorful painting on the walls.

For the Christmas holidays in 1965, Elsa went to visit her brother Aldo, then the director of the Banca Commerciale in Mexico City. She spent several months in Mexico and traveled to the Yucatán. She fell in love with the country and would return to visit several times. On one of her trips Elsa claimed to have tried psychedelic mushrooms and she even, she said, managed to smuggle a peyote button back to Italy, which she kept on her desk. Later, Elsa was to say that these trips to Mexico were some of the happiest times in her life.

On the same day that Patrizia Cavalli showed me Elsa's clothes, she let me listen to a recording of Elsa's voice. The tape was old and scratchy but one could hear Elsa clearly reciting her poems in a deep, sonorous voice. Patrizia started to laugh: Elsa, she said, was speaking in an unnatural, self-conscious way, as if speaking by rote. Also, she had put on a pretentious Roman accent and she did not talk at all like that in real life. On the tape, Elsa was saying: *"Solo chi ama conosce. Povero chi non ama!"* ("Only the one who loves knows. Unfortunate the one who does not love!") and I closed my eyes and listened as carefully as I could. No matter what Patrizia said, I thought it was amazing to hear Elsa Morante's voice.

ten

THE WORLD SAVED BY CHILDREN

The Living Theater opened at the Teatro Eliseo in Rome in 1965 with *Mysteries and Smaller Pieces*, which was both an instant success and an enormous shock. The Italian audiences were unaccustomed to this American avant-garde troupe's revolutionary stance, which broke down the barriers between art and politics, challenged sexual assumptions and confronted the audience, often forcing it to participate. Elsa Morante first saw a performance with a young American friend who was living in Rome. Peter Hartman was a musician as well as a poet and an actor who had once worked with the Living Theater back in New York. Not surprisingly, since she was so attracted to the American counterculture of the time, Elsa loved the Living Theater and, right away, she befriended Julian Beck and his wife, Judith Malina, its founders. To this day, Judith Malina, who had just turned eighty when I interviewed her, has happy memories of how Morante and Moravia welcomed them with open arms. In particular, she remembered the day Elsa took them on their first tour of Rome. As they were about to round the corner and enter Piazza Navona, Elsa told them, "Now, you are going to see the most beautiful piazza in the world." [1] Elsa was deeply connected to the city, Malina said; she had a wonderful relationship with every stone, every street, and an uncanny ability to find beauty and splendor everywhere. Elsa introduced Judith and Julian to her friends and, for once, Judith Malina said, they felt appreciated.[2] Certainly, all the Italians (most Europeans, as a matter of fact) Malina and Beck met, although still conservative, were very impressed by the avant-garde company, with its lack of inhibitions regarding nudity, sex and the use of drugs. Elsa must have supported and agreed with the Living Theater's anarchist imperatives, which stated that the plays should be performed in the street, outside of institutionalized theaters, and for the benefit of the proletariat—the poorest of the poor. Probably too, according to her coexecutor Carlo Cecchi, Elsa Morante must have made an unconscious connection between Bill Morrow and the Living Theater.[3]

I first met Carlo Cecchi, an actor and the director of a theater company, in Iesi, a city near the Adriatic coast, where he was both directing and acting in Pirandello's *Six Characters in Search of an Author*; when we met again the following year, I took a bus to the hill town of Urbino, where he was rehearsing a production of Molière's *Tartuffe*—as a result, I got to see some beautiful Italian countryside, especially the region known as Marche, thanks to Cecchi's willingness to share his memories of Elsa. Carlo Cecchi met Elsa, in 1965, when he was twenty-three—almost a boy, he said—and he, too, had been deeply affected by the Living Theater. He had studied at the Accademia in Rome and was acting; with friends, he had already put together a small underground theater called A la Lettera near Piazza di Spagna, where he had produced Rolf Hochhuth's *The Deputy*. The play had been banned and the newspapers in Rome had been full of the controversy. Next, while he was rehearsing *Woyzeck* by Georg Büchner, the telephone rang one day and he heard Elsa Morante's voice for the first time. A "singing" voice was how he described it—not very crystalline but filled with resonance. The Living Theater was having problems with the police—someone had gone onstage naked—and since she knew he had had a similar sort of problem, she had telephoned to ask for his advice. She also knew he was a friend of Peter Hartman. When she learned that he was directing *Woyzeck,* Elsa became very enthusiastic and animated. She had seen the play several times and felt it was a masterpiece. In general, she spoke with great passion about the theater. The way she spoke to him, too, Carlo Cecchi could not help but remark, was curious, as if they had known each other for a long time. Finally Elsa said, "Come, it is better that we meet and talk about all these things."

Carlo Cecchi went to see Elsa Morante in her apartment on via dell'Oca on an autumn morning. The apartment consisted of two floors and she had asked him to come directly to the apartment's studio on the top floor, which had its own entrance. Her studio, he remembered, was quite dark and furnished simply; there was an enormous desk, her record player and record collection and some photos on the walls. Outside was the bright terrace and it was like going from night to day, with the explosion of light on the terrace, which was full of plants—sunflowers, bougainvillea and lemon trees—and the view below of Piazza del Popolo, with the Egyptian obelisk and the domes of three churches: Santa Maria del Popolo, Santa Maria di Montesanto and Santa Maria dei Miracoli.

Carlo Cecchi found Elsa Morante very beautiful. He had no idea how old she was—he thought she was forty, no more than forty—and he described her hair as "not too long, red brown, more brown than red." She was slim and wore slacks and a beautiful sweater. Elsa asked Carlo if he wanted something to eat—he was then poor and thin. "No, just coffee," he answered. They sat out on the terrace and spoke about the Living Theater and many other things as well. When it was time for him to leave, Elsa told him that she was going to New York and Mexico soon. After this, his first encounter with her, Carlo did not see Elsa again for another year.[4]

Elsa Morante made a point of avoiding the literary set, the more social and political crowd Moravia belonged to. She did not see Moravia often—he and Dacia Maraini lived across the river in an apartment on Lungo Tevere delle Vittoria—but when she did, their relationship was always quite cordial. She defended him and spoke of him with tenderness, although sometimes she made fun of him a little—of his stinginess, for example. By then, too, in Rome, Elsa had created her own circle of friends, who were for the most part younger and with whom she felt an affinity: Paolo and Stella Graziosi, Angelica Ippolito, Dario Bellezza, Patrizia Cavalli, Carlo Cecchi, Peter Hartman, Allen Midgette, Fleur Jaeggy, Piergiorgio Bellocchio, Ginevra Bompiani, Giorgio Agamben, Grazia Cherchi, Linuccia Saba and Paolo Volponi. Later her friends included Goffredo Fofi, Tonino Ricchezza and Alfonso Berardinelli. Her presence, according to the critic Alfonso Berardinelli, was charismatic and she had the effect of being like a guru to her friends.[5] Apparently, she was very astute at figuring out people's weaknesses and their hidden sides. She was also fiercely loyal and very generous. Adriana Asti remembers how Elsa always gave her presents: jewelry, scarves, once a bit of opium inside a carved wooden box![6] Another friend, Charis Vivante, remembered how Elsa brought her back a beautiful silk kimono from Japan.[7] She also had an uncanny ability to know when to help. Allen Midgette recalls how sometimes he was so poor he would go three or four days without food and just as he thought he was going to starve to death, Elsa would appear and take him out to lunch. Another time, Allen found a broken piggy bank lying on the floor of his tiny apartment in Trastevere with a 20,000 lire note next to it. Elsa, he guessed, had thrown the piggy bank through his window.

Another young man Elsa befriended was William Edwards, a handsome Englishman who was wandering around the world aimlessly and who now would probably be diagnosed as bipolar, as he alternated between states of being docile and violently aggressive. Clearly Elsa was very fond of Edwards. She wrote a poem about him with the line "Happiness does not exist without a boy / Without a boy, it is pointless to drag through life."[8] When Edwards was arrested for deliberately breaking things in an antique store and was taken by the police to a mental hospital, Elsa enlisted Allen Midgette's help to get him out. It was a very rainy day and Elsa and Allen could not find a taxi so when a horse and carriage came clip-clopping by, out of desperation, they hired it and got in. Allen Midgette remembers how on the way to the hospital they both began to laugh hysterically at the surreal picture they must have made: arriving at the loony bin in the pouring rain in a horse and carriage to try to get someone in there out.

Elsa Morante was always very attracted to handsome, young, homosexual (or perhaps bisexual) men. The most obvious reason for this attraction, of course, is that women—particularly women of a certain age—feel safe with homosexual men because there is no possibility of sex between them. Also, it is certainly not unusual for artistic women to be attracted to homosexuals and feel a kinship to them, the result of similar sensibilities and interests. In Morante's case, however, I would venture that her attraction to young gay men had more to do with her maternal instincts and her desire to have a son. The young men Elsa was drawn to were for the most part slightly childlike in the sense that they had a certain innocence or purity about them (as Allen Midgette still does), a kind of naïveté that translates itself into a sweetness and a trust in life and in other people to help them and an optimism that somehow everything will turn out all right. Elsa's love for these young men can be compared to the love that she might have felt for a child of her own. However, her love for, say, Bill Morrow, Allen Midgette or William Edwards—unlike the many archetypal and mythological figures of mothers who fall in love with their sons—could manifest itself without the specter of incest.

Nor was Elsa a demonstratively physical person. She never kissed anyone and if someone tried to kiss her she drew back. As she grew older, she said that kissing her was like "kissing a rotten apple." She always gave Patrizia Cavalli her hand, which was odd since they were close friends. One Christmas day—and this impressed Patrizia enormously—when Patrizia was all alone, she had had a misunderstanding with her family, and, during lunch, she asked Elsa whether they were going to also have dinner together that evening. Elsa, who must have sensed how upset Patrizia was, did something she had never done before. She took Patrizia's chin in her hand and said, *"Ma certo tesore"* ("But of course, darling").[9] Patrizia was very moved by this little gesture of tenderness and affection.

The only member of her family whom Elsa liked and included in her group of friends was Daniele Morante, the oldest of Marcello's ten children. (Interestingly, she always introduced him as a friend and never as her nephew.) Of the other nine, she had formed a negative impression that did not make much sense. (For instance, Elsa once heard Daniele's sister Laura, who was fourteen at the time, humming a popular song that she could not stand and based on that little incident decided that she did not want anything more to do with Laura.) For the most part, she and

Daniele maintained a warm relationship. In 1966, when Daniele was newly married and studying in Rome, Elsa Morante lent him and his wife her studio apartment on via Archimede. In the end, however, because Elsa's maid Lucia went there from time to time to tidy up and must have reported back to Elsa what a terrible mess the apartment was in, Elsa asked them both to leave. Having to do this upset her so much that she began to cry and, as compensation, she gave Daniele and his wife some money.[10]

Elsa Morante was always very outspoken, she had a mania for truth-telling, no matter how hurtful or aggressive, and she often made very provocative demands. She could also be witty and sarcastic; one of my favorite of her purported sayings occurred after the Italian soccer team won a match at the 1968 Olympics in Mexico and, hearing people screaming and shouting in the streets of Rome, she asked, "Do they shout like that because they have just been told that the latest book by Sandro Penna has been published?"[11] She did not like being photographed, nor did she like being interviewed. "If someone wants to know something about me," she would say, "they should read my books."[12] She hated to give information about herself, and she rarely said the same thing twice; instead she liked to create something that was real but not necessarily true, or the other way around—that was true but not real.[13] She also refused ever to go on television; she hated television. She did not even own a TV until she bought a small black-and-white set to watch the moon landing in 1969, but then she never watched television again.[14]

Although she rarely inhaled, Elsa Morante was a heavy smoker. She smoked North Pole menthol cigarettes, and she used a long cigarette holder—always the same one. She insisted on lighting her own cigarettes because, as she liked to say, "the pleasure of smoking lies in lighting up the cigarette. I hate those people, who out of kindness, rob you of that pleasure." Occasionally, she tried drugs. Allen Midgette remembers her telling him over the phone that she had taken some LSD. Elsa said the only effect she felt was a headache, but, worried, Allen went over to her apartment anyway—Elsa was then still living on via del Babuino. When he got there Elsa asked him whether he would mind if she lay down on the floor for a while, which was not like her at all— although not prudish, Elsa was proper in her way and she was not a flirt. Lying on the floor, she began to talk about the apartment as if it were not hers: how it was ugly and looked like a doctor's office. She discussed the paintings on the walls with him. One painting was a portrait of Elsa by her friend Leonor Fini, and it was beautiful but Elsa did not like it; the other was a Braque, a small landscape of a beach by the sea, very simple and also very beautiful and that painting Elsa said she did like. She then said that she wanted to go out and see the architecture of Rome. Allen and Elsa walked to Piazza del Popolo and when she saw the cars (cars were then permitted on the piazza), she said how she had never realized before how dirty cars were. When she saw the obelisk in the middle of the piazza, she said, "It's all made of dust." Afterward Allen walked her home and Elsa said, "Good night, Allen, you are an angel." [15]

Elsa's truth-telling proved helpful to him, Daniele said, when he went to see his aunt soon after he was divorced. Instead of trying to console him, Elsa told Daniele that his wife had done the right thing to leave him and for him not to come back and see her until he had put his own life in order. Elsa's outspokenness proved less useful a few years later, when Daniele took his second wife to meet her. Elsa noticed that Daniele's wife did not shave her armpits. As a result, Elsa imagined that she was an angry feminist, a kind of militant, which she was not at all. Elsa made a huge scene, telling Daniele's wife never to come again with that hair hanging from under her arm. The wife, who was very sensitive and proper, never went to see Elsa again.[16]

Ginevra Bompiani, the owner of the beautiful necklace Elsa coveted when they used to play Murder in the Dark, recalled how she and her friends, who were young and impressionable at the time, learned a great deal from Elsa. They learned not to use euphemisms and to say things the way they were—in other words, they learned not to lie. Conversations with Elsa, Ginevra recalled, were never trivial; they never talked about worldly things, which was also a useful lesson.[17] Patrizia Cavalli remembered how Elsa was almost superstitious about telling the truth and how she would make pronouncements and judge things in absolute terms: *"Questo e molto bello"* ("This is very good") or *"Questo e bruto"* ("This is bad"). In this sense, she was reassuring because Patrizia felt that if Elsa agreed or if she said something was good or beautiful, it was, and she should believe it. As a result too, her friends developed a kind of *sostanza etica* ("ethical essence") or a way of behaving.[18] Ginevra also remembered what a wonderful storyteller Elsa was. She would tell all sorts of stories about herself and her life and she never told the same one twice. Ginevra described what a beautiful way Elsa had of making contact with people, simple people, and how, for instance, in the summer, when Ginevra, Giorgio Agamben and Elsa went to the island of Ponza together, Elsa would talk to the old women on the island. She would talk to them for hours and make them talk to her as well. She had a real sense of people and could tap into their "fairy tale" side. It was really beautiful to see, and the word Ginevra used was *fabuloso*.[19]

· · ·

The next time Carlo Cecchi met Elsa was in 1966 at a screening of an experimental film called *The Blind Fly (A mosca cieca)*, based loosely on Camus's *The Stranger*, in which he played the protagonist. Elsa was very much moved by the film, telling Carlo Cecchi, "You know, you've made my day!" From then on, they saw each other quite often, usually with Peter Hartman, Bernardo Bertolucci and others connected to or interested in the Living Theater.

One day Carlo mentioned that he was going to Venice to see the Berliner Ensemble, the theater company founded by Bertolt Brecht. Elsa said that she wanted to go as well but that it was always difficult to find a place to stay in Venice. Cecchi drove to Venice with friends, and since he had no money he stayed at a youth hostel, but once there, he managed to get two tickets for all the performances as well as find a room for Elsa in a pensione. He then telephoned Elsa and told her, "Come." It was his telling her to come and that he would pick her up at the airport that convinced her. On the appointed day, Cecchi went to the airport. He was early and because it was a beautiful sunny day, he lay down on the runway in the sun to wait for Elsa's plane. (During our interview, we both laughed at the image of Carlo sunbathing on the runway and at how impossible that would be to do today.) When Elsa arrived they took the bus into Venice. On the bus, Elsa opened her purse and handed her money to Cecchi, saying: "Look at all the money I brought. Take it—*senza complimenti*." ("With no strings attached" is the English expression that comes closest to match this Italian idiom).

But what truly changed him, Carlo Cecchi said, was what Elsa told him one day during that trip. They were in a gondola on the Grand Canal and she began talking about the nonexistence of time as the fourth dimension of space. As an example, she told him a parable—a favorite and one that Bertolucci used in his 1964 film *Before the Revolution*. Two men are walking together in the desert. When they stop to rest, the older man tells the younger man to fetch him some water. The young man sets off to the nearest village; at the fountain there he sees a beautiful young woman. He falls in love with her, kisses her and marries her. They have several children. One day, a terrible plague afflicts the village and the man's wife dies. His children die. Distraught, he leaves the village and wanders, for days, in the desert. All of a sudden he comes across the old man, who is sitting in the same spot where he left him when he went to fetch the water. The old man asks, "Where is the water? I've been waiting for you all morning."

Elsa talked to Cecchi about the Upanishads and how their philosophy related to contemporary physics, and it was the first time he had been introduced to these ideas. Elsa, he said, opened up his framework of cultural references—references that hitherto had been tied to a humanism based on the Italian philosopher Benedetto Croce's idealism, and to *storicismo*, a belief in history as an instrument of knowledge. Elsa, Cecchi also said, had unconsciously chosen Venice as the living proof, where one could literally touch the reality of years, to introduce him to these new concepts. It was a very important time for them both—and not just because it deepened and solidified their friendship.[20]

Elsa Morante wrote most of *The World Saved by Children and Other Poems (Il mondo salvato dai ragazzini e altri poemi)* in 1966. She finished the book the next summer and it was published in 1968. That was the year Italian students revolted, marking the beginning of a large protest movement in Italy (never as intense as the May student uprising in France, but more profound and long-lasting).[21] By the late 1960s, the total number of students entering university in Italy had grown tenfold since the 1920s, but the system itself had not undergone any corresponding expansion. There were shortages of classrooms, textbooks, teachers, etc. To make matters worse, the new open access to education also meant that there was a great disparity within the student body itself, between the rich and poor. The working-class students, too busy trying to make ends meet so they could afford their education, often could not pass the exams, get a degree or, later, find jobs. In 1967, eight students under the direction of Don Lorenzo Milani* wrote *Lettera a una professoressa (Letter to a Professor)*, an extraordinary document, in which they blamed the triumph of individualism and consumerism, said to be modeled on the American ideal of free enterprise. They wrote, "You care nothing for society or its needs. . . . The lift is a machine for avoiding your neighbors, the car for ignoring people who go by tram, the telephone for not talking face to face." [22] A powerful indictment of the injustices of the school system as well, *Lettera a una professoressa* became a best seller in several languages and the cult text for the protesting students. In addition, by 1968, an entire generation of Italians, disgusted and disillusioned by the Vietnam War, had jettisoned their admiration of the United States to embrace the counterculture, the black-power movement and the legacy of Che Guevara. [23]

The student revolutionaries came mostly from the wealthier upper and middle classes (the working-class students did not have the luxury or leisure to protest), yet the fact that they were anti-capitalists as well as anti-Communists created a certain amount

---

* Milani was a dissident Catholic priest who in 1954 founded the Barbiana School, outside of Florence, dedicated to the education of disadvantaged working-class boys.

of political confusion. This confusion manifested itself primarily through violence—rioting in the streets and confrontations with the police. One of the people to object to this contradiction was Pier Paolo Pasolini, his objections fueled no doubt by his espousing the cause of the proletariat and by his contempt for the student bourgeoisie. On June 16, 1968, he published a poem mocking the students in the newspaper *L'Espresso*. It read in part:

> *Now the journalists of all the world (including*
> *those of the television)*
> *are licking your arses (as one still says in student slang).*
> *Not me, my dears.*
> *You have the faces of spoilt rich brats. . . .*
> *You are cowardly, uncertain and desperate. . . .*
> *When, the other day, at Villa Giulia you fought the police*
> *I can tell you I was on their side.*
> *Because police are the sons of the poor.*
> *They come from subtopias, in the cities and countryside . . .*[24]

The trade unionist Vittorio Foa took particular exception to Pasolini's poem, accusing him of missing the point. "In my opinion," Foa wrote, speaking on behalf of both the students and the workers, "everything is being done to isolate the youth movement. . . . In all this concerted action only the voice of the poet was missing."[25]

Although *The World Saved by Children* was not intended as a political statement, it took a strong moral stance. In the preface to an early edition, Elsa Morante stated that she believed that no conscious person was allowed not to know. Modern technology enabled even the most average man to be conscious of the immense misery and destruction that is present everywhere in the world.

Three years earlier, in 1965—first in Turin at the Teatro Cari-
gnano, then in Rome at the Teatro Eliseo—under the auspices of
the Italian Cultural Association, Elsa Morante had given a lecture
called "For or against the Atomic Bomb." * It was a kind of *J'accuse*
aimed at the Italian middle class and at their consumer-driven society over which the atomic bomb had cast a large shadow. The
atomic bomb, Morante claimed, was the "flower" or the natural
expression for contemporary society (as were the Platonic dia-
logues for the Greeks, Raphael's Madonnas for the Italian human-
ists, and so forth) and the sign of approaching disintegration. Art,
however, she also maintained, was the opposite of disintegration,
because its function was precisely to prevent it and to restore the
integrity of reality. The duty of poets was to open their own consciousness and the consciousness of others to reality and the reason for the presence of poets in the world was to find an answer for
themselves and for others.[26]

Described by the publisher as a "novel," a "memorial," a "manifesto," a "ballet," both a "comedy" and a "tragedy," a "dialogue,"
an "autobiography," a "cartoon" and, finally, a "magic key," [27] *The
World Saved by Children* is unquestionably Morante's most unusual
work. An odd and difficult (and nearly untranslatable) collection
of songs, poems, and a play, it is hard to classify. In a review that
appeared in the journal *Paragone*, Pasolini came the closest. Writing in free verse, the same form used by Morante, he said the book
was certainly a political manifesto but written like a fable, with
humor and joy. He coined the phrase *nonna bambina* ("grandmother child") to describe the author and praised her ability to
scandalize not only bourgeois society but all social classes and her

---

* Also the title of her collection of essays, published posthumously in 1987
by Adelphi.

refusal to follow literary trends. He admired her willed childishness as well as her love for children and the adults who remain like them.[28] Bernardo Bertolucci hailed the book as well, saying that the poems were written in a state of great freedom.[29]

The World Saved by Children begins with a long poem, "Addio" ("Good-bye"), which was written as a sad farewell to Bill Morrow. One can hear the influence of the beat poets Allen Ginsberg and Gregory Corso, as well as the autobiographical self-scrutiny and anarchistic spirit of Walt Whitman:

> *and when, competing with the blackbird*
> *you threw yourself off the roof*
> *to try to fly. . . .*
> . . . .
> *"Who is there? Samarkand? London? Persepolis?*
> *Is it you!? It's me, from New York City!! Can you hear my*
> *voice?*
> *How are you? Here one is bored to death! There, too? When*
> *are you coming back?*
> *Hey! I've got the cat here sitting on my belly*
> *Who greets you! Can you hear her, her voice?*[30]

The Evening at Colonus (*La serata a colono*), a one-act play, is a parody of Sophocles' *Oedipus at Colonus*. Here, Oedipus is not the king of Thebes but a small blind Italian landowner accompanied by Antigone, who speaks to him in dialect (the same dialect, Carlo Cecchi said, spoken by Lucia, Elsa's maid). Meanwhile, the chorus speaks in satiric tones making allusions to a number of disparate sources: documents transcribed from Nazi concentration camps, ancient Aztec songs, the Vedas, Hölderlin, the Dead Sea Scrolls, blues sung by slaves, and so on. (Carlo Cecchi also said how he hoped, one day, to produce this play.)

The style of the last section, "Canzoni popolari" ("Popular Songs"), most resembles twentieth-century experimental writing. A lot of the text is printed crosswise on the page. Handwritten "words" such as "BUMM," "THUMPA" and "KRASH" fill other pages, musical scores and the words *pandemonio generale* ("general pandemonium") surrounded by exclamation and question marks fill another. The section ends with the disclaimer (in large letters) that, anyway, it is all a "GAME."

The title *The World Saved by Children* was not chosen lightly. In the poem titled "La canzone degli F [elici]. P [oci]. e degli I [nfelici]. M [olti]." ("The Song of the Happy Few and the Unhappy Many"), perhaps the most important and revelatory section of the book, Elsa Morante divides the world into two groups: the Happy Few and the Unhappy Many (or Multitude). The Happy Few, the group to which children belong, are the salt of the earth, the breath of fire, the true revolutionaries. They are said to have a great sense of reality, which must not be confused with practicality, usefulness or convenience. In addition to the children, the Happy Few who inhabit Morante's pantheon are Spinoza, Antonio Gramsci, Arthur Rimbaud, Giordano Bruno, Joan of Arc, Simone Weil, Mozart, Giovanni Bellini, Plato and Rembrandt. Their names are placed in boxes that include the date and cause of death (Rimbaud, for example, died of gangrene, both Giordano Bruno and Joan of Arc were burned alive and Bellini died of old age) that fill a page and that Morante arranged in the form of a cross. At the other end of the spectrum are the Unhappy Many, who are the rest of us. According to Morante, we or them, as the case may be, live abandoned by the spirit and practice the degrading vice of power, which makes us blind to reality.

On a hot summer night not long after *The World Saved by Chil-*

dren was published, Elsa Morante and Cesare Garboli had dinner
together. Garboli recalled,

> Rome was deserted. Like two loyal dogs, we met in an
> old trattoria on via della Vite. We got into an argument. I
> have to confess that in that ovenlike temperature, I felt de-
> pressed, bitter and unhappy. I can't remember what we or-
> dered. I do remember that at one point I began to predict
> that the destiny of the world would be both sinister and op-
> timistic. I told Elsa that all our complaints about our present
> civilization were the result of our shortsightedness. . . . His-
> tory is only a parenthesis. Life is quantifiable. . . . Once
> nature will be defeated, we will lean over our own hearts
> (which we will no longer have) just in time to say, along
> with the poet, "you have beaten enough."* And perhaps
> the earth will explode then. Yet the button for the catastro-
> phe will not be pushed by us but by beings who are equal to
> death, by beings for whom life or death will no longer pres-
> ent a fundamental alternative.
>
> I remember now that Elsa was eating buffalo mozzarella.
> She told me that she was surprised that I could talk such
> nonsense. Death, she objected, does not exist, it is a physi-
> cal appearance. What truly is, she said, never began and
> will never end. We see only an insignificant aspect of real-
> ity. I, in turn, accused her of spiritualism. I told her that she
> was a mystic, and that all the oriental philosophies seemed
> to me to be therapies to treat incurable diseases. I insisted
> on telling her that the revolt against technology, welfare,

---

* Cesare Garboli is quoting the nineteenth-century Italian poet Giocomo
Leopardi.

consumerism, the establishment arose from the same set of neurosis that produced this civilization: the symptoms vary but the disease is the same. And it is the consciousness of death. The moment man differentiated himself from animal confusion by becoming cognizant of death, man began to both build civilization and rebel against it. . . . The disease of man, I told Elsa, sounding in spite of myself like a Nietzschean, is not his inability to escape from a diminished reality but his inability to escape religion. It is time to do it. But the price for escaping religion is to embrace death. Your Happy Few, I concluded, are not happy at all.

Elsa then suggested we get some fresh air and move to the bar in the garden. I realized that she had decided to ignore my nonsense. I was filled with shame. We got up and went to the bar. I was grateful that she had changed the subject. I ordered a yogurt. Then she told me that I had never read *The World Saved by Children* and it was useless for me to lie and say the contrary. It was clear that I had a complex about that book. . . . It was true. I had read *The World Saved by Children* quickly and poorly.

I forget how the evening ended. Elsa returned to our argument (she always had the last word), but only for an instant. "Let's be clear," she concluded, "I already know what I will do when I die. You will find a note in an envelope on which there will be written: *'torno subito'* ('I will be right back')." Then, tilting her head back and lifting her chin in a childish gesture of defiance, she looked at me fiercely as if checking to see the effect she was producing. She anticipated me by only a fraction of a second with a burst of hilarity which echoed like applause amongst the empty tables, before we found ourselves laughing together.[31]

eleven

HISTORY

I should be grateful to Mussolini," Elsa once said. "By introducing the racist laws in 1938, he made me realize that I myself was a Jew; my mother was Jewish, but the thought had never crossed my mind that there was something peculiar about having a mother whose father and mother used to pray in a synagogue. At first, the Fascists were very loose in the enforcement of discrimination. But when the Germans took over Rome in 1943, I learned a great lesson, I learned terror. I was afraid for myself, but even more for Moravia. His father was Jewish. Actually, I was the real Jew, because you inherit from your mother's side. But the Fascists were so illiterate that they did not know, and then Jewishness to them was a race, a breed; they explained it through the barbaric, regressive imagery of 'blood.' And all this went through my mind, over and over. We escaped, Moravia and I, to the mountains of Ciociaria. On the way, the people we had to be afraid of were the middle classes, teachers, civil servants—the prejudice was with them, they would have reported us to the Gestapo. We were finally given shelter by a peasant family. To them, Jewish or non-Jewish, we were all *cristiani*.* I learnt a lot from terror." [1]

In the early 1970s, while she was working on her novel *His-*

---

* In popular Italian *cristiani* means "man" in general.

tory: A Novel (La storia), Elsa Morante took many long walks through the old Roman Ghetto, the Testaccio and San Lorenzo districts, entering buildings, inspecting rooms, peering closely at objects (after all, she was very nearsighted). She took copious notes and Luca Fontana, a friend who often accompanied her on these walks, found this very uncharacteristic. One day, although he knew he was transgressing the writer's code as Elsa never spoke about the specifics of a novel she was working on, he could not resist asking, "What sort of book are you writing?" Elsa's reply was cryptic: "I'm writing a book for the illiterate."[2] And in fact, the epigraph for *History*, Elsa Morante's best-known novel, is a line from the militant Peruvian poet César Vallejo: *"Por el analfabeto a quien escribo"* ("To the illiterate for whom I write").

Above all, Elsa Morante wanted the book to reach beyond the small circle of literary readers and be accessible to and read by the general public—the *poor* general public. When the book was published in 1974, she insisted that her publisher, Einaudi, bring it out in paperback right away, and she herself fixed the price at 2000 lire (then equivalent to about five dollars), thus giving up a large portion of the royalties she could have earned. For the cover, Morante had originally thought to use a painting by Bill Morrow but, instead, decided on a Robert Capa photograph that had a more dramatic effect. *The Fallen Partisan*, which Capa took during the Spanish Civil War, turned out not to be an actual photograph but a photomontage. Colored red, it showed a young man, presumably dead, lying in an almost Christ-like position on top of a pile of rubble. A tagline underneath the photograph sent out a fiery message: "A scandal that has lasted ten thousand years." (On the cover of the most recent edition of the novel, published by Einaudi in 1995, a little boy sits forlornly on a pile of rubble. Although poignant, this photograph is more sentimental than

Capa's. The price of this later edition is thirteen euros, approximately nineteen dollars.) In any event, Elsa Morante got her wish: within a year of the publication, *History* had sold 800,000 copies.

In a letter dated November 1, 1974, to Bill Koshland, who was now Elsa's editor at Knopf, her literary agent described how well the book was doing. Erich Linder had sold the foreign rights to several countries, including Spain, "with an advance of $15,000, which, I believe, is almost unheard of from Spain—and certainly unheard of for an Italian novel." In addition, the novel was still on top of the best-seller list in Italy and was selling at the rate of several thousand copies a week. Linder continued, "We no longer know who still buys the book, since there appear to be copies in every Italian household by now . . ."[3] That same year, Paul Hofmann, writing an "Arts Abroad" dispatch from Rome to *The New York Times*, reported, "For the first time since anyone can remember, people in railroad compartments and espresso bars discuss a book—the Morante novel—rather than the soccer championship or latest scandal. The critics write endlessly about the meaning of *La storia* and the reasons for the exceptional stir it is causing."[4]

The idea for *History* came to Elsa Morante from her reading of the Greek classics—she wanted the novel to be a kind of "modern-day *Iliad*"[5]—and from her reading of Simone Weil's "The Iliad or The Poem of Force." (Elsa Morante's statement about being grateful to Mussolini for teaching her "terror" echoes Simone Weil's own famous perversely logical one when the German troops occupied Paris: "This is a great day for Indo-China.") Weil's essay, which first appeared in the December 1940 and January 1941 issue of *Cahiers du Sud*, and was published under the near acrostical pseudonym Emile Novis (the essay was later translated by Mary McCarthy and appeared in November 1945 in

Politics, which was edited by Dwight Macdonald), is a powerful meditation on the uses of power in history and it corresponded with Elsa Morante's own views on the subject. It begins:

The true hero, the true subject, the center of the *Iliad* is force. Force employed by man, force that enslaves man, force before which man's flesh shrinks away. In this work, at all times, the human spirit is shown as modified by its relations with force, as swept away, blinded, by the very force it imagined it could handle, as deformed by the weight of the force it submits to. For those dreamers who considered that force, thanks to progress, would soon be a thing of the past, the *Iliad* could appear as an historical document; for others, whose powers of recognition are more acute and who perceive force, today as yesterday, at the very center of human history, the *Iliad* is the purest and the loveliest of mirrors.[6]

In the *Iliad*, according to Simone Weil, the distress and misery caused by force never ceases and each side is made to suffer in turn like "a continual game of seesaw." The death of Hector, for instance, "would be but a brief joy for Achilles" and likewise "the death of Achilles but a brief joy to the Trojans, and the destruction of Troy but a brief joy to the Achaeans."[7] (The critic George Steiner's response was to complain that Weil's reading of the *Iliad* as a poem of suffering was a "bizarre interpretation" and that she was "blind to the wild joy and ferocity of archaic warfare which makes the epic blaze."[8]) But man's suffering and man's fate are of little importance to Simone Weil: either way man will be destroyed—by his own self-destructive power or by that of others.

"Force is as pitiless to the man who possesses it, or thinks he does, as it is to its victims; the second it crushes, the first it intoxicates." And again: "Thus violence obliterates anybody who feels its touch. It comes to seem just as external to its employer as to its victim."[9] For Simone Weil, force is equally harmful to those who inflict it and to those who bear it.

Elsa Morante held Simone Weil in great esteem. She admired her pure mind, which, as she put it, was the mind of a great contemplator of truth while her own mind, she complained, was in a state of continual metamorphosis.[10] She must also have been attracted by Simone Weil's determination to live out her "truths," first by enlisting in the Spanish Civil War, then working in a Renault factory assembly line so that she could write a firsthand account about working-class conditions. Less appealing to Morante, probably, were Weil's highly charged sense of personal accountability for the world's suffering, her self-loathing, her eccentricities, her untimely rejection of Judaism and her enforced starvation—what George Steiner called her "mystical anorexia"[11]—which eventually led to her death.

Although no ascetic, Morante, at the time she was writing *History*, made the conscious decision to grow old. She had turned sixty and she deliberately put on the mask of an old lady by dressing like one and wearing a scarf over her head. Also she gave up on love. Claiming that she had been young for a long time, she said, "Enough. Enough of youth; the others are young but I am not."[12] According to Cesare Garboli, the appearance of old age for Elsa was terrible and traumatic; "like the explosion of a hurricane."[13] It affected her in such a way that she could not reconcile herself to the transformation it produced on her physically. She could no longer recognize or love herself in her own body. In addition, Garboli proposed his male-centric theory about how her body grown old and altered came also to signify for Elsa its failure to create, its unfulfilled and denied maternity.

Old or not, Elsa Morante still needed and craved life, and, for her, life mostly took place in restaurants. She enjoyed eating well (apparently, she never ate at home and although she had a large, well-appointed kitchen, she never used it); she particularly liked seafood and rarely ate meat, only chicken. According to her friend Patrizia Cavalli, Elsa's day would begin around ten or eleven in the morning, when she would start telephoning friends to set up an appointment for lunch (she never made arrangements the day before) and she would go about putting people together— she hated it when people did not get along. There were always at least five or six people at table in the restaurant; all were young, poor and worshiped Elsa. Carlo Cecchi remembers how she used to quote Plato and say, "Those who love are close to God, those who are loved are far from God," and then laugh. (Elsa had a very infectious laugh but since she did not take care of her teeth, they had turned brown and she usually covered her mouth with her hand when she laughed.) During lunch, she advised and encouraged her friends in their work. And, always generous, Elsa paid for everyone. She herself ate a lot, and afterward she took a pill, probably benzadrine, which helped her stay awake. Then she went home, turned off her phone and wrote all afternoon and most of the night.[14]

History is divided into nine chronological sections marked by years ("19**," 1941, 1942 and so on through 1947, followed by a last "19**"). Each begins with a flat, uninflected summary of the important events of that year, which constitutes the official History, history with a capital *H*; but it is the commonplace events that follow, the stories of ordinary people, which of course constitute the *real* history, albeit history with a small *h*. Along with these two disparate narratives, Morante included snatches of songs, verse, diary entries (cited as anonymous but in fact taken from Gramsci's well-known prison letters), all of which combine to create a "newsreel" effect reminiscent of John Dos Passos's technique in *U.S.A.*, his collective portrait of America. And, unlike her other novels, *History* is narrated by the author herself, in the tone and timbre of her own voice, which gives it the form of a neighborhood chronicle. The narrator is gathering information about actual events that occurred in the Testaccio and San Lorenzo districts of Rome; in some instances, she appears to be an eyewitness. Her reporting on actions and motivation is detailed, meticulous and for the most part dispassionate. It is a neutral voice that has abandoned the musical quality of *House of Liars* and the fablelike echoes of *Arturo's Island*; instead, Morante writes from that distant place that she claimed renders the dead and the living equal.[15]

The plot of the novel is based on an event that was reported in a Roman newspaper in June 1947: a mother, her six-year-old boy and their *maremmana* (a big white sheepdog from the Maremma region of Italy) were discovered in an apartment in the Testaccio; the boy was dead, the mother insane with grief, the dog so aggressive in its attempt to protect its owners that it had to be killed in order for the authorities to gain entrance into the apartment. What, the writer of the newspaper piece asked, brought this poor little family to such a tragic end? In order to try to answer this question, Elsa Morante begins the novel proper in 1941, with a young German soldier named Gunther, on leave for the day, who wanders around San Lorenzo, drinks too much and rapes a young schoolteacher who is on her way home with her bag of groceries. Ida Mancuso (née Ramundo), the young teacher, is a timid widow who lives in fear of being discovered to be half Jewish. (The character has been compared to Elsa's mother, Irma Poggibonsi, a schoolteacher who likewise was afraid of being discovered to be Jewish.) Ida is so afraid that she is relieved that instead of denouncing or deporting her, the soldier rapes her. The rape scene is depicted as a kind of an Annunciation: during it, Ida has an epileptic fit, which the soldier mistakes for orgasmic pleasure. He tells her that he comes from the town of Dachau and is an electrician. Before leaving, he repairs a light fixture in Ida's apartment (thus, by impregnating Ida with the little boy Useppe, the German soldier has symbolically also brought her light). Gunther will then be killed on his way to Libya.

Examining this rape scene in an essay that deals with how novels and short stories begin, the writer Amos Oz has astutely observed that right away there is a fundamental ideological paradox in *History*. The novel begins with a summary of political events that focuses on the struggle between the oppressed poor and the powerful masters; it posits the simple axiom that the rich are evil and the poor good. "And thus in a novel whose opening contract has insisted that the reader recognize the world's evil as caused by the establishment in its various guises, and that the fount of grace and mercy is children, peasants, laborers, women, the simple folk, the plot actually results from a brutal act of rape committed by an innocent child, a simple fellow." How could this be? Oz asks. How could one good, simple soul (Gunther) inflict pain on another good simple soul (Ida)? So where does evil come from? From the same source as good? The answer he suggests lies in the epigraph of the novel, which is taken from Luke 10:21: "[T]hou hast hid these things from the wise and prudent, and hast revealed them unto babes . . . for so it seemed good in thy sight." Oz claims that this concept integrates Morante's Christian sentiments with her leftist beliefs. Gunther may be a monster but he is a simple monster, not a political one, and thus he can be redeemed.[16]

Ida, who already has a handsome but truant teenage son named Nino, gives birth to Giuseppe, known as Useppe (he cannot pronounce the *G*—like Elsa Morante's little nephew, Luca). He, too, suffers from epilepsy or grand mal attacks. (A comparison has been made between the way Elsa Morante uses epilepsy or a grand mal attack for the physical consequences while Dostoevsky, in *The Idiot* specifically, uses it for its psychological ones. For Dostoevsky, epilepsy is a means of achieving Truth; it has the function of giving knowledge. In Morante, its function is destructive; epilepsy brings death.)[17] Useppe is a child who is too strange, too ill equipped and too beautiful for this world. A natural poet, he observes the world with joy and wonderment and turns everything into a source of delight: '

> A merrier baby than he had never been seen. Everything he glimpsed around him roused his interest and stirred him to joy. He looked with delight at the threads of rain outside the window, as if they were confetti and multicolored streamers. . . .
>
> The color of a rag, of a scrap of paper, suggesting to him the resonance of all prisms and scales of light, was enough to transport him to awed laughter. One of the first words he learned was *ttars* [stars].
>
> Even the things that, in general, arouse aversion or repugnance, in him inspired only attention and transparent wonder, like the others. In his endless journeys of exploration, crawling on all fours around the Urals and the Amazon and the Australian archipelagoes which the furniture of the house was to him, sometimes he no longer knew where

he was. And he would be found under the sink in the kitchen, ecstatically observing a patrol of cockroaches as if they were wild colts on the prairie. He even recognized a ttar in a gob of spit.[18]

Useppe is the poet of joy and innocence. He is close to nature, to animals and birds. The novel is full of dogs and cats who have been anthropomorphized into compassionate companions and whom Useppe understands and can speak to. He recites his poems to Nino's dog, Bella (*a maremmana*), and she answers him back.

The war continues in *History* as it did in fact with its inevitable and disastrous consequences. By 1943, Ida's modest apartment is bombed and destroyed, Nino has joined the Fascist Blackshirts (later Nino becomes a Communist partisan, then a black-market racketeer) and she and little Useppe are reduced to seeking refuge with other fugitive families in a dormitory set up for the homeless. "Almost all the people ahead of her or following her carried bundles or suitcases or household goods, but except for Useppe, she had absolutely nothing to carry. The only property left her was the shopping bag hanging from her arm . . ." The dormitory, a cement hovel, "consisted of a single ground-floor room, rather vast, with low grilled windows, and one exit which opened directly onto a ditch; but it boasted some conveniences truly rare those days in the outlying slums, namely a private latrine with cesspool, and a cistern feeding a water tank on the roof. . . . Now, however, at the end of summer, the cistern was dry."[19]

Into the homeless dormitory comes the disruptive voice of Davide Segre,* initially known as Vivaldi Carlo. He has escaped

---

* Segre is a well-known Italian Jewish family name.

from a German prison camp, where he was tortured. A poet, but a poet of anguish, he is the Jew, the intellectual, the anarchist (also, the victim of drug abuse). He is the prophetic voice of suffering, and of the apocalypse: "History, of course, is all an obscenity from the beginning; however, years as obscene as these have never existed before," Davide Segre shouts out in one of his many tirades. Later—never mind that by then the war is over and no one in the crowded tavern listens to him—he continues his harangue:*

> [A]ll History is a history of fascisms, more or less disguised . . . in the Greece of Pericles . . . and in the Rome of the Caesars and the Popes . . . and in the steppes of the Huns . . . and in the Aztec Empire . . . and in the America of the pioneers . . . and in the Italy of the Risorgimento . . . always and everywhere . . . free men and slaves . . . rich and poor. . . . And so, here we are . . . this poor matter, material for work and labor, become fodder for extermination and destruction. . . . *Extermination camps.*[20]

By the spring of 1947, Ida has resumed teaching; her hair is white and she has turned into an old woman. Useppe's epileptic seizures are more frequent and severe; Davide Segre has died and Nino too has been killed, in an accident. Bella, Nino's dog, reappears to look after Useppe. The boy and the dog take walks and during one of them they discover a place along the banks of the Tiber River, a place where grass grows green and birds sing (the

---

* Garboli writes that Elsa Morante gave all of herself to Davide Segre—her love, her ideas, her masochism. But it would seem more likely that Davide Segre's feverish dreams of an anarchistic utopia combined with his evangelical Christianity were modeled on Simone Weil's tortured philosophy.

birds sing: "It's a joke / a joke / all a joke")—an elysian field where time ceases to exist—and here, the novel takes a strange turn. For more than six hundred pages, Morante's narrative has portrayed a poor people's struggle for everyday existence and now, all of a sudden, it depicts a kind of eden. Only this eden cannot last. Despite the protection of his magical and marvelous dog, despite having found a paradise, Useppe is beset by a band of pirates—or so he believes (the pirates turn out to be boys like himself). In the battle that ensues he has an epileptic fit, which presages his death the following day. But, first, Bella—who, while battling with the pirates, has transformed herself from a gentle shepherdess into "a terrifying monster," "her jaws wide and her fierce teeth bare, her big eyes resembling two pieces of volcanic glass,"—delivers a triumphant report not unlike one of Mussolini's war bulletins on the events of the day: "THE DE-FEATED WOLVES HAVE RETREATED IN FLIGHT, ABANDONING THE SIEGE OF THE HUT AND THE ENGAGEMENT ENDED WITH THE SENSA-TIONAL VICTORY OF USEPPE AND BELLA."[21] The two, Useppe and Bella, are no different from the others. They self-destruct. According to Morante, nothing can survive in this corrupt and violent world—not reality, not fantasy and certainly not poetry.

With the death of Useppe, Ida goes mad. When finally the authorities break down the door of her apartment, they will find her physically frozen, a state of paralysis that, according to the narrator, will last for another nine years and until her death. Thus, Ida plays out the same tragic drama originally reported in the newspaper article that was Morante's inspiration for the story.

In the final section of the novel, the events of the years 1948 through 1967 are summarized; beginning with the crimes committed by southern landowners against the Italian peasants and workers and ending with "Three thousand six hundred and twenty-one aerial bombardments in Vietnam in a six month period, the United States declares.—In Greece, army officers seize power and suspend the constitution. Mass deportations and arrests." The novel ends with the words ". . . and History continues . . ." [22]

Elsa Morante was meticulous in her research. She knew Rome intimately and was obsessed with accuracy. She spent hours, for instance, in a garage learning about motorcycles and how they function since Nino owns a Triumph. She was also a perfectionist. When she was going through the final galleys of *History*, she asked Patrizia Cavalli to read them out loud to her. She instructed her to read mechanically, without inflection or without giving a sense to the words. It took Patrizia several days and when the novel was published she could not, she said, read it again. [23]

Rereading *History* now, admittedly, would be a very different experience from reading the novel when it first came out in 1974. That year, the atmosphere on the Italian political scene was highly charged. The early seventies had seen the election of Enrico Berlinguer as national secretary of the Communist Party, and it appeared to those on the left—including many academics, writers and artists—that new solutions to Italy's social and economic problems might be in sight. Berlinguer launched the concept of the "historic compromise" between the three major political parties—the Communists, the right-wing Christian Democrats and the Socialists—as well as a convergence of Catholic and Communist morality in the name of a greater political good (for Berlinguer himself, the latter was the most important goal). He hoped that the Communists and Catholics could find, in historian Paul Ginsborg's words, "a shared moral and ethical code on which to base the political and social salvation of Italy. The Catholic emphasis on solidarity would combine with the

Communist practice of collective action to produce a new political order."[24]

Although Berlinguer's project ultimately failed for a number of reasons—the main one being that it was too vague—the Italian left in the early 1970s was riding along on a wave of great optimism and it viewed Elsa Morante's novel as far too pessimistic a vision of the world and out of sync with the dominant Marxist ideology of the period. As a result, the novel polarized the Italian intellectual community. The debate was carried on in literary journals: *La Fiera Letteraria* devoted two issues to trying to decide whether *History* was or was not a masterpiece. The Communist newspaper *Il Manifesto* published an "invective-letter" composed in concert by four writers. The book, in fact, was as divisive for Italian intellectuals as Lampedusa's *Il gattopardo* was when it was published in 1958. And in 1976, *History* was banned in Franco's Spain.[25] The resistance and hostility from some Italian critics and a part of the Italian public to the novel was due, on the one hand, to their failure to understand the author's ideology and, on the other, to Morante's own refusal to align herself with any one political party. Nonetheless, the novel's huge sales record was testimony to the fact that controversy may not always be such a bad thing.

One writer who greeted *History* enthusiastically was Natalia Ginzburg. In a review in *Corriere della Sera*, she said that she was happy to live in a world where there was also Elsa Morante. Nonetheless, Elsa harbored suspicions about the review; she thought Natalia Ginzburg's enthusiasm was excessive. She complained that it was a hidden way of being aggressive. Although, the psychology is a bit simplistic, it has also been suggested that Natalia envied Elsa's literary genius while Elsa envied Natalia's maternity. Natalia had children.[26]

Inexplicably, Pier Paolo Pasolini did not follow suit. He wrote a most damning and cruel review of *History*. The review appeared in two separate installments in *Tempo Illustrato*, a newspaper where he had begun writing a weekly book review and where he had already reviewed such writers as Marianne Moore, John Ashbery, "the best of the New York school," [27] Céline, Gabriel García Márquez, E. M. Forster and Italo Calvino, to whom he gave a rave for *Invisible Cities*. The review began with admiration for the novel's huge scale and subject: "And it is difficult to imagine a subject more ambitious than this." However, Pasolini felt Morante should probably have spent another year or two working on it. Then, dividing Morante's novel into three books, he wrote that the first book was "extraordinarily beautiful . . . I read it while I was in the middle of rereading *The Brothers Karamazov* and it stood up to the comparison marvelously well." Yet the criticism that followed was not so laudatory. The second book "misses the point completely; it is nothing more than a mass of haphazard thrown together information; the third book is beautiful although discontinuous and with many of the same confusions as those of the middle book."

Pasolini became harsher still when he commented on Morante's use of dialects:

> The Roman language spoken by Nino and his friends (Morante will forgive me but I must be blunt) resembles that used by the scribblers of *Il Messagero*; whereas Davide speaks in an unrecognizable way: the boy presents himself as from Bologna, while in fact he is from Mantua, but talks as if he were from Venice. There is not a single place in the whole of Alta Italia where *"cadere"* [to fall] is said *"cader."* There, in northern Italy, it is *"cascare"* that has won out over

other current forms or variations. That Davide says *"cader"* is offensive to the reader: but, above all, it is offensive to him. Where is Morante's great love for him if she is too lazy to make the slightest effort to listen to the way he talks?

Pasolini aggressively pressed on with his attack: all but Ida were false characters, constructed arbitrarily and founded on abstractions. Nothing they said or did seemed plausible. What, for instance, was Morante's logic in having an important character like Nino disappear from the story while, instead, she supplied a lot of irrelevant and useless information about minor characters the reader did not care about? Pasolini attacked the "mannerism" of her writing and mocked how she portrayed Useppe and how she described animals. In addition, he objected to the way the events that are summarized at the beginning of each section reappeared as part of the narrative and thus, he claimed, lost their vitality and reality. Finally, Pasolini went after Morante's ideology, maintaining that it was not possible to separate the History of the victims of Power from the History of Power. Morante's philosophical-political framework was merely a construct, a pastiche. He ended his review, "When such an ideology is transformed into the 'theme' of a popular novel—voluminous by definition, full of facts and information, predictable, coming full circle to closure—it loses all credibility: it becomes a feeble pretext that ends by undermining the disproportionate narrative structure which it intended to put in motion." [28]

It is not difficult to imagine how devastated Elsa Morante must have been by Pasolini's review. And how angry. Although, over the last few years, their relationship had become more distant and difficult—they had very different views on politics and Pasolini's life was very public while hers was very private and perhaps, too, Elsa disapproved of his obsessive and dangerous sexual encounters—Elsa prided herself on her loyalty to her friends. If anyone ever spoke against Pasolini, she always defended him. Thus she could not understand or reconcile herself to the animosity in the article and the violence of his attack. Their friendship came to an abrupt end. Elsa Morante and Pier Paolo Pasolini never spoke to each other again.

A year later, in 1975, Pasolini was found brutally murdered on a deserted beach in Ostia. Photographs show him lying on his back, one arm bloody and twisted, his hair matted, his jaw fractured, his nose flattened, his ear cut in half; worse still, and not apparent in the photos, Pasolini's testicles were badly bruised, his sternum and ten ribs were broken, his liver was lacerated and his heart had burst. Giuseppe (Pino) Pelosi, a seventeen-year-old boy whom Pasolini had picked up that night, was accused and eventually convicted of his death, the result of beatings with a plank studded with nails and running Pasolini over, perhaps even twice, with his own car, an Alfa.

The investigation of the murder, however, was seriously mishandled: the police waited too long, the site was not secured and soon after heavy rains obliterated tire tracks, footprints and other evidence; and much of the testimony at the trial was based on conjecture and contradictory confessions. The newspapers were full of articles: some made Pasolini out to be a hero and a martyr, others a whipping boy.

The day of Pasolini's funeral, ten thousand people lined the streets around the Campo dei Fiori in Rome to bid Pier Paolo farewell. The coffin was brought on foot from the Communist Party's Casa di Cultura near Piazza Venezia, where the body had lain in state, and his friends, including Bernardo Bertolucci, carried it. Another friend, Sergio Citti, had tied Pasolini's red soccer jersey around it—number eleven. At the sight of the coffin, the crowds applauded, fists rose in the traditional revolutionary salute, people threw flowers. One journalist wrote, "On such a Roman November afternoon, the day begins to end and the birds rise toward a sun justly called blood-red." [29] At the funeral, Alberto Moravia spoke movingly about Pasolini, saying that he was the most important Italian poet of the second half of the century and that he should not be marginalized by his sexuality. He finished with the words "Few poets are born . . . only two or three in a century." Grief-stricken and devastated, Elsa, who attended the funeral, was said to have howled like an animal. [30]

While he was translating *La storia* into English, William Weaver complained that Elsa Morante would call every morning at ten thirty—the time he had once mentioned to her that he took a break for coffee. She asked questions or else she would say things like "Now on page 379, when I use the word so-and-so, how will you translate that?" And Weaver would answer: "Elsa, I'm on page 123. I've got no idea!" But that never stopped her and she called almost daily, ruining his mornings. Finally, Weaver could stand it no longer. He sat down and wrote her a letter: "Dear Elsa, I'm giving up the job. I think you better find somebody else, I don't think that this is working." He made a copy for the publisher and another for his agent and sealed the envelopes to mail the next morning. Just at that moment, Elsa called him once more: "I'm calling to say that this is the last time I'm going to call you because I realize that this is not helping you." Elsa, Weaver said, had read his mind. He tore up the letters and finished the translation. Even so, she was the hardest person he had ever worked with. [31]

When *History* was published in the United States in 1977 by

Knopf, the reviews were mixed. In *The New York Times*, Robert Alter, a professor of comparative literature at Berkeley, compared the novel's setting, "a vast war-scarred landscape of rubble" to that of grainy black-and-white neorealist films and described the plot as a "progress of disasters." He wrote, "It is of course pernicious nonsense to reduce all history to such a grossly leveling common denominator. All that remains of historical experience is the pangs of victimhood; and those, after abundant repetition and heavy insistence, are likely to leave readers numbed—and with a sense that the sharpness of authorial indictment has finally been eroded by sentimentality." The novel, he felt, fails as a whole despite some "arresting moments" when Morante "manages to carry out wonderful forays into the uncanny, moving from bleak earthbound things to metaphysical vistas." [32]

Stephen Spender, in his review in *The New York Review of Books*, was more positive, although his praise seemed a bit faint-hearted. He did praise Morante's style and compared her treatment of Ida to that of Flaubert's Félicité in *A Simple Heart*. Although the novel is full of doomed characters, Spender noted, "it is also full of enchanting surprises, showing the immense vitality of the poor and oppressed." He ended his review by calling William Weaver's translation "a fine achievement." [33]

Notwithstanding the faint praise, a passage from Morante's novel describing the last days of the German occupation of Rome was excerpted in *The New York Times*. Twice the novel appeared on *The Times'* noteworthy lists: first on May 8 as an "Editors' Choice" and on June 5 in "Fiction" (presumably, the recommended summer reading for that year). Along with *History*, some of the other novels on the latter list were: *Amateurs* by Donald Barthelme, *An American Romance* by John Casey, *A Book of Common Prayer* by Joan Didion, *The Castle of Crossed Destinies* by

Italo Calvino (also translated by William Weaver), *Falconer* by John Cheever, *Fools Say* by Nathalie Sarraute, *Henry and Cato* by Iris Murdoch, *In the Miro District and Other Stories* by Peter Taylor, *Junky* by William S. Burroughs, *Lancelot* by Walker Percy, *October Light* by John Gardner, *The Street of Crocodiles* by Bruno Schulz and a new translation of *The Tale of Genji* by Murasaki Shikibu—an impressive array of books.

As a result, no doubt, of the mixed reviews, Morante's novel did not do particularly well in the United States nor, in the words of Erich Linder, did it fulfill Knopf's expectations. However, in France, it was a huge success and, in spite of a "doubtful" translation, Gallimard, the publisher, reprinted *History* three times and sales approached fifty thousand copies.[34]

Large, sprawling, messy, ambitious, strange, *History* is difficult to judge. Although it appears realistic, the novel breaks with conventional storytelling tradition. There is very little plot, most of the action appears random and disconnected and, instead of heroes, there are only poor human beings motivated by hunger and the search for shelter. There is no narrative center, only a web of stories, each leading away from the others. Morante's discourse is self-conscious, her tone aggrieved and often cynical. The novel is a sustained dolorous cry against injustice at the same time that it is deeply pessimistic about art. Like the serpent that devours its own tail, *History* tells the story of its own demise. Cesare Garboli was quite right when he wrote that *History* is based on antiphrasis and expresses itself through antithesis and negation. Contrary to what the reader expects, the end of the war does not bring euphoria or happiness but, instead, transforms the novel into one about the impossibility of sustaining any kind of creativity.[35]

The tragedy of war is the actual protagonist of Elsa Morante's novel; it is the grand mal from which Useppe suffers and which affects us all. Conceived both as a literary work and a political action, the novel also makes quite clear the impossibility and futility of fictionalizing an event of such historical magnitude as World War II (in Italian, the war's *non-romanzabilità*). Writers such as Primo Levi and Elie Wiesel have written actual testimonies, but not fictional accounts. This, more than anything else, is Elsa Morante's difficult legacy. At once self-reflective and political (a combination quite new in Italian postwar fiction), her novel, by putting into question the future of the human race by depicting the recent terrible past, places the onus of responsibility for "change" on the reader.[36] In Morante's own words, *History* is both a "work of poetry" and "an act of accusation against all the fascism of the world."[37]

In the introduction to an American limited edition for the members of the First Edition Society, in 1977, she outlined her goals, which daily become more relevant and urgent:

> In this book, I—who was born at such a horrible time in the twentieth century—wanted to leave behind a testimony that described my actual experience of the Second World War, one that would expose it as the ultimate and bloodiest example of man's inhumanity to man in the history of the past thousand years. Thus, here is History for you, just as it is and just as we all contributed to making it.

She went on to say,

> Since I am by nature a poet, I could not do anything else but a work of poetry. And in view of this, experience has taught me that, unfortunately, for many, even poetry can be used as an alibi. As if poetry should content itself with its

own beauty, as if it were only an elegant arabesque designed on paper.

So I must warn you that this book, before it is a work of poetry, first, must be an act of accusation and a prayer.[38]

A courageous prayer.

twelve

ARACOELI

In 1976, during the Christmas holidays, Elsa Morante
and Carlo Cecchi went to Spain together. Elsa was
looking for a setting for *Aracoeli*, the novel she had begun work
on—specifically, for a little village she would make the home of
her eponymous character. At Elsa's insistence, Carlo Cecchi had
randomly put his finger on the map and it fell on the province of
Almería. From the airport, they took a taxi and the driver, as
luck would have it, spoke Italian. His name was Angel and he
truly was "an angel," Elsa Morante said, because after explain-
ing to him what they were looking for, he took them to a village
called El Almendral, which was exactly how she had imagined it
should be.

The actual inspiration for Morante's last novel may well have
been something that had occurred when she met Cecchi years
earlier in Venice. Together they had gone to the Accademia
d'Arte to look at two paintings; a Madonna and child by Giovanni
Bellini and *The Tempest* by Giorgione. Somehow, standing in
front of those paintings, Elsa felt as if she could traverse time and
see the young girl who had posed for the Madonna in the Bellini
painting as well as the girl who had posed for the woman nursing
the baby in the Giorgione painting, and both would become the
inspiration for the character Aracoeli. It was a moment that, later,
she could see contained everything that would be important in

the novel.[1] It was also a recurring theme in her life: this sense of having been someplace before, of having lived another, earlier life, combined with the often obsessive pull and inexplicable significance of certain scenes and objects.

Earlier on the same trip to Spain, Elsa and Carlo Cecchi had gone on a tour of Andalucía. Cecchi said he was always amazed at how energetic Elsa was and how she wanted to go everywhere and see everything. One night in Granada, they were sitting in a popular café when a very poor family arrived. The wife was quite short and she had a girl of about ten and a little boy of four; they were waiting for the father whose job was to guard a car park. Elsa began talking to them, half in Spanish, half in Italian. She may have found something of Useppe's innocence in the little boy, whose name was Casper Muñoz, because she took down their address. The next day she and Carlo went to find them in a very poor section of the city, bringing a number of presents, including a toy piano for the little boy. They went inside the family's house, which was very simple but clean. They sat together at the table and Elsa talked to them as if she were an old friend and had known them for a long time.[2]

Elsa Morante was like that—impetuous and generous. The same sort of thing happened with Tonino Ricchezza, a boy from Naples whom she befriended. He too was from a poor family, he worked cleaning streets, but he was intelligent and Elsa wanted to help him, which she did.[3] He, in turn, viewed Elsa as a kind of fairy godmother—a lady who was part ugly old woman and part beautiful young one—who, according to a dream he had when he was a boy in school, would come and rescue him from his hard life. Elsa and Tonino met in the 1970s and spent time together—first on the island of Procida, then Tonino came to stay with Elsa in

Rome, where she took him to visit museums, to the Villa Borghese and to all the places in *History* where Useppe had lived. According to Tonino, Elsa Morante looked after him because she understood that life had not offered him much thus far. In a short paean to her, he touchingly described their time together and their friendship, ending it with "the fairy tale continued for several years then, as the saying goes, the best things always have to come to an end."[4]

Alfonso Berardinelli was another young man who was grateful to Elsa and regarded her as his teacher. To talk to her was a form of therapy as well as an antidote to a culture that, he felt, was becoming more and more alien. Elsa, Berardinelli said, lived between heaven and hell. Sometimes her face had a look of tragedy as if she was condemned to see nothing but darkness but then she would suddenly laugh. She could see the comedy beneath the tragedy. Being with Elsa always gave Alfonso the impression that ancient Greece, Italy of the Renaissance, Shakespeare, Mozart, the Mayan civilization, India, Naples, Paris, London and the Yucatán were right there all around them as they were sitting outdoors having coffee and talking. Elsa could remove herself from the world, she could be elsewhere. In one of the books she inscribed to him, she wrote, "To Alfonso, who knows from where."[5]

Nonetheless, the mid-1970s was a time when Elsa Morante became more and more reclusive. She broke off with some of her friends and did not want to bother with casual relationships. She let her hair go white. When asked in a questionnaire what she considered to be the pinnacle of happiness, Elsa answered "solitude"; when asked what she considered to be the pinnacle of unhappiness, Elsa answered the same thing, "solitude." The questionnaire also asked what she loved best in the world and Elsa replied the three Ms—in Italian, *Mozart, mare, gelato al mandarino*—"Mozart, the sea and tangerine ice cream." [6]

Morante began writing *Aracoeli* in 1977, when she was reading Proust's *A la Recherche du temps perdu*, Dante's *Divine Comedy*, Michel Tournier and Salvatore Satta, a Sardinian writer. She also turned to the letters between Baudelaire and his mother for inspiration about the character of Aracoeli.[7] Although she rarely spoke about what she was working on, she did tell her friends that she thought it was strange that for the first time in her life she was writing about a character, Manuel, who was so ugly and unhappy. Up until then all her characters had been young and beautiful— she was speaking about her male characters—or if they were not handsome, at least they were charming and fascinating. It was as if the character Manuel needed to have his story told, she said.[8]

On March 16, 1978, however, her work was interrupted by an event that would prove to be a severe blow to Italy's government and its people. Aldo Moro, the former prime minister and the head of the Christian Democratic Party, was kidnapped by the Red Brigades. The kidnappers demanded the release of thirteen Red Brigade members who were on trial in Turin but Prime Minister Giulio Andreotti refused to negotiate. On May 9, the kidnappers shot and killed Aldo Moro. Moro had worked hard with Enrico Berlinguer to implement the "historic compromise," which, for the first time, would have brought together the Communist Party and the Christian Democrats. With his death, all attempts to achieve solidarity between the two parties ended.

Meanwhile, two days after Aldo Moro was kidnapped, Elsa drafted a letter to the Red Brigades.

I know very well that this letter, by the standards of today's objective judgments, may seem pointless, ridiculous, idiotic and scandalous. But these are extreme times when intelligence is no longer of use and all that can be done is to follow the dictates of one's despairing conscience . . . even though one is aware of how futile that is.

In addressing myself to you, members of the Red Brigades . . . I will try, at least, not to doubt that you are convinced in good faith *by the motives that you promote by your acts*; that is to say that you are truly, in your own eyes, *revolutionaries*. I admit that it repels me to repeat . . . that word—*revolution*—when I think of the use it has been put to—up to this present day—in history. Nonetheless, this word . . . still has a primary and authentic significance: that of a great popular action whose goal is to install a more worthy society. Now, too many equivocal flags have been waved over this definition which nevertheless is clear.

And the first equivocation was to write on this flag the national slogan: *the end justifies the means*.

This principle (which Benito Mussolini and his cohorts also espoused for their "revolutions") is a false sign which one recognizes without even firing a shot. For contrarily, it is in its opposite that one finds the truth: the means betray the end. And, the means you are actually pursuing . . . is founded on a single, basic fact: the total contempt for human beings.

A society based on the total contempt for a human being, no matter what name it gives itself, can only be an obscene Fascist society.

Because of your youth, you have not physically experienced the history of this century. Perhaps you have not even studied it enough. . . .

But whatever judgment one may make on our actual inept and corrupt societies, I hope I will not live long enough to participate in a new totalitarianism.[9]

In the end, Elsa Morante neither finished nor sent the letter because, as she confided to a friend, she knew that it would not be understood. Nevertheless, the letter was a beautiful declaration of her principles, principles that were neglected and ignored to the great and tragic detriment of the Communist Party movement. The subsequent murder of Moro contributed to Italy's so-called Years of Lead, which were dominated by both the threat and fear of terrorism.

Aracoeli,* the beautiful name Elsa Morante gave her character, is the Latin word for "altar of heaven." It was the name of one of Morante's Spanish acquaintances, Aracoeli Zambrano, whose sister was the Spanish philosopher Maria Zambrano. Muñoz, Aracoeli's last name, Elsa borrowed from the poor Spanish family she befriended in Granada and she used it twice: "It so happened that both her father and mother were born with the same surname: Muñoz. And so, following the Spanish usage, she bore the double family name Muñoz Muñoz." About his mother's name, Manuel, who is both the narrator and protagonist, says: "I learned later that in Spain it is common to baptize girls with such names, even Latin ones. . . . Nevertheless, gradually, as I grew up, that name Aracoeli became stamped in my memory as a sign of distinction, a

---

* The church of Santa Maria in Aracoeli in Rome, which dates from the sixth century, stands on the Capitoline Hill.

unique title in which my mother remains separate and enclosed, as in a heavy tortile [*sic*] frame painted with gold." [10]

Aracoeli is written in the form of one long and emotional quest, which also doubles as a memoir, and, except for a few space breaks, no chapters or divisions mark or separate its pages. At the start, Manuel is a forty-three-year-old ineffectual homosexual and recovered drug addict who is filled with self-loathing; he works as a reader in a small, dull publishing house, work that he also loathes. On an impulse, he decides to set out for the village of El Almendral, in Spain, and visit his mother's birthplace to "look for her"—by which he means not merely to evoke her as a memory but to resurrect her "carnally" from the dead. The date he gives at the start of his journey is All Saints' Day 1975. (The day and year are mentioned quite specifically and it has been pointed out that this date corresponds exactly to that of Pier Paolo Pasolini's gruesome murder on the beach in Ostia.) A small portion of the novel is devoted to Manuel's actual journey; the rest and greater part is written in the form of flashbacks to his childhood and to his mother's life and death.

His mother, Aracoeli, is a beautiful, illiterate, young Spanish girl who, like Nunziata in *Arturo's Island*, epitomizes the primitive, natural woman: "[I]t would be difficult for nature, with all its variety, to produce a more beautiful face. And yet . . . there are certain irregularities and flaws in that face. . . . And similarly, of her body . . . a certain asymmetry, or clumsiness, . . . the stocky, rural legs, with their overdeveloped calves . . . , in contrast with the still-frail arms and body; a certain awkwardness in her walk . . . the short, broad feet, the toes uneven and a bit twisted, the toenails ill-formed." [11] Often, and especially when she is pregnant, Aracoeli is compared to an animal.

Eugenio, Manuel's father, is a handsome, blond navy ensign

who, in spite of the disapproval of his bourgeois northern Italian parents, falls in love with and marries Aracoeli. Right away, they have a son. Manuel's early years are idyllic. His father is away a great deal, his young mother dotes on him, sings to him, kisses him, kisses that remind the reader of the ones Arturo longed for, and that "snapped like little pennons [*sic*] or minuscule castanets, and they left a tiny furrow moist with saliva, which she wiped away, caressing me with one finger. It was as prompt as a gesture of healing, that caress of hers, and yet as silly as a joke, and in fact we laughed at it together." [12]

Until the age of four, Manuel has his mother to himself. He does not distinguish himself from her or that he is male; he has no memory of his father. He and Aracoeli live in the still rural Monte Sacro section of Rome, their house surrounded by fields. They play games, together they learn to read and write. The mother is chaste and modest—once, when she leaves menstrual blood on the sheet, she tells Manuel she has had a nosebleed. He never sees her naked and she hides all her bodily functions from him.

The idyll is shattered when they move to a more elegant and socially prominent neighborhood and Aracoeli has to learn the ways of the bourgeois world and act like a lady. She also becomes pregnant and gives birth to a longed-for little girl, Encarnación. Manuel's feelings of displacement and jealousy are exacerbated by the fact that he is growing older and uglier; he now also has to wear glasses. "Undoubtedly [Aracoeli] had to realize then, invincibly, that her son, as he grew up, was becoming ugly; and that to blame only the eyeglasses would have been at least in part an alibi. To tell the truth: on the original mold of my face, which so inspired her love, that obscure and malignant thumb was already at work, to make it irreparably misshapen, to my eternal misfortune." [13]

The world, too, no longer appears beautiful to Manuel. "But the worst was awaiting me outside the shop: where the crowded street, rutilant [*sic*] with neon and headlights, struck me with its never-before-seen spectacle of horror." [14]

On each of his father's brief visits home, Manuel feels alienated from him as well as jealous of his mother's love for him. "I, on the contrary, was never the son of a father. When I was with him, I always avoided calling him Papà: the very sound of these two syllables gave me a sense of something ridiculous, almost indecorous. The two syllables Ma-ma, on the other hand, sounded very sweet and natural to me, like the very sounds of my own flesh." [15]

Encarnación dies soon after she is born, and the heartbroken and grieving Aracoeli is sent away to recover. When she returns she is completely changed. From a lovely, chaste young woman she has inexplicably—the result of an unnamed illness, presumably syphilis—been transformed into a nymphomaniac. She has gained weight and is slovenly as well as sexually promiscuous. Manuel watches as Aracoeli obsessively masturbates and as she indiscriminately seduces men in the street. In one scene, Aracoeli makes love to a workman in the elevator of her building as it travels between floors. Her behavior becomes more and more aberrant and erratic; eventually she runs away from home, to a brothel, and Manuel is sent away to live with his strict, disapproving grandparents. He sees his mother one last time as she is dying in the hospital. An operation on her brain has left her semiconscious and horribly disfigured.

Her head was all wrapped in a thick gauze bandage. But at one point, between two strips of bandage, I thought I could glimpse, beneath, the scalp, naked, with a faint shadow of down, as if shaven. Moreover (or so it seemed to me), the gauze—along one strip between ear and the nape—was bloodstained.

And the face, framed by the bandages, seemed so diminished that it was almost unrecognizable. Thin, shrunken between the prominent cheekbones and the tiny chin, it resembled the triangular snout of a little animal. And like wild animals, when they fall ill, it seemed oblivious to the whole universe except for its illness. Between her teeth, the tip of her tongue protruded. The great, prominent eyes had sunk considerably into their sockets.[16]

This description of Aracoeli becomes more chilling still in the light of Ginevra Bompiani's account of her visit to Elsa, a few years later, in the hospital: "I saw her exactly like Aracoeli when she came out of the operation."[17] And although it is difficult to believe that Morante could have been so prescient, many of those who knew her may think otherwise.

Thus, by the end of the novel, Aracoeli, the source of life for Manuel, has become the threat of death. On finally reaching El Almendral, Aracoeli's birthplace, Manuel conjures her up for the very last time. However, she is no longer a woman, but a "kind of minuscule sack of shadow" that soon crumples and dissolves in the wind, and—as if to further emphasize the futility of his quest—laughs and tells him, "But niño chiquito, there's nothing to be understood." Manuel realizes that "after all, this encounter was an invention of mine. Mine and alcohol's. Alcohol is a notorious pander; and Aracoeli is a wh—."[18]

Manuel's quest then is futile. "There is nothing to see" or find. Unlike Arturo in *Arturo's Island*, who seeks to free himself from his island home and his family, Manuel seeks the very opposite. He can be said to be a travesty of a hero—and the novel a parody of the mother-son relationship. Instead of wanting freedom or any kind of personal autonomy, Manuel's one desire is to return to his mother's womb, a place of safety and happiness for him. Early in the novel, he declares that he was never happier in his whole life than when he was there. Forty-three years later, Manuel still regrets the day and the hour of his birth: "my first separation from her, when alien hands tear me from her vagina to expose me to insult. . . . I didn't want to be separated from her. I must have already known that this first, bloodstained separation of ours would be followed by another, and another, until the last, the most bloody of all." [19]

As a writer Elsa Morante always focused on the traumas of despotic, egotistical and narcissistic love. And it is difficult to resist the temptation of looking for biography in her work and making certain connections, especially in *Aracoeli*—her last and by far darkest novel. Conjectures begin with the already mentioned fact that the date that marks the start of Manuel's journey coincides with that of Pier Paolo Pasolini's murder, which raises the possibility that Manuel is, in part, a portrait of Pasolini and the novel a way for Morante to interpret his death and console herself. When Manuel speaks of his homosexual love affairs the description of his lovers bring to mind exactly Pasolini's *ragazzi di vita*: "Assuming various names or nicknames: Antonello, Cherubino, Tiger, Rock: sounds that, by themselves, could arouse tumult and clangor in the blood, like supreme formulas. . . . Doubles of real existences [*sic*]; and their living doubles roamed around in the city, among bars, work sites, dance halls, the river front. They were all adolescent and, for the most part, lovers of women. And in my films our encounters, all of them following custom, culminated in my murder." [20] In addition, some of Manuel's insights about himself are said to belong to Pasolini as when, for example, at the end of the novel, Manuel, in a complete reversal, discovers that he loved his father more than he loved his mother.[21]

The pages of *Aracoeli* are filled with dreams, each dream aptly described as one that, in the words of a critic, "grips and throbs like a late van Gogh painting, all magic and menace,"[22] which also brings to mind Elsa Morante's *Diario 1938*. Manuel echoes Elsa when he says, "I have always been an enormous factory of dreams."[23] And many of those dreams resemble hers, referring as they do to her contradictory feelings for her mother, Irma. Another recurrent theme has to do with the absent or missing father; this, of course, can be attributed to Morante's own singular family history.

What also strikes the reader in *Aracoeli* is Morante's unflinching brutal descriptions of the deterioration of the body and the decrepitude of old age. Here Manuel is looking at himself:

> Of average stature, my legs too short for my trunk, my appearance is an unhappy combination of fragility and corpulence. Below the chest with its thick black pelt, the stomach and abdomen with their sedentary bloat protrude over the skinny legs and overhang the genital parts (the "virile attributes") from which I immediately shift my humiliated gaze. The feet, quite dirty, are broad, with misshapen toes. The somewhat large head with its curly hair is crudely joined to the short, thick neck, all of a piece with the bovine nape. The shoulders are broad but weak and sloping. And the arms, thin and poorly muscled, turn downright scrawny between elbow and wrist. I become almost spellbound staring.[24]

Nor are her descriptions of female body parts for the faint of heart: "she widened her legs and pulled the short slip up over her naked sex . . . . I had never seen, exposed so closely to my eyes, a woman's sex; and this, revealed to me today, appeared to me an object of massacre and horrendous suffering, like the mouth of a slaughtered animal. I could just glimpse, between two patches of poor flabby flesh, bare and grayish (so it seemed to me), a kind of bloody wound, darker at the edges; and my stomach twisted with revulsion, so I turned my gaze away." [25]

These graphic descriptions may well suggest Morante's own extreme fear and loathing at growing old, her inability to reconcile herself with her aging body and her appearance. She herself was the first to admit that the coming of old age affected her more deeply than it did other people. "It altered her body and left it occupied by a person Elsa did not recognize as herself. Above all, it left a person Elsa did not love." [26] Manuel's nearsightedness, too, which signals the onset of his adolescence and his ugliness and results in the loss of his mother's love, can be compared with Elsa's own nearsightedness, always a source of worry for her since she feared going blind.

The first time I read *Aracoeli*, I found it almost pointlessly disturbing and shocking. On rereading it, I still found it disturbing and shocking, but I have also grown to admire it—perhaps because it is so dark and resists any attempt to classify it. In writing this novel, Morante may have knowingly sacrificed clarity and logic in order to express her vision of a chaotic world. Manuel's bitter, self-revelatory journey into memory seems almost unjustifiably painful and unnecessary, as does Aracoeli's transformation from virginal beauty to voracious sexual predator. Yet, at the same time, there is something almost inevitable if one regards Manuel as the last progression in a long chain of lost boys beginning with Arturo and continuing with Useppe. These are the boys who once, according to Morante, could save the world but now no longer can. The themes of maternity and identity too are rejected and abandoned, and at the novel's end—never mind that one may not understand Aracoeli's experience, her degradation and illness—one is left with the terrifying awareness that nothing matters any longer for the protagonist or, perhaps, for the writer as well. Old age and the decay of the body have taken their toll and the impossibility of achieving any kind of redeeming love has been proved. Only death remains.

Early on, Manuel tells us, "As a boy I was in doubt, on certain nights, about the real existence of the myriad of stars that appear to us in the sky. In my opinion, there existed perhaps only a single star, created in the beginning, then multiplied to infinity by an illusory game of mirrors. Today, I am offered an autobiographical variant of this childhood cosmogony." [27]

In March 1980, while Elsa Morante was with her friend Tonino Ricchezza and two other young men, she missed a step—no doubt because she was so nearsighted—going from one room to another in Portico di Ottavia, a restaurant in the Ghetto. She broke her femur. (In Elsa's version, the accident took place on her way out of a movie theater after seeing a Woody Allen film.[28]) She was operated on and spent several weeks in the hospital. The next month, while she was recuperating at home, Ginevra Bompiani and Giorgio Agamben went to visit, hoping to cheer her up. Elsa, Ginevra remembered, was lying in bed in beautiful, clean sheets, and Caruso, her cat, was lying next to her. Joking, Giorgio Agamben remarked how the cat looked just like the comic actor, Eduardo De Filippo. Since, according still to Ginevra, Caruso, of course, must have understood what Giorgio had said, he got up and peed on the bed. The beautiful, clean sheets had to be changed and Elsa, Ginevra said, was furious at them.[29]

A year and a half later, in December 1981, the entire manuscript of *Aracoeli* was sent to a typist; for Elsa Morante, this signified that it was the finished draft. Right after that, she suffered terrible pains in her legs, which forced her back to bed, where she remained for months, almost unable to move. By then, too, Elsa had undergone an enormous change. Carlo Cecchi, who saw her frequently, later described this change as something between madness and despair. She became exceedingly combative and went from being gentle one minute to being extremely violent the next. She would no longer listen to reason and everything turned into a conflict. One day when Cecchi ran into Elsa in the street, he barely recognized her. Elsa was walking with a cane and looked like someone out of a Goya painting—either mad or homeless. Seeing him, Elsa said, "Carlo, you look surprised but you have just met my soul." It was a strange and troubling exchange. However, after Morante finished writing *Aracoeli*, Cecchi had known something would happen—it was almost as if through her book, she felt the menace—and her brain, he thought, must already have been affected. He had a terrible premonition.[30]

Aracoeli was published in 1982.* That same year her beloved Caruso died. Erich Linder, her good friend and agent, died the following year. In 1984, the year before Elsa's own death, *Aracoeli* won the prestigious French prize Prix Médicis Etranger.

---

* Since then *Aracoeli* has sold 122,000 copies; in 1989, when it was reissued in paperback it sold 38,000 copies. Apparently, in Italy, unlike in the United States, hardcover books sell better than paperbacks, the result of having a more elite readership who prefer to buy a better-looking book.

thirteen

ELSA'S DEATH

On April 6, 1983, five months after the publication of *Aracoeli*, Elsa Morante tried to commit suicide. She swallowed three different kinds of sleeping pills, then shut all the windows of her apartment and turned on the gas. Her maid found her just in time. Lucia had worked for Elsa for over thirty years, and her only defect was that she was always late for work. A sort of miraculous instinct, Elsa later told a friend, must have propelled Lucia to arrive at via dell'Oca much earlier than usual that day.[1] Elsa Morante had really wanted to die, she said; she was sick, she was unhappy, she was desperate.

Elsa Morante was brought unconscious to San Giacomo Hospital. While undergoing treatment there, she was also diagnosed with hydroencephalitis, or water on the brain. The pressure of this buildup of the cerebrospinal fluid, if not treated, can cause brain damage, and an operation with its attendant risks was discussed. Alberto Moravia and Maria Morante, Elsa's sister, were in favor of the operation while Elsa's friends, familiar with her wishes and her fear of becoming an invalid or of having anyone tamper with her brain, were opposed to it. Moravia and Maria Morante overruled the others and the operation took place at the Villa Margherita clinic; it was not considered a success. Her friends Ginevra Bompiani, Goffredo Fofi, Alfonso Berardinelli and Patrizia Cavalli, as well as Moravia, who were all waiting for her to emerge from the surgery, were deeply shocked when they finally saw her—shocked, too, that life should so cruelly imitate art (with her head bandaged, Elsa looked exactly like Aracoeli).[2]

Elsa Morante lived for another two and a half years. During this time she rarely left the clinic or her bed, except to be wheeled down the corridor to look out at the trees in the garden. For a long time, too, she remained comatose. To make matters worse, her medical expenses had become so burdensome that Moravia— who, as her husband, was ultimately responsible for them— worried that if Elsa remained unconscious for a long time her own funds would run out and he might not have enough money to pay the clinic. Since there is a law in Italy, the Legge Bacchelli, to help artists in need, Moravia decided to solicit the help of President Alessandro Pertini to obtain money for Elsa. Again, all of Morante's friends objected and they tried to persuade Moravia not to proceed, as news of Elsa's deteriorating condition and depleted finances would inevitably get into the newspapers. Fortunately, Elsa Morante regained consciousness just in time and was able to resolve her financial problems herself by putting her affairs in order and by selling the rights to *History* to television.*

While Elsa was in the clinic, she was not always lucid but when she was, she appeared to be quite calm. She sat with a book, Dante's *Inferno*, in her lap, which she read and reread; she spoke only when spoken to. Her hair, which had been cut for the surgery, was short. When asked by a friend if she planned to ever write again, Elsa Morante answered, "To write, I have to be able to walk. If I stay here, I will die."[3] Moravia, no doubt suffering

---

* The television version of the novel, directed by Luigi Comencini, starring Claudia Cardinale as Ida (a strange choice) aired in 1986, after Morante's death.

from remorse, went to see her often; he sat quietly in the room next to her bed. One time when both he and Ginevra Bompiani were visiting, Elsa started to say, "To think that—" and Ginevra right away understood that Elsa was referring to her having to go through all of this suffering for Moravia to come and spend time with her. Moravia, however, did not understand.[4]

Many of Elsa's friends visited her in the clinic. Certain ones, however, did not. Daniele Morante, her favorite nephew, later told me how he deeply regretted that he had not gone to see her more often but he could not bear to see Elsa suffering and so diminished. Another great friend, Alfonso Berardinelli, also said how he felt guilty and he tried to justify himself by saying that he thought of life as a great gift that should not be destroyed by the presence of death.[5]

A happier note about visiting Elsa in the clinic was struck by Dacia Maraini, the woman Alberto Moravia left Elsa for and who always, she said, maintained a friendly relationship with Elsa. At the time of Dacia's visit, Elsa was lying in bed, hardly able to move or speak. Nonetheless, the moment she saw Dacia, Elsa asked, "Shall we play the guess-who game?" Carlo Cecchi was also in the room. Dacia Maraini said, "We both tried to guess who the person Elsa was thinking of through analogies and by asking: 'If he or she was a piece of music what sort of music would he or she be?' Elsa would reply 'A Bach fugue.' 'If he or she was something to eat?' Elsa would say, 'Goat cheese from the mountains,' and so on. Neither Carlo nor I were able to guess and, each time, Elsa would burst out laughing. Then, after a good fifteen minutes, we both gave up and Elsa told us the person was Pier Paolo Pasolini. That was the last time I saw Elsa and that is the last memory I have of her."[6]

Carlo Cecchi remembered other visits to Elsa during her last two years. Lucia, Elsa's loyal maid, was always there. Lucia lived in the clinic, never once leaving and sleeping in Elsa's room, on a sofa that every night she made up into a bed. According to Cecchi, Elsa was sedated much of the time, thus she appeared remote and detached. Together, they would sit in the lounge in front of the garden or in good weather, outside in the garden, Elsa in the wheelchair. A few times they managed to go to a nearby café. In the lounge, they were allowed to smoke and Elsa had started smoking again. But mainly she seemed to be in a kind of limbo. She tired easily and wanted to go back to her room.

In mid-1984, however, Elsa seemed to suddenly become more present and she started to entertain the hope that she would get better and go back to normal life. She worked with a physical therapist and managed to take a few steps. Carlo spent that Christmas with Elsa and she talked of going home (in anticipation, her friend Ida Einaudi repainted her apartment walls). She talked of starting a new novel—one about which she had been thinking. On New Year's Day, 1985, she maintained her tradition of writing something at the beginning of each year: "Only today have I awakened to the memory of that enchantment which has in fact left a few signs on my life. Between then and now there has been an interval of darkness and total oblivion as if the River Lethe had completely swallowed me up." [7]

It was the last thing she wrote. At the end of the month, she suddenly had to have emergency surgery for a perforated ulcer. This resulted in peritonitis and in her being catheterized. From then on, her physical condition worsened. She would not accept being a cripple. She barely answered when spoken to and withdrew to an inaccessible place. When her pain abated and she was not sleeping, she seemed quite absent. According to the doctors, this state of hers might last for a very long time. [8]

Alberto Moravia, although conflicted emotionally about Elsa Morante, was very astute about her character. Recalling her behavior during the war when they were in hiding together, he said, "She was a person who, so to speak, lived in the exceptional and not in the normal." In fact, she was always someone who responded well to danger; ordinary and routine situations tended to make her impatient. He also remembered how she was always torn between her ideal of innocence and lightness and that aspect of her temperament she likened to Simone Weil's—an aspect which she defined as "a heaviness." Moravia compared this duality in her nature to "Ariel and Caliban . . . but an Ariel as incapable of ridding himself of Caliban as Caliban [is] of Ariel." [9]

Describing how, in the early 1960s, they would both meet regularly for tea at Babington's on the Piazza di Spagna, Cesare Garboli reinforced the notion of a duality in her nature: "Each time, our meetings were either a fight or a reconciliation. Elsa was a cannibal, waging war was her way of living; with her one had to attack or retreat, bite or be bitten." According to Garboli, her moods would alternate quickly between being hurt or wanting to hurt, between being generous and kind and being cruel, but always, during this time, she laughed, she played. [10] As time passed, however, and Elsa grew older and she was forced to live alone, she began to hate herself and she wanted to disappear. She felt she lacked a fundamental quality of the soul which again translated itself into "heaviness." A little simplistically, Garboli again attributed this heaviness to Morante's not having had any children. (Although Elsa always claimed to love children, to love their innocence and purity, it is difficult in retrospect to imagine how she would have pursued her career as a writer had she had children or, for that matter, difficult to imagine what sort of mother she might have been.)

• • •

The night of November 24, 1985, Elsa's condition in the Villa Margherita clinic deteriorated. Her blood pressure fell to below 70, although she rallied and slept peacefully through the night. For the last few days, Maria, her sister said, Elsa had no longer been able to recognize anyone—only Macalousse, a nine-year-old Libyan boy diagnosed with cancer who occupied the room next to hers. Over time together in the clinic, they had gotten to be friends; according to a nurse, Elsa helped Macalousse learn Italian and she gave him a copy of *Peter Pan*. "Come here, my little one," she would say to him. "You are the only light in this dismal place."

The following morning, however, Elsa was worse. She had trouble breathing and she was given oxygen. In the early afternoon, the doctor came to do an electrocardiogram and her visitors—Maria Morante, Carlo Cecchi and Stella Graziosi—were asked to leave the room. All but Lucia, who never left her side and who was like a shadow to her. After a few seconds, the doctor called everyone back in the room and told them, "It's over. A heart attack. Her heart gave up."

Elsa Morante died at 1:20 P.M. on November 25, 1985. Her head resting slightly to the left, a blue chiffon scarf tied under her chin, she lay in bed looking as if she were merely sleeping. Hanging from the headboard was an old-fashioned toy, a little wooden bear puppet; on her nightstand were three tangerines and a daisy inside a bottle of mineral water; piled up high on a bedside table, there were at least twenty unread books. The book on top of the pile was Moravia's most recent novel, *The Voyeur (L'uomo che guarda)*—an apt title. Underneath it was her story collection *The Andalusian Shawl* in the German translation.

• • •

Lucia dressed Elsa Morante in a long white cotton Mexican dress decorated with bright colored embroidered flowers. Carlo Cecchi replaced the dreary red roses provided by the funeral home with wild flowers, daisies and miniature tangerine plants, the sort of flowers that Elsa loved and that grew on her terrace.[11] Marcello Morante, Elsa's brother, came to the funeral parlor and sat alone with her for a long time. In his memoir he described how she looked: "She was very beautiful, she looked like a child again. It seemed as if her face had freed itself from the mask that had covered it throughout her final years of physical pain and suffering. The mask had reproduced the face of her mother with a striking, uncanny similarity, and, now, in death, this mask had disappeared."[12] Alberto Moravia, who had been away in Germany when Elsa died, came back in time to view her body lying in the coffin. Like Marcello Morante, he, too, said how Elsa's face had been transformed by old age and suffering but "[w]ith death, it had regained an almost childish aspect, serene, perhaps smiling."[13]

Elsa Morante's death could be seen as a release from great suffering and as a blessing. Moravia wrote, "Her death made me think about the big question of euthanasia. . . . [F]or two years and eight months, Elsa lived a long agony. In my opinion the doctor knew very well that she would not recover from the surgery that followed her first attempt at suicide; the surgery could have been 70 percent successful so I gave permission for it because I was her husband. The operation was not successful and from that moment the doctor knew she would never recover. So they kept her alive without curing her. It would have been better not to let a person condemned to die survive."[14]

The day after her death, November 26, all the leading newspapers in Italy wrote long obituaries devoted to Elsa Morante and her oeuvre (in *La Repubblica's* case, there were three full pages). Their headlines read, FROM A LIE IS BORN THE TIME OF DREAMS, GOOD-BYE ELSA OF A THOUSAND SPELLS and ELSA MORANTE, ROMANTICIST OF OUR TIME.[15] Photographs showed her both young and old, with her cats, with Moravia, with Pasolini and Berardinelli. Her work was excerpted; a letter to Giacomo Debenedetti in which she wrote how she always wanted to be a boy was reprinted; drawings she did as a child were reproduced; her opinions on love, women, fame and writers were quoted, as well as one on life and literature:

I am a little old lady who wants to be left alone. I have put on weight, I have white hair, I am sick. What could anyone say about me? The private life of a writer is gossip and gossip no matter about whom offends me. Novels are more autobiographical than anything else one could say about oneself. My life is in *House of Liars* and *Arturo's Island* . . . not in the facts of my life. But it does not matter. It does not matter how the facts occur in life, it matters how they are told. In books, the facts always have a disguise, conscious or unconscious, but that disguise is their truth. It occurs in novels the way it occurs in dreams: a magical transposition of our life that is perhaps even more significant than life itself because it is enriched by the strength of the imagination. As far as I am concerned, I don't want to be considered a living person.[16]

The funeral took place at 11:00 A.M. on November 27, at the Church of Santa Maria del Popolo. Located on Piazza del Popolo, a stone's throw away from her apartment on via dell'Oca, the beautiful old church must have been very familiar to Elsa Morante. According to legend, Santa Maria del Popolo was built on the Emperor Nero's ancient grave site after he was disinterred and his remains were thrown into the Tiber. It is one of Rome's first Renaissance churches and both Bernini and Raphael had a hand in its design. Two of Caravaggio's paintings, *The Conversion of St. Paul* and *The Crucifixion of St. Peter*, hang in one of the chapels. Elsa Morante, who claimed that she no longer loved God— despite the general rule that as one gets older one becomes more religious, the reverse, she said, was true for her [17]—loved Jesus Christ and she must have looked at those Caravaggio paintings that depict religious experience with such vigorous realism a thousand times. During the service, the church of Santa Maria del Popolo was packed with mourners while outside a large crowd waited patiently in the cold and damp to watch Morante's simple wooden coffin covered with wreaths of flowers drive away.

The day after the funeral service Elsa was cremated. Cremation is not an accepted Catholic practice, yet it is tolerated now for practical reasons: the growing lack of cemetery space. The Rome crematorium then must have been brand-new and it was, as Alberto Moravia justly noted, "a strange building, very modern and very hermetic, not suggesting any idea of death." During the cremation Moravia sat outside in the sun waiting for everything to be over. He could see a farm with cows grazing, a peaceful scene, so that his last impression was "that Elsa had faded into the air, on a sunny day. An impression, all things considered, in harmony with Elsa's special spirituality." [18] Her remains were buried in the Prima Porta Cemetery, located a few kilometers north of central Rome, on the via Flaminia.

Elsa Morante's story does not quite end there, however. One night six months later, an unidentified small group, led by a loyal and intrepid friend, managed to break into the cemetery, whose high walls are strewed with broken glass and whose iron gates are locked, to dig up Elsa Morante's remains (a highly illegal act—if caught, the leader of the group might well have had to serve a prison sentence of up to seven years). The rest can easily be imagined. With the box containing her ashes set carefully in the trunk of the borrowed car, and while none of them dared hardly breathe or speak, they drove at breakneck speed to Naples. There, again under cover of darkness, a local fisherman, his cap half hiding his rugged face, waited for them. A full moon lit their way across the Bay of Naples, prescribing a shiny, phosphorescent path for the boat as it made its determined way across the water toward the little island of Procida, to keep a promise and a last wish. When they reached the island, the wind had picked up quite a bit, tossing the small boat back and forth in the choppy waves, but that was a good thing—an excellent thing, really—for it meant that Elsa Morante's ashes would spread farther, scatter farther out into the world.

EPILOGUE

"There does not exist in all of Italian literature a writer who is more loved and hated, more read and more ignored, than Morante," wrote her friend Cesare Garboli.[1] Certainly, as a writer, she was, for a long time, ignored. She refused to write within a specific ideology, which made it difficult to categorize her or include her in the literary canon. She was isolated as a writer and her work was deemed both exceptional and extraneous. Her themes, which focused on homosexuality, incest and narcissism, were ahead of her time and her style was an unclassifiable mix of the postmodern disjunctive and the traditional. Her stance as a writer—that she had to be a witness as well as be the intellectual conscience of the world—was often didactic and may have alienated her readers. Her refusal to ally herself with any one political group or define herself within the feminist movement created resentment among her female peers. And, finally, an innately private person, she rarely made appearances or granted interviews, which made her less visible to the public.

As time went by, however, Morante's reputation grew (inversely to Moravia's, which has declined). This growing interest was based primarily on a reevaluation of her work, which until then, with the exception of *History* and *Arturo's Island* (the latter was always considered a cult book), had not been widely read. By the early 1990s, a number of critical and scholarly monographs on Morante began to appear in Italy. In particular, her cause was taken up by Italy's foremost critics (also, Morante's friends): Giacomo Debenedetti, Cesare Garboli and Alfonso Berardinelli. Elsa Morante's oeuvre was collected in two handsome volumes, published by Meridiani Mondadori, in 1988 and 1990 respectively. They contained all but the very early stories and essays and featured a very detailed chronology.

To celebrate the twentieth anniversary of Elsa Morante's death, a number of tributes to her were organized in 2005 by the Commune of Rome libraries. The opening conference took place at the Campidoglio on March 15; the participating speakers were Enzo Siciliano, Alfonso Berardinelli, Patrizia Cavalli and Carlo Cecchi. A roving exhibit showed photographs by Federico Garolla of Elsa Morante taken between the years 1956 and 1961. (Unfortunately, in most of the photographs, Elsa is not seen to her best advantage, since she wears a scarf around her head; nor are the stunningly beautiful photos of her as a young woman included). Over the next eight months, a number of conferences and lectures were held at various schools, libraries and other public venues throughout Rome. The subjects ranged from the transition from novel to movie (*Arturo's Island*), to her stormy relations with Pier Paolo Pasolini, and to the influence of Judaism on her work. To accompany these conferences, *A Woman after My Own Taste: Elsa Morante and Others (Una signora di mio gusto: Elsa Morante e le altre)*, a group of short essays comparing and contrasting her work with that of other twentieth-century women writers such as Simone Weil, Maria Zambrano, Virginia Woolf, Marguerite Yourcenar and Anna Maria Ortese, was published in book form. During the entire month of April, the RAI broadcasted a daily reading by Maria Paiato of *History* (one can still listen to these radio shows online).

More recently, in 2006, the Biblioteca Nazionale Centrale di Roma mounted a comprehensive exhibit of Elsa Morante's work, which included a large display of photos, letters, newspaper articles and manuscript pages. The accompanying illustrated catalogue, entitled *Elsa's Room (La stanze di Elsa)*, contains essays on both her life and work and two bibliographies. That same year, a collection of critical scholarly essays called *Under Arturo's Star: The Cultural Legacies of Elsa Morante* was published in English by Purdue University Press; its editors, Stefania Lucamante and Sharon Wood, are both professors who have written extensively on Italian literature and women writers.

During the past two years and some that I have spent writing and thinking about Elsa Morante, I have, not surprisingly, often wondered what my impressions of her would have been had I known her. My guess is that I would have—certainly at first— been intimidated by her, but I would also like to think that my admiration and respect for her would have overcome my reticence. Elsa Morante's life was never easy. She was a serious artist who wanted, through her work, to change the world, even as she knew quite well that it was impossible. She was a passionate, deeply spiritual person who despised authority under any form. She was immensely well read, she had great intellectual curiosity, she appreciated the finer things in life—good food, pretty clothes, art, theater—she had a great sense of fun, she adored animals and children, Mozart, Rimbaud, Stendhal.

According to people who knew her, Elsa Morante never stopped loving Alberto Moravia. A love that was often expressed in an ambivalent, disingenuous and belligerent fashion, no doubt because Elsa Morante felt that she had to both protect and defend herself from Moravia's indifference. And Alberto Moravia must have loved her in his fashion, too. A few years later, after Elsa had died and he was married to Carmen Llera, Moravia was vacationing in Capri with his friend and biographer, Alain Elkann. Elkann asked Moravia to show him the very simple house Moravia often talked about where he and Elsa had lived during the war. A bit reluctant at first, Moravia finally agreed and the two men took a taxi up to Anacapri. But instead of a simple house, Alain Elkann said, there stood a big Napoleonic villa with a beautiful view of the Bay of Naples. Moravia became very abrupt, the way he did when he was embarrassed or did not know what to do, before he admitted that this was in fact the house where they had lived and that Elsa had had a huge room with a terrace. Then, all of a sudden, turning to Elkann, Moravia said in a gloomy voice, "You know they spread Elsa's ashes in the sea between Capri and Procida." By then, too, Moravia was visibly upset, he was red in the face and perspiring. "There she is again," he said to Elkann. "Ashes, you know, move, move in the air and I thought I was liberated from Elsa and here we are." [2]

NOTES

For full citations of books by Elsa Morante (EM), see the listing on page 245. If an English-language version is listed, that was consulted; otherwise, the original Italian edition is the source.

1. TWO UNCLES

1   EM, *Opere*, 1:xx (chronology).

2   EM, "Avventura," *Alibi*, p. 67. Unless otherwise noted, the translations from the Italian are by Giulia Ruggiero.

3   EM, *Opere*, 1:xix.

4   Ibid., 1:xx.

5   Interview with Paolo Morante, Princeton, N.J., May 2005.

6   Marcello Morante, *Maledetta benedetta* (Milan: Garzanti, 1986), p. 18.

7   Ibid., p. 12.

8   Ibid., pp. 42–43.

9   Ibid., p. 39.

10   Ibid., p. 46.

11   Ibid., pp. 62–63.

12   Ibid., p. 33.

13   Ibid., p. 37.

14   Interview with Maria Morante, Rome, January 2006.

15 Ibid.

16 Interview with Daniele Morante, Rome, April 2005.

17 Interview with Patrizia Cavalli, Rome, January 2007.

18 EM, *Aracoeli*, pp. 124–25.

19 Marcello Morante, *Maledetta benedetta*, p. 28.

20 Paolo Morante interview.

2. SECRET GAMES

1 EM, *Opere*, 1:xxi. Thanks to Carlo Cecchi for showing me Elsa's school notebook.

2 EM, "Prima della classe," in *Cahiers Elsa Morante*, ed. Jean-Noël Schifano and Tjuna Notarbartolo (Naples: Edizioni Schientifiche Italiane, 1993), p. 67.

3 EM, *Opere*, 1:xxii.

4 The letter, dated February 8, 1957, was published as "una lettera inedita del Febbraio 1957 a Giacomo Debenedetti," in *Corriere della Sera*, November 26, 1985, p. 3.

5 *Opere*, 1:xxvi–xxvii.

6 Marcello Morante, *Maledette benedetta* (Milan, Garzanti, 1986), p. 35.

7 Ibid., p. 79.

8 Carlo Levi's characterization, which originally appeared in a magazine article in May 1960, is reprinted in EM, *Opere*, 1:xxix.

9 Alberto Moravia and Alain Elkann, *Life of Moravia*, trans. William Weaver (Hanover, N.H.: Steerforth Italia, 2000), p. 134.

10 Rocco Capozzi, *Contemporary Women Writers in Italy*, ed. Santo L. Aricò (Amherst: University of Massachusetts Press, 1990), p. 16.

11 EM, "Domestiche," *Oggi*, November 11, 1939.

12 The essay was published posthumously in 1987, in a collection called *Pro o contro la bomba atomica (For or Against the Atomic*

Bomb). For an interesting critique of it, see Marco Bardini, "Poetry and Reality in 'The Aesthetics of Our Time,' " in *Under Arturo's Star: The Cultural Legacies of Elsa Morante*, ed. Stefania Lucamante and Sharon Wood (West Lafayette, Ind.: Purdue University Press, 2006), pp. 67–71. "Mille città in una" was originally published in *Prospettive*, nos. 4–5 (1938).

13   Cesare Garboli, preface to EM, *Racconti dimenticati*, p. ix.

3. DIARY 1938

1   Dante, *Purgatory*, Canto XV, l. 31–33; translation by Henry Wadsworth Longfellow.

2   Alba Andreaini, preface to *Diario 1938*, by EM, p. viii.

3   Elisa Gambaro, "Strategies and Affabulation in Elsa Morante's 'Diario 1938,' " *in Under Arturo's Star: The Cultural Legacies of Elsa Morante*, ed. Stefania Lucamante and Sharon Wood (West Lafayette, Ind.: Purdue University Press, 2006), p. 24.

4   Interview with Ginevra Bompiani, Rome, April 2005.

5   Alberto Moravia, *Conjugal Love*, trans. Marina Harss (New York: Other Press, 2007), p. 11.

6   Alberto Moravia and Alain Elkann, *Life of Moravia*, trans. William Weaver (Hanover, N.H.: Steerforth Italia, 2000), p. 86.

4. THE WAR YEARS

1   Alberto Moravia and Alain Elkann, *Life of Moravia*, trans. William Weaver (Hanover, N.H.: Steerforth Italia, 2000), p. 138.

2   Luca Fontana, "Elsa Morante: A Personal Remembrance," *Poetry Nation Review* 14, no. 6, p. 20.

3   EM, *Opere*, 1:xxviii.

4   Moravia and Elkann, *Life of Moravia*, p. 137.

5   Robert O. Paxton, *The Anatomy of Fascism* (New York: Alfred A. Knopf, 2004), p. 166.

6   Moravia and Elkann, *Life of Moravia*, p. 143.

7   Ibid., pp. 135–37.

8   Ibid., pp. 137–38.

9   John Middleton Murry, ed., *Novels and Novelists* (London: Constable, 1930), p. 32.

10 Nicoletta Di Ciolla McGowan, "Elsa Morante: Translator of Katherine Mansfield," in *Under Arturo's Star: The Cultural Legacies of Elsa Morante*, ed. Stefania Lucamante and Sharon Wood (West Lafayette, Ind.: Purdue University Press, 2006), p. 62.

11 Moravia and Elkann, *Life of Moravia*, p. 160.

12 Alberto Moravia, *Bitter Honeymoon and Other Stories*, trans. Frances Frenaye (New York: Signet/New American Library, 1958), p. 154.

13 Ibid., p. 155.

14 Ibid., p. 158.

15 Ibid., p. 175.

16 Moravia and Elkann, *Life of Moravia*, p. 103.

17 Ibid., p. 215.

18 Ibid., pp. 166–67.

19 Ibid., pp. 168–70.

20 Ibid., p. 171.

21 Carlo Levi, *Christ Stopped at Eboli*, trans. Frances Frenaye (New York: Farrar, Straus and Giroux, 1963), p. 4.

22 Ibid., p. 22.

23 Ibid., pp. 76–78.

24 Moravia and Elkann, *Life of Moravia*, pp. 172–76.

25 Davide Marrocco, "Un ricordo indelebile," *Latina Oggi*, May 21, 1989, p. 12.

26 Tonino Tornitore, afterword to *Two Women*, by Alberto Moravia, trans. Angus Davidson and Ann McCarrell (Hanover, N.H.: Steerforth Italia, 2001), p. 348 (quoting AM's letter of December 24, 1956).

27   Moravia and Elkann, *Life of Moravia*, p. 189.

28   Ann McCarrell, afterword to Moravia, *Two Women*, p. 335.

29   Moravia, *Two Women*, p. 39.

30   EM, *Lo scialle andaluso*, p. 138.

31   Robert Katz, *The Battle for Rome* (New York: Simon & Schuster, 2003), p. 6.

32   EM, *History*, pp. 362–64.

33   Alfred de Grazia, "Memoir of a Strange Battle Encounter," in *The Taste of War* (Princeton, N.J.: Quiddity Press, 1992), unpaginated. The author is a political theorist and historian. Although his book is out of print, it is available at www.grazian-archive.com.

34   EM, *Opere*, 1:li–lii.

5. HOUSE OF LIARS

1   EM, *Opere*, 1:lii–liii.

2   Giuliana Zagra and Simonetta Buttò, eds., *La stanze di Elsa: Dentro la scrittura di Elsa Morante* (catalogue of exhibition at Biblioteca Nazionale Centrale di Roma, April 27–June 3, 2006) (Rome: Editore Colombo, 2006), p. 27.

3   Michel David, "Interview with Elsa Morante," *Le Monde*, April 13, 1968, p. viii.

4   Ibid.

5   Alberto Moravia and Alain Elkann, *Life of Moravia*, trans. William Weaver (Hanover, N.H.: Steerforth Italia, 2000), p. 191.

6   EM, *House of Liars*, p. 90.

7   Ibid., p. 11.

8   Ibid., p. 12.

9   Ibid., p. 11.

10   Ibid., p. 179.

11   Ibid., p. 281.

12   Ibid., p. 9.

13   Ibid., pp. 198–99.

14   Ibid., p. 78.

15   Ibid., p. 8.

16   Ibid., p. 462.

17   Ibid., p. 463.

18   Ibid., p. 509.

19   David, "Interview with EM," p. viii.

20   EM, *House of Liars*, p. 563.

21   Ibid., p. 565. The poem is titled "Canto for Alvaro the Cat."

22   Nadia Fusini, "Menzonga e sortilegio: 50 anni dopo," *La Rivista dei Libri*, December 1994, pp. 6–7.

23   Cesare Garboli, "Menzonga e sortilegio: 50 anni dopo," *La Rivista dei Libri*, December 1994, p. 6.

24   Laura Furman, "An Interview with Natalia Ginzburg," *Southwest Review* 72, no. 1 (1987), p. 37.

25   Quoted in EM, *Opere*, 1:lv.

26   Moravia and Elkann, *Life of Moravia*, p. 198.

27   Ibid., p. 185.

28   Ibid., p. 213.

29   Interview with Daniele Morante, Rome, April 2005.

30   Maeve Brennan, "Lives in Limbo," *The New Yorker*, February 9, 1952, pp. 106–9.

31   William Weaver, ed., *Open City: Seven Writers in Postwar Rome* (Hanover, N.H.: Steerforth, 1999), p. 19.

6. ROME

1   Pier Paolo Pasolini, *Stories from the City of God: Sketches and Chronicles of Rome, 1950–1966*, ed. Walter Siti, trans. Marina Harss (New York: Handsel Books/Other Press, 2003), p. 147.

2   William Weaver, ed., *Open City: Seven Writers in Postwar Rome* (Hanover, N.H.: Steerforth, 1999), pp. 2–4.

3   Sybille Bedford, *Quicksands* (Berkeley, Calif.: Counterpoint, 2005), pp. 11–12.

4   Thomas Erling Peterson, *Alberto Moravia* (New York: Twayne, 1996), p. 56.

5   Norman Lewis, *Naples '44* (New York: Carroll & Graf, 2005), p. 159.

6   Weaver, *Open City*, p. 26.

7   Alberto Moravia and Alain Elkann, *Life of Moravia*, trans. William Weaver (Hanover, N.H.: Steerforth Italia, 2000), p. 203.

8   Ibid., p. 204.

9   Weaver, *Open City*, pp. 17–18.

10   Moravia and Elkann, *Life of Moravia*, p. 191.

11   Weaver, *Open City*, p. 16.

12   Ibid., p. 23.

13   Moravia and Elkann, *Life of Moravia*, p. 188.

14   Ibid., p. 190.

15   Interview with Patrizia Cavalli, Rome, January 2007.

16   EM, *Opere*, 1:lvii. Morante's "Rosso e bianco" essays were published posthumously in 1989, in *Pro o Contro la bomba atomica*.

17   EM, *Opere*, 2:1465.

18   Ibid., 2:1476.

19   Interview with Bernardo Bertolucci, Rome, January 2007.

20   Interview with Ginevra Bompiani, Rome, April 2005.

21   Gaia Servadio, *Luchino Visconti* (London: Weidenfeld and Nicolson, 1983), p. 128.

22   Franco Zeffirelli, *Autobiografia* (Milan: Mondadori, 2006), p. 110.

23   Ibid., p. 165.

24   Interview with Adriana Asti, Naples, January 2007.

25   Servadio, *Luchino Visconti*, pp. 129, 220–21.

26   Moravia and Elkann, *Life of Moravia*, pp. 222–23.

27   Ibid., pp. 186, 183–84, 214.

28   Ibid., pp. 234–35.

29   Asti interview.

7. ARTURO'S ISLAND

1   Jean-Noël Schifano, *Désir d'Italie* (Paris: Gallimard, 1990),
          p. 384.

2   EM, "Una lettera inedita del Febbraio 1957 a Giacomo Debene-
          detti," *Corriere della Sera*, November 26, 1985, p. 3.

3   Schifano, *Désir d'Italie*, pp. 377–78.

4   Lesley Chamberlain, *Nietzsche in Turin* (New York: Picador
          USA, 1999), pp. 96–98.

5   EM, *Opere*, 1:1ix–1xii.

6   Ibid., 1:1xiii.

7   Ibid., 1:1xiii–1xiv.

8   Ibid., 1:1xv.

9   Renata Propper, graphology report, June 2006.

10   EM, *Arturo's Island*, p. 4.

11   Schifano, *Désir d'Italie*, p. 404.

12   EM, *Arturo's Island*, p. 3.

13   Giacomo Debenedetti, "L'isola della Morante," *Nuovi Argu-
          menti*, 26 (1957), pp. 43–61.

14   EM, *Arturo's Island*, p. 12.

15   Ibid., p. 35.

16   Ibid., p. 20.

17   Ibid., pp. 28–29.

18   Ibid., pp. 32, 34.

19   Ibid., pp. 38, 39.

20   Ibid., pp. 61, 137–38, 131, 121.

21   Ibid., pp. 125, 123, 145.

22   Ibid., p. 213.

23   Ibid., p. 291.

24   Debenedetti, "L'isola della Morante."

25   Cesare Garboli, *Il gioco segreto: Nove immagini di Elsa Morante* (Milan: Adelphi Edizioni, 1995), p. 19.

26   EM, *Arturo's Island*, pp. 348, 349.

27   Blanche Knopf to EM, July 31, 1957, Harry Ransom Center, University of Texas at Austin.

28   EM to Blanche Knopf, August 18, 1957, ibid.

29   Memo from Judith B. Jones, September 8, 1958, ibid.

30   Raleigh Trevelyan (of William Collins Sons) to Blanche Knopf, September 2, 1958, ibid.

31   EM to Blanche Knopf, August 17, 1959, ibid.

32   Gilbert Millstein, "Books of the Times," *The New York Times*, August 18, 1959, p. 27.

33   Frederic Morton, "His Idyl," *The New York Times Book Review*, August 16, 1959, p. 4.

34   EM to Blanche Knopf, October 29, 1959, Harry Ransom Center.

35   Frederic Morton, "A Talk with Elsa Morante," *The New York Times Book Review*, October 25, 1959, p. 57.

8. WITHOUT THE COMFORT OF RELIGION

1   Interview with Allen Midgette, Woodstock, N.Y., February 2007.

2   Ibid.

3   Barth David Schwartz, *Pasolini Requiem* (New York: Vintage, 1995), p. 502.

4   Francine Virduzzo's 1961 interview is reprinted in EM, *Opere*, 1:1xxiii–lxxiv.

5   Ibid., 2:1497–1520 (questions on pp. 1573–75), reprinted from *Nuovi Argomenti*, no. 38–39 (May–August 1959).

6   Ibid., 1:1xix.

7   Enzo Siciliano, *Campo de' Fiori* (Milan: Rizzoli, 1993), p. 49.

8   Alberto Moravia, invitation to the opening of Bill Morrow's show *Vernissage*, Galerie Lambert, Paris, December 1, 1961.

9   Ibid.

10   Alberto Moravia and Alain Elkann, *Life of Moravia*, trans. William Weaver (Hanover, N.H.: Steerforth, 2000), p. 255.

11   EM, *Opere*, 1:1xxvi–lxxviii.

12   Blanche Knopf to EM, March 19, 1963, Harry Ransom Center, University of Texas at Austin.

13   Blanche Knopf to EM, February 9, 1965, ibid.

14   Blanche Knopf to EM, May 18, 1965, ibid.

15   Erich Linder to Blanche Knopf, July 26, 1965, ibid.

16   Giulio Einaudi to Blanche Knopf, September 2, 1965, ibid.

17   Cesare Garboli, *Il gioco segreto: Nove immagini di Elsa Morante* (Milan: Adelphi Edizioni, 1945), p. 128.

18   Concetta d'Angeli, "A Difficult Legacy: Morante's Presence in Contemporary Italian Literature," in *Under Arturo's Star: The Cultural Legacies of Elsa Morante*, ed. Stefania Lucamante and Sharon Wood (West Lafayette, Ind.: Purdue University Press, 2006), p. 218.

19   Garboli, *Il gioco segreto*, pp. 206–7.

9. POETRY AND PASOLINI

1   Patrizia Cavalli, *Poesie (1974–1992)* (Turin: Einaudi, 1992), p. 32.

2   Interview with Patrizia Cavalli, Rome, April 2004.

3   Sandro Penna, "Watching a Boy Fall Asleep," *Confused Dream*,
        trans. George Scrivani (Madras and New York: Hanuman
        Books, 1988), p. 47.

4   Lietta Tornabuoni, "La difficile scelta di essere 'contor,' "
        Corriere della Sera, November 3, 1975, p. 3.

5   Enzo Siciliano, *Pasolini*, trans. John Shepley (New York:
        Random House, 1982), p. 237.

6   Filippo La Porta, "The 'Dragon of Unreality' against the
        'Dream of a Thing': On Morante and Pasolini," in *Under Artu-
        ro's Star: The Cultural Legacies of Elsa Morante*, ed. Stefania
        Lucamante and Sharon Wood (West Lafayette, Ind.:
        Purdue University Press, 2006), p. 291.

7   Barth David Schwartz, *Pasolini Requiem* (New York: Vintage,
        1995), p. 297.

8   Pier Paolo Pasolini, *Selected Poems*, trans. Norman MacAfee
        and Luciano Martinengo (London: John Calder, 1984), p. 3.

9   Cesare Garboli, *Il gioco segreto: Nove immagini di Elsa Morante*
        (Milan: Adelphi Edizioni, 1995), p. 91.

10   EM, *Alibi*, preface.

11   Hans Werner Henze, *Bohemian Fifths*, trans. Stewart Spencer
        (Princeton, N.J.: Princeton University Press, 1999), p. 200.

12   Fondo Alberto Moravia, Lungotevere della Vittoria 1, Rome.

13   EM, *House of Liars*, epigraph. (The existing English-language
        translation uses "illusion" in the opening line, but "fiction" is
        more accurate.)

14   Pier Paolo Pasolini, *The Scent of India*, trans. David Price
        (London: The Olive Press, 1984), p. 38.

15   Ibid., p. 43.

16   Walter Siti, "Elsa Morante and Pier Paolo Pasolini," in *Under
        Arturo's Star*, p. 271.

17   Luca Fontana, "Elsa Morante: A Personal Remembrance,"
        Poetry Nation Review 14, no. 6, p. 19.

10. THE WORLD SAVED BY CHILDREN

1   In a lighthearted essay called "My Navona" published in *Illust-
        razione Italiana* in February 1962, EM wrote that of all the
        squares in the world Piazza Navona is the most beautiful.

2   Interview with Judith Malina, New York, March 2007.

3   Interview with Carlo Cecchi, Iesi, January 2006.

4   Ibid.

5   Interview with Alfonso Berardinelli, Rome, April 2005.

6   Interview with Adriana Asti, Naples, January 2007.

7   Interview with Charis Vivante, Florence, via telephone, 2006.

8   EM, *Opere*, 1:lxxvi–lxxvii.

9   Interview with Patrizia Cavalli, Rome, January 2007.

10   Interview with Daniele Morante, Rome, April 2005.

11   Sandra Petrignani, *Le signore della scrittura: Interviste* (1984;
        repr., Milan: La Tartaruga Edizioni, 1996), pp. 113–14.

12   Daniele Morante interview.

13   Interview with Patrizia Cavalli, Rome, April 2005.

14   Daniele Morante interview.

15   Interview with Allen Midgette, Woodstock, N.Y., February
        2007.

16   Daniele Morante interview.

17   Interview with Ginevra Bompiani, April 2005.

18   Cavalli interview, April 2005.

19   Bompiani interview.

20   Cecchi interview.

21   Paul Ginsborg, *A History of Contemporary Italy: Society and
        Politics, 1943–1988* (New York: Palgrave Macmillan, 2003),
        p. 298.

22   Ibid., p. 301. Scuola di Barbiana, *Lettera a una professoressa*
        (Florence: Libreria Editrice Fiorentina, 1967), pp. 112, 116.

23   Ginsborg, *History of Contemporary Italy*, p. 302.

24   Ibid., p. 307; *L'Espresso*, June 16, 1968.

25   Ginsborg, *History of Contemporary Italy*, p. 308.

26   EM, *Opere*, 1:lxxx–lxxxi.

27   Description on the back cover of the 1995 Einaudi edition.

28   Rocco Capozzi, *Contemporary Women Writers in Italy*, ed. Santo L. Aricò (Amherst: University of Massachusetts Press, 1990), p. 15.

29   Interview with Bernardo Bertolucci, Rome, January 2007.

30   EM, *The World Saved by Children*, pp. 9–10.

31   Cesare Garboli, *Il gioco segreto: Nove immagini di Elsa Morante* (Milan: Adelphi Edizioni, 1995), pp. 148–52.

11. HISTORY

1   Luca Fontana, "Elsa Morante: A Personal Remembrance," *Poetry Nation Review* 14, no. 6, p. 20.

2   Ibid.

3   Erich Linder to William Koshland, November 1, 1974, Harry Ransom Center, University of Texas at Austin.

4   Paul Hofmann, "Rome: 'La Storia,' Literary Sensation," *The New York Times*, September 5, 1974.

5   EM, *Opere*, 1:lxxxii.

6   Simone Weil, "The Iliad or, The Poem of Force," trans. Mary McCarthy, *Politics Pamphlet*, no. 1 (November 1945), p. 3.

7   Ibid., pp. 13, 16.

8   George Steiner, "Sainte Simone: The Jewish Bases of Simone Weil's Via Negativa to the Philosophic Peaks," *TLS*, June 4, 1993, p. 9.

9   Weil, "The Iliad or, The Poem of Force," pp. 9, 16.

10   Cesare Garboli, program on RAI produced with students of the Liceo Classico Orazio, Rome, April 23, 2002.

11   Steiner, "Sainte Simone," p. 3.

12   Interview with Alfonso Berardinelli, Rome, April 2005.

13   Cesare Garboli, *Il gioco segreto: Nove immagini di Elsa Morante* (Milan: Adelphi Edizioni, 1995), p. 196.

14   Interviews with Patrizia Cavalli and Ginevra Bompiani, Rome, April 2005.

15   Garboli, *Il gioco secreto*, pp. 188–90.

16   Amos Oz, *The Story Begins: Essays on Literature*, trans. Maggie Bar-Tura (New York: Harcourt Brace, 1999), pp. 73, 87.

17   Ferdinando Camon, "Il grande male," in *Cahiers Elsa Morante*, ed. Jean-Noël Schifano and Tjuna Notarbartolo (Naples: Edizioni Schientifiche Italiane, 1993), pp. 91–95.

18   EM, *History*, pp. 132–33.

19   Ibid., pp. 193, 197–98.

20   Ibid., pp. 655, 637.

21   Ibid., pp. 573, 710, 713.

22   Ibid., p. 734.

23   Cavalli interview.

24   Paul Ginsborg, *A History of Contemporary Italy: Society and Politics, 1943–1988* (New York: Palgrave Macmillan, 2003), p. 356.

25   Stefania Lucamante and Sharon Wood, "Introduction: Life and Work," in *Under Arturo's Star: The Cultural Legacies of Elsa Morante* (West Lafayette, Ind.: Purdue University Press, 2006), p. 5.

26   Berardinelli interview.

27   Barth David Schwartz, *Pasolini Requiem* (New York: Vintage, 1995), p. 598.

28   Pier Paolo Pasolini, *Tempo Illustrato*, July 26, 1974, and August 2, 1974.

29   Schwartz, *Pasolini Requiem*, p. 87.

30   Bompiani interview.

31 Willard Spiegelman, "William Weaver: The Art of Translation III" (interview), *The Paris Review*, issue 161 (Spring 2002).

32 Robert Alter, "The Setting, Rome 1941 to 1947," *The New York Times*, April 24, 1977.

33 Stephen Spender, *The New York Review of Books* 24, no. 7 (April 28, 1977).

34 Erich Linder to William Koshland, September 12, 1977, Harry Ransom Center.

35 Garboli, *Il gioco secreto*, pp. 170–71.

36 Gregory L. Lucente, *Beautiful Fables: Self–consciousness in Italian Narrative from Manzoni to Calvino* (Baltimore: The Johns Hopkins University Press, 1986), p. 264.

37 EM, "La censura in Spagna," *L'unità*, May 15, 1976; " '*La Storia*' secondo Elsa Morante," *Corriere della Sera*, May 15, 1976.

38 EM, *Opere*, 1:lxxxiii–lxxxv.

12. ARACOELI

1 Interview with Carlo Cecchi, Iesi, January 2006.

2 Ibid.

3 Ibid.

4 Tonino Ricchezza, "La favola continua," in *Cahiers Elsa Morante*, ed. Jean-Noël Schifano and Tjuna Notarbartolo (Naples: Edizioni Schientifiche Italiane, 1993), p. 77.

5 Alfonso Berardinelli, speech at conference "Elsa Morante in Rome, 1912–1985," in "Today's Program at 9:30 at Protomoteca, Campidoglio," *Il Foglio*, March 15, 2005.

6 Interview with Carlo Cecchi, Urbino, January 2007.

7 Interview with Alfonso Berardinelli, Rome, April 2005.

8 Cecchi interview, January 2006.

9 "A Letter to the Red Brigades" was finally published ten years later, in *Paragone*, no. 456 (February 1988).

10 EM, *Aracoeli*, pp. 3, 10.

11   Ibid., p. 12.

12   Ibid., p. 42.

13   Ibid., p. 165.

14   Ibid., p. 166.

15   Ibid., p. 174.

16   Ibid., p. 282.

17   Interview with Ginevra Bompiani, Rome, April 2005.

18   EM, *Aracoeli*, pp. 291–92.

19   Ibid., p. 17.

20   Ibid., p. 91.

21   Walter Siti, "Elsa Morante and Pier Paolo Pasolini," in *Under
        Arturo's Star: The Cultural Legacies of Elsa Morante*, ed. Stefania
        Lucamante and Sharon Wood (West Lafayette, Ind.: Purdue
        University Press, 2006), p. 286.

22   Gabriele Annan, "Give Him a Break!," *The New York Review of
        Books* 32, no. 4 (March 14, 1985).

23   EM, *Aracoeli*, p. 276.

24   Ibid., pp. 99–100.

25   Ibid., p. 80.

26   Cesare Garboli, *Il gioco segreto: Nove immagini di Elsa Morante*
        (Milan: Adelphi Edizioni, 1995), p. 196.

27   EM, *Aracoeli*, p. 131.

28   Jean-Noël Schifano, *Désir d'Italie* (Paris: Gallimard, 1990),
        p. 378.

29   Bompiani interview.

30   Cecchi interview, January 2007.

13. ELSA'S DEATH

1   Jean-Noël Schifano, *Désir d'Italie* (Paris: Gallimard, 1990),
        p. 378.

2   Interview with Ginevra Bompiani, Rome, April 2005.

3   Schifano, *Désir d'Italie*, p. 388.

4   Bompiani interview.

5   Interview with Alfonso Berardinelli, Rome, April 2005.

6   Dacia Maraini, e-mail message to author, March 4, 2006.

7   EM, *Opere*, 1:xc.

8   Carlo Cecchi, e-mail message to author, October 21, 2006.

9   Alberto Moravia and Alain Elkann, *Life of Moravia*, trans. William Weaver (Hanover, N.H.: Steerforth Italia, 2000), pp. 174, 191.

10   Cesare Garboli, *Il gioco segreto: Nove immagini di Elsa Morante* (Milan: Adelphi Edizioni, 1995), pp. 206–7, 213.

11   Laura Laurenzi, " 'Sono stanca di vivere' è finita l'agonia: Così si è spenta Elsa Morante," *La Repubblica*, November 26, 1985, p. 19.

12   Marcello Morante, *Maledetta benedetta* (Milan: Garzanti, 1986), p. 7.

13   Moravia and Elkann, *Life of Moravia*, p. 344.

14   Alberto Moravia, "Amore e morte," in *Cahiers Elsa Morante*, ed. Jean-Noël Schifano and Tjuna Notarbartolo (Naples: Edizione Schientifiche Italiane, 1993), p. 65.

15   *Il Messaggero* and *Corriere della Sera*, November 26, 1985.

16   *Il Messaggero*, November 26, 1985, p. 5.

17   Luca Coppola, "Letter," in *Cahiers Elsa Morante*, p. 99.

18   Moravia and Elkann, *Life of Moravia*, p. 344.

EPILOGUE

1   Cesare Garboli, *Il gioco segreto: Nove immagini di Elsa Morante* (Milan: Adelphi Edizioni, 1995), p. 23.

2   Interview with Alain Elkann, Rome, January 2006.

WORKS BY ELSA MORANTE

Il gioco segreto (The Secret Game). Milan: Garzanti, 1941.

Le bellissime avventure di Caterì dalla trecciolina e altre storie (The Marvelous Adventures of Cathy with the Long Tresses and Other Stories). Turin: Einaudi, 1942.

—Republished as *Le straordinarie avventure di Caterina (The Extraordinary Adventures of Catherine)*. Turin: Einaudi, 1959 and 2007.

Menzogna e sortilegio. Turin: Einaudi, 1948.

—In English, *House of Liars*, translated by Adrienne Foulke with the editorial assistance of Andrew Chiappe. New York: Harcourt Brace, 1951.

L'isola di Arturo. Turin: Einaudi, 1957.

—In English. *Arturo's Island*, translated by Isabel Quigly. New York: Knopf, 1959.

—Reissue, Hanover, N.H.: Steerforth Italia, 1998.

Alibi (Alibi). Milan: Longanesi Editions (then called Domenico Landini), 1958.

—Reprinted by Garzanti in 1990.

—*Lo scialle andaluso (The Andalusian Shawl)*. Turin: Einaudi, 1963.

—Reprinted by Einaudi in 2007.

Il mondo salvato dai ragazzini e altri poemi (The World Saved by Children and Other Poems). Turin: Einaudi, 1968.

—Reprinted by Einaudi in 1971 and in 2006.

La storia. Turin: Einaudi, 1974.

—Reprinted by Einaudi in 1986 and in 2005.

—In English, *History: A Novel*, translated by William Weaver. New York: Knopf, 1977.

—Reissue, Hanover, N.H., Steerforth Italia: 2000.

—Reissue, Zoland Books, an imprint of Steerforth Press, Hanover, N.H.: 2007.

Aracoeli. Turin: Einaudi, 1982.

—Reprinted by Einaudi in 2005.

—In English, *Aracoeli*, translated by William Weaver. New York: Random House, 1984.

Pro o contro la bomba atomica (For or Against the Atomic Bomb). Milan: Adelphi Edizioni, 1987.

Diario 1938 (Diary 1938). Turin: Einaudi, 1989.

—Reprinted by Einaudi in 2005.

Racconti dimenticati (Forgotten Tales). Turin: Einaudi, 2002.

—Reprinted by Einaudi in 2004.

Elsa Morante Opere (Elsa Morante: Complete Works). Edited by Carlo Cecchi and Cesare Garboli. 2 vols. Milan: Mondadori, 1988 and 1990.

ACKNOWLEDGMENTS

Many people helped me write this book.

Silvia Valisa, a Ph.D. candidate at the University of California at Berkeley, answered my first query and set me on the right track with a long, passionate, informative e-mail, which was soon followed by the names of people I should contact as well as copies of Elsa Morante's hard-to-find early published work. I am deeply grateful to Silvia for this initial as well as for her continual support, her enthusiasm for my project and her generosity in sharing her greatly superior expertise.

My research assistant, the beautiful and talented Veronica Raimo, made persistent phone calls, set up interviews and accompanied me to them, translated and recorded texts, took me on a tour of the San Lorenzo and Testaccio districts of Rome and accompanied me to the Biblioteca Nazionale Centrale di Roma, where she charmed recalcitrant and uncooperative librarians into searching archives and producing documents. She also accompanied me to the State Archives in Turin, where again she charmed recalcitrant archivists into producing documents. *Mille grazie*, Veronica.

I am most thankful to Giulia Ruggiero, who translated Morante's early stories, Marcello Morante's memoir and Cesare Garboli's and Giorgio Agamben's essays, and who generously and rapidly responded to my many, many queries. Also, to Paola

Basirico, my teacher, who patiently tried to improve my mediocre Italian and who graciously allowed me to distract her from lessons in grammar with readings and discussions of stories by Morante, Moravia and Verga (her favorite).

This book would not exist without Carlo Cecchi, Elsa Morante's coexecutor, who at first was elusive. I telephoned him a dozen times before I realized that, not so surprisingly, there was, on the part of Elsa's friends and relatives, a certain amount of resistance to me. After all, why would an American who did not speak fluent Italian want to write about Elsa Morante? Just as I was ready to give up, Carlo answered the phone and agreed to see me. To do so, I had to cross the width of Italy. On the day we were to meet for lunch, I was both lost and late (each time I called to say that I was still lost, I could hear increasing irritation creep into his voice). I will never forget how when finally I drove up to the door of his hotel and saw him—a handsome man, dressed entirely in black, a shock of white hair falling over his forehead, looking stern and impatient—my heart sank. Since then, we have spoken and seen each other several times and Carlo has been more than forthcoming and candid with his memories, as well as generous in giving me access to material and allowing me to use his photographs of Elsa. I hope that this account of the woman he so admired and loved will not disappoint him. I am immensely grateful and thank him with all my heart.

For granting interviews, I want to thank Adriana Asti; Alfonso Berardinelli; Bernardo Bertolucci; Ginevra Bompiani; Alain Elkann; Dacia Maraini; Allen Midgette, a newfound friend (thanks to Bernardo Bertolucci) who knew both Elsa and Bill Morrow well; Daniele Morante; Maria Morante; and Paolo Morante. I especially want to thank Patrizia Cavalli with whom I spent several afternoons, including a memorable one sorting through a suitcase filled with photographs.

For their cooperation and help, my thanks also go to Toni Maraini and Alberto Cau at the Fondo Moravia; Mauro Bersani at Einaudi; Luigi Bernabó; Marco Cassini at Minimum Fax; Dr. Margherita Breccia Fratadocchi at the Rare Books and Manuscript Room, Biblioteca Nazionale Centrale di Roma; Dr. Marsaglia at the State Archives in Turin; Danielle Sigler at the Harry Ransom Center at the University of Texas at Austin; and finally to Flora Ghezzo, assistant professor at Columbia University, who graciously agreed to speak to me about nineteenth- and twentieth-century Italian women writers.

My special thanks to the American Academy in Rome for thrice providing a beautiful roof over my head, and to Adele Chatfield-Taylor, Carmela Franklin, Dana Prescott, and Pina Pasquantonio. I would also like to thank the gatekeeper, Norman Robertson, for cheer, directions and transportation, and, in particular, Romano Migliarino, who notwithstanding the fact that we were late and lost, drove me ten hours to Iesi and back. I also want to thank Terzo Giovanni of Procida for the gift of a lemon.

For their friendship and advice, I am grateful to JoAnne Akalaitis, Anselma dell'Olio, Paul Elie, Louisa Ermelino, Molly Haskell, Shirley Hazzard, Susan Minot, Renata Propper, Maria Tucci, LuAnn Walther and Beverley Zabriskie. For still more friendship, advice and for a close reading and rereading of these pages, I am very much indebted to Michelle Huneven and Frances Kiernan. Most of all, I want to express my enormous gratitude to Trent Duffy for his keen-eyed fact checking and masterly editing of this book. As always I thank Georges and Anne Borchardt, my guardian angels and friends. Finally, I thank Terry Karten and Julia Felsenthal.

INDEX

Grateful acknowledgment is made to Elsa Morante's Estate, and to Carlo Cecchi in particular, for permission to quote from the works included in *Opere Morante* (Mondadori) and from interviews with Elsa Morante.

"To the Story" from *House of Liars*, copyright © 1948 by Elsa Morante, English translation copyright © 1951 by Adrienne Foulke, reproduced by permission of Harcourt, Inc.

"Watching a Boy Fall Asleep" by Sandro Penna from *The Complete Sandro Penna Poems*, © Sandro Penna, reproduced by permission of Garzanti Libri Spa.

"Untitled Poem" by Patrizia Cavalli from *Poesia*, © Patrizia Cavalli, reprinted by permission of Einaudi.

All photographs are courtesy of the Elsa Morante Estate, with the exception of the following:

Photographs of manuscript pages from Elsa Morante's *House of Liars (Menzogna e sortilegio)* are reproduced by permission of the Biblioteca Nazionale Centrale di Roma.

Photograph of Elsa Morante holding a hat in Capri by Elia Capri.

Photograph of congratulatory telegram from Italo Calvino © 1963 by Italo Calvino. Reprinted with the permission of The Wylie Agency.

Photograph of Elsa Morante at work in her studio © Federico Garolla, reprinted by permission of Isabella Garolla.